America Speaks

America Speaks

BY PHILIP GIBBS

DOUBLEDAY, DORAN AND COMPANY, INC.
GARDEN CITY 1942 NEW YORK

PRINTED AT THE *Country Life Press,* GARDEN CITY, N. Y., U. S. A.

Contents

America Speaks

I

By Clipper to New York

IT WAS BURNING HOT in Lisbon, where a crowd of British and American people waited for their chance of getting onto the Clipper. It seemed easier to get a first-class ticket to Paradise than a place on this Pan-American air liner which was now the only safe way of escape from a world at war to a world at peace. Refugees from many countries now captured by the Germans had had desperate adventures in getting as far as Lisbon and then found that they had to wait weary weeks and sometimes months before they could get a seat under the wings of that great bird. While they waited they were held up for ransom in Portuguese hotels until all their money had gone.

It was very expensive in Lisbon, I found. The Hotel Aviz, suitable for princes and grand dukes of the prewar world, a little palace in a great garden built by an architect with a passion for eagles in brass and stone, rapidly absorbed certain funds which had been placed to my credit in a Lisbon bank. When they went, what? British regulations had allowed me to bring only ten pounds in English money, and at the Hotel Aviz that was a pauper's dole.

I possessed a magic password without which the Clipper is unapproachable, except with a long delay. "Priority." "Have you priority?" I was asked a score of times by fellow travellers. There were degrees of priority. Film stars, diplomats, government officials on urgent national business, and American newspaper correspondents seemed to be in the first category. As a private individual with a lecture tour as my mission in the United States, I was not among those exalted few. But I had pulled every wire I could think of for two and a half months of desperate endeavour. I was put back only three times before I passed through the gates of the airport.

I had only eight days of waiting. They were days of intense heat under a sun which blazed out of a blue sky until night brought a little cool breeze under the stars in a velvet darkness. I saw the beauty of Lisbon and Estoril and Cintra, with their white palaces and churches and villas, and with the purple-flowered bougainvillea spilt like wine on old white walls beneath a sky of cloudless blue. I saw the strange international life of Lisbon, a sanctuary for the refugees of many nations and the rendezvous of international espionage. In the restaurants of hotels at Estoril I avoided the eyes of Germans whom I had known before the war. One of them was a well-known diplomat who spoke English perfectly and was familiar in the clubs of Pall Mall. Now he was an enemy and an agent of Hitler.

I caught the Lisbon bug. Most English visitors fell a victim to it. It was very disintegrating to one's internal mechanism.

One paid for meals which one could not eat. A little lady, very thoughtful and very kind, led me to a chemist's shop and asked for a bottle of white liquid which tasted like zinc ointment. "This will help you," she told me, "but it will take weeks and weeks."

I had the microbe with me when at dawn one morning the telephone rang in my bedroom and a voice gave me a welcome message.

"You start today."

In the hall was a friend of mine, a tall, long-limbed Scot who had also received the message, Sir Alexander MacFadyn. He was in trouble. It appeared that he had to pay a small fine for staying in Lisbon a day longer than his *permis de séjour* allowed without notification. He had spent all his Portuguese money. Without that he could not pass. I was able to come to his help with the last few pesetas which remained in my banking account, for which I had a scarlet chequebook. A car was waiting for us at the office of the Pan American Airways. Each of us had been presented with a little bag of blue and white linen in which we had to carry our shaving tackle and the few things we needed for the transatlantic crossing. There was lively conversation among my fellow travellers. A Swiss diplomat was gay and high spirited and appeared to know everybody of importance in the world as he exchanged reminiscences with Sir Alexander MacFadyn.

I sat rather silent and rather thoughtful. That Lisbon microbe was making me uneasy. But I was thinking back to things and thinking forward. How astonishing that I should be about to fly the Atlantic! It seemed only yesterday that a boy named Lindbergh had come like a young god—Mercury —on swift wings across the great grey sea. It had seemed like a miracle. Now there was a regular service keeping its time-table. I thought of England and of a little village there called Shamley Green which I had left eight days before. My friends and neighbours had wished me good luck and I had left them with a guilty feeling. They would have to go through another winter of war. They would hear the drone of German bombers again. High explosives would fall in their fields and gardens. In London, where I had been in many air raids, there had been a respite from bombing because of Germany's attack on Russia. But it might not last much longer. I should be out of all that for some months. Was it possible that in a few hours I should be in New York? How did the war affect the American people? What were they thinking about it? Or were they failing to think of it except as a far-off conflict in the old European jungle from which they were infinitely remote, and which only interested them now and again between baseball matches and private affairs as a bloody drama providing good material for the radio and the movie? I should have to find out all that. It would be a study in unknown psychology, vastly interesting.

There was the Clipper moored alongside the landing stage, a thing of beauty and power, with silver wings and body like a great lovely bird. We stood watching it for something more than an hour while we chatted to each other.

"A fine-looking craft," said the Swiss diplomat. "I have no sense of apprehension. What strength! What marvellous power! In a few hours—how incredible!—we shall be across the Atlantic."

Someone told a story which I heard afterwards in New York:

The Clipper was overladen by too many passengers and too much mail. One of the pilots addressed the passengers.

"Very sorry, ladies and gentlemen, but we must ask three of you to sacrifice yourselves for the sake of the others. I will open the door. Three of you must go overboard to lighten our load. The bravest will volunteer."

Instantly an Englishman rose, saluted, said, "God save the King!" and went through the door.

A Frenchman rose, saluted, said, "*Vive la France!*" and went through the door.

A German rose, gave the Nazi salute, said "Heil Hitler!" and pushed out two Italians.

A barber in New York, telling me this story, varied it slightly. He said the Englishman rose, saluted, said, "There'll always be an England!" and pushed out two Greeks. He was an Italian barber.

We took our places in the Clipper. We heard the vibration of its engines. We soared into the blue sky above Lisbon. We were away.

Strangely enough—so odd is human psychology—the flight across the Atlantic seemed extremely long, though it was only twenty hours with two stops of nearly three hours each— at the Azores and Bermuda. One's mind—or mine—flew much faster than this aircraft. Each hour seemed long drawn out, and it seemed to me that I was a week in the Clipper, making new friendships which seemed like old friendships, having endless conversations, watching a drama with many acts and incidents.

We travelled in luxury. This flying boat was like a small

hotel. It was divided into little drawing rooms, each one a few steps lower than the other. One walked from one to another, joining different groups. Light refreshments were served from time to time. There were rooms in which one could smoke. Those strong wings of the Clipper flew so steadily that there was hardly any sense of movement. Only the vibration of the engines thrilled through one's body and brain.

There were women and children with us. One of them was a famous little lady named Jessie Matthews, woman and child too. She was like quicksilver in all her movements and flitted through the plane like a ray of sunshine. Her hands, her eyes, and her body were always restless and expressive of gaiety and good will. She was a born actress in every fibre of her being, and every gesture was pleasant to watch. She became the little mother of a small boy who was sick, now and then, and whose own mother was preoccupied with a tiny daughter. Jessie Matthews folded him in her arms, crooned little songs to him, wiped his forehead with a little handkerchief, and was his fairy godmother. She had time to make many people fall in love with her, including one stout fellow who went dippy about the little wrinkle on her nose when she laughed. She was good enough to sleep for a time with her head against my shoulder. The icy finger of death touched her in America.

There were also Bebe Daniels and her husband Ben Lyon, who had been working hard in England to cheer up the troops. I joined their table a number of times, and it was in their company that I heard a conversation led by a young American physicist who was a serious young man obsessed with the facts of science and the refusal of his mind to believe anything which could not be proved by measurement. He did not believe in future life for which he could find no evidence.

But he believed in life and liked it. He liked life so much—his pursuit of scientific knowledge as part of it—that he was intensely hostile to war which demanded the sacrifice of life. He spoke very sombrely against the idiocy of war and the killing of young men who allowed themselves to be dragged into it with death as their penalty.

"I cannot understand," he told me, "why so many millions of men allow themselves to be killed, when they only have one life."

I mentioned the word "liberty."

He didn't think much of that word.

"Liberty is not worth so much as life," he said. "I want to keep living. I want to enjoy life with a wife and children."

"Would you care for life," I asked him, "if you had to submit to the rule of Hitler, who might prohibit your scientific career and who would prevent the freedom of your mind?"

He thought over this and was silent for some moments.

"I only have one life," he said. "I don't believe in all this spiritual business—a better world next time. There is no evidence. I know that when I'm dead I'm dead. If Hitler didn't like my science I should take up some other interest. I'm keen on music. I would rather be alive under Hitler than dead with liberty."

Bebe Daniels and her husband were shocked. They argued with this young man hotly. Bebe Daniels became eloquent and passionate and stated the other side of the case with a little flame in her eyes. She had been playing to men who believed in liberty and were willing to die for it. She had been in London bombardments. She had seen the courage of the English. Life was senseless without spiritual values, she said.

"Life is life," said the young physicist. "It's all we have.

I'm going to keep alive if possible. This war is a crime against life."

Bebe Daniels and her husband spoke to me in low voices when the young man went to another table.

"Don't take any notice of what he says," they told me. "That young man has got it all wrong. American boys don't think like that."

We dropped down to the Azores and had lunch in the sunshine under an azure sky.

Somebody quoted the ballad of Sir Richard Grenville.

"The Americans will take over the Azores before much more history has passed," said someone else.

The sea was aglitter with gold. We were in an enchanted island. It would be good to stay here in another dream of life.

We returned to our places in the Clipper again. Sir Alexander MacFadyn had made friends with the tiny sister of the small boy who was mothered by Jessie Matthews. He was very good with children, and the little girl was happy on his lap watching his comical tricks.

Darkness crept into the sky. The stars came out. We were flying through the night on strong wings.

We dropped down in Bermuda, next morning, and had another meal. Some journalists desired my views about the war and asked questions about the morale in England. One was a Scotsman and a very pleasant fellow who had somehow drifted to Bermuda and found life good there though a bit dull. I saw the low-lying hills and the golden shore. I should have liked to spend three weeks there. I should find friends among the censors who read all our letters and cut out little bits which seemed quite harmless. But the Clipper does not wait as long as three hours, and we had to fly away.

We flew along the American coast. It was raining heavily. Presently we saw New York with its tall towers touching the clouds. They tilted sideways crazily as we came down. We had flown from one dream to another.

I was in the United States.

II

The Soaring City

O N THE NIGHT of my arrival in the early days of September I walked in New York City with my son Anthony, who had met me at the Customs. It seemed to me that I was walking in a strange, fantastic dream. A few days before I had been in England, an island fortress whose people had been through a fiery ordeal and had suffered dreadful casualties, most of whom were women and children. They were severely rationed for food, with only just enough and never too much at any meal. Before darkness came every window was blacked out and not a chink of light showed from one end of the land to the other. The news of war came as a direct message from which they could estimate their chances of life and liberty. They thought of the war and dreamed of the war, and the ring of a telephone bell or some wired words might bring at any moment, to a cottage or house, the news that some boy of ours in the R.A.F. or the Royal Navy had been killed or wounded. Here in New York I felt incredibly remote from all that. Here in New York it was a different world, as though I had come to a different planet. The lights were on—millions of lights from millions of windows reaching to the stars in those tall towers of steel which climbed above the clouds. Lighted signs flashed and winked and spun and dazzled. The shops on Fifth Avenue were all ablaze. A ceaseless traffic of cars poured in tides down the streets, held up for a few moments by red signals, while crowds on the sidewalks crossed in a leisurely way before the light changed and the tide bore down. What was moving in the minds of those people? I wondered. Were any of them thinking about the war—so far away from them, so utterly distant from their own interests? Was any shadow of it creeping nearer?

On that September night it was very warm. I found it suffocating and weakening. With that Lisbon bug still biting me I could hardly drag my feet from one block to another. Yet my mind was alert and excited. It was nearly twenty years since I had been in New York. Even in this first walk by night I saw many changes. New towers had soared up, topping the old ones. Immense new blocks, bigger than any giant castle in any fairy tale, had been built since my last visit.

"We ought to stagger as far as Radio City," said my son. "It's worth an effort."

We stood below Radio City, and I threw my head back and looked up and gave a kind of gasp, and felt a little frightened and awed. It was astonishing in its immensity and in its beauty. The central tower, flanked by two vast wings, shot up as a tall shaft to pierce the high dome of the night sky, darkly blue and star spangled. It was floodlit and was dazzling white above a great gulf of darkness to the pointed tower on top. Some fellow had had a dream: here it was in steel and stone, yet still it seemed insubstantial and dreamlike.

"It's a very amusing place," said my son. "Round the fountains in that courtyard they had a lot of penguins until a few days ago. And sea lions the week before that. Look at those flowers."

We went into a great courtyard, with terraces above the central court, where there were chairs and tables and coloured sunshades. All around the terrace were massed flowers—hydrangeas, I think—strangely coloured by the artificial lights. Many people were moving about in the shadow world down there; American girls came past laughing and talking. Two lovers stood near us, with the girl's hand on the man's arm and her head leaned against his shoulder. On this September night in Radio City peace-minded people were sipping iced drinks, talking about baseball, making love, having a good time after a day's work, while over in Russia—that other world—corpses were piling up on the roads to Moscow, and over in Poland and Yugoslavia and Czechoslovakia and France and Holland and Belgium and Norway undernourished people, suffering under a harsh tyranny, with their minds soaked in agony and tragedy and despair, whispered a few fearful words to each other, afraid that they should be overheard. Here it was different. It was truly another world.

I went back to the Plaza Hotel. It was almost twenty years since I had been there before, for the first time, after the World War which had ended in victory for us. We had believed for a time that it was the war to end war. Germany had been crushed, disarmed, and freed from her old rulers. President Wilson had established his League of Nations, aban-

doned on the doorstep like an illegitimate child by his own
people, who repudiated him, but supported by nearly all
the other nations of the world, who professed its noble ideals
with certain mental reservations. One day it would work.
There would be a long peace. . . .

The Plaza was filled with ghosts for me. It was hardly
changed, I noticed with pleasure. It all came back to me as I
had remembered it. There were the elevators in which I had
doffed my hat, according to American ritual, after coming
back from lectures in the Carnegie Hall and New York
theatres, where I had talked about the horrors of war and
the ideals of peace. There was the lounge where I had met
David Davies, chief apostle of the League and founder of
the League of Nations Union, at great expense to himself.
In those days we had been filled with idealism and had never
dreamed, even after late suppers, of another war happening
in twenty years or of ruins in London and other English cities.
I had dedicated my pen to peace. In all my books, beginning
with *Now It Can Be Told,* called in England *Realities of War,*
I had tried to create better understanding between the peoples
and had been a hater of war and a lover of peace. Now I
was coming to talk to the American people about another war,
worse than the last, more horrible because of its attacks on
civilians, not incompatible, as it seemed to me, without inconsistency with those ideals of peace because the Spirit of Evil had
come out of its old lairs and was menacing with frightful power
and ruthless cruelty all the decent code of civilised minds, all
the liberties for which men have struggled since the beginning
of history, and all the spiritual values of life. We had made
ghastly mistakes. We had blundered into this war because
of those errors, but our leaders had gone to the ultimate

limits in trying to keep the peace. What did the American people, among whom I now found myself, think of all this? How closely did it touch their minds and souls? That, really, was what I had come to find out, though as a means to this enquiry I was on a lecture tour.

My first encounters were friendly, warm, and sympathetic. The American friends who had come to meet me had expressed their profound admiration for England, for British courage, for all that our people had endured so stoically during the long bombardment from the air, from which recently there had been a respite owing to the German war on Russia.

"Your people have been wonderful," said one of these friends. "We're out to help you to the uttermost limit—this side of an expeditionary force."

That was the first time I heard of a very definite limitation in the American mind regarding the extent of their aid to Britain. Later I encountered it in every section of American life, in every state. It was a fundamental reluctance in the American mind.

Within half an hour of my arrival in New York I was being put wise to the internal situation and the political divergencies of thought in this new world to which I had come.

"What do the English people think of our American effort?" I was asked by one of my friends. "What do they think of our President? Do they know much of what is happening over here—our dillydallying while the world is on fire, our labour troubles—all these strikes—and the opposition of the isolationists?"

"We have had a good interpreter of the United States," I told him. "Every Saturday night the whole nation listens to Raymond Gram Swing, who has kept us well informed. He has done a fine job for both nations, with a finely balanced judgment and a sincerity in which we believe. As for the President's foreign policy—most of us think he has been marvellous in leading the American people as far as they have come. We think him one of the world's idealists and our greatest friend."

"Now I'll tell *you*," said my American friend.

He told me a lot about President Roosevelt upon which I reserved judgment, having something like hero worship for that statesman. It was not favourable. It was unfavourable to the President, his wife, his sons, his associates, and his social policies. It was bitter, scathing, and ironical. The President, he assured me, has made an unholy mess of things. He was playing into the hands of revolutionary labour. He was a twister, a double-crosser, and other unpleasant things. His foreign policy was not bad—a lot of fine words—but if Wendell Willkie had been in power, there would have been more than words. There would have been acts. Things would have been done.

I listened to all this and made a mental note that the critics of President Roosevelt were still criticising, with considerable, though suppressed, passion. I held to my own belief that whatever may have gone wrong with his New Deal and much of his social legislation, he was a great leader in a time of world crisis.

"We're all for England," said my friend after his monologue. "You'll find the American people deeply sympathetic."

Before leaving New York I heard other points of view. I heard the voice of the man in the street and the man in the shop and the man in the taxicab.

I have come to have an admiration for the cabdrivers of

New York and other American cities. They are friendly
fellows, very shrewd and humorous, and willing to deliver
their views on life while they thread their way through surging
traffic or halt with the red light against them.

"From England?" asked one of them when I gave him an
address.

"Yes. Just out."

"I could tell by your accent. Maybe you can't help it.
Your natural way to talk, I guess. Well, you must have been
having a rough time. I've read about it. I've seen it on the
newsreels. Jesus!"

At Forty-eighth Street, Fifth Avenue, he turned his head
slightly in my direction.

"The isolationists are all dumb. They don't know yet that
Hitler won't leave us alone if he gets England down."

"Are there many of them?" I asked.

"They shoot off their mouths," he told me. "But they're on
the losing side. I can't think what bug is biting that fellow
Lindbergh. Then there's Senator Nye. Hell, they're against
geography! These United States are only thirty-six miles away
from Russia up here beyond Alaska. Bombing planes don't
make much account of distance. In my judgment England
is fighting our war. We've just got to beat Hitler or lose our
own liberties. That's how I see it. But then my mother was an
Englishwoman. Yes sir, born in London."

Another New York cabdriver was more argumentative. He
was driving me to the house of Dr. Nicholas Murray Butler.

"English?" he asked.

I admitted it.

"Yeah?" he answered. "Well, this war is all England's
fault."

"How do you make that out?"

"Hell! England was dumb in letting Hitler get ahead with his rearmament. There wouldn't have been a war if England had gone in with France when Hitler first began. The policy of appeasement was what caused the present state of things."

I put up a slight defence, but he was not interested.

"Do you want me to tell you the truth?" he asked.

I was in search of truth.

"Well, it's like this," he said when the red lights were against us. "We don't feel so friendly towards England as we did in the last war."

"I'm sorry to hear that. Why not?"

"Well, I'll tell you. England didn't pay back her debt. Only little Finland paid. England didn't even say she was sorry. Just refused to pay and called us a nation of Shylocks. It was a contract, wasn't it? Same as when I hire this cab? I have to pay so many dollars a week. I don't tell my company I can't pay any more and I ain't going to. That wouldn't wash with them. Jeepers creepers! A contract is a contract, and we thought England was honest! It makes us kinda sore. We've been fooled once and we won't be fooled twice. That's how many of us think. Though—mind you—we want England to win. We've no use for that fellow Hitler."

He stopped his cab outside the house to which I had directed him.

"Nicholas Murray Butler's house," he said. "I've been here often before. A well-meaning old guy, maybe. Well, I daresay he'll give you a good dinner. Have a nice time!"

He held out his hand and grasped mine in a tight grip.

"I speak my mind," he said, "but quite friendly. It's best to tell the truth. No offence meant."

We parted the best of friends and I went up the steps to Dr. Nicholas Murray Butler's front door. I had been there before, and I had had a painful moment in this house twenty years ago, if it was the same house. Dr. Butler had given a very fine reception in my honour. I had put on full evening dress and thought I looked beautiful. But it was not so. When I advanced into a drawing room filled with elegant ladies and gentlemen a footman had come up to me and whispered a rebuke.

"Say! You got your gums on!"

I had put on rubbers, or what we call galoshes, on a snowy night. I had forgotten to kick them off. I was a scandal in Dr. Nicholas Murray Butler's drawing room.

This night I was in a tuxedo and black tie. There was a party of professors and their wives. Dr. Butler introduced me and spoke of the times when we had met in England. He had been a great idealist. I had believed in his ideals—the League of Nations, the intelligent construction of peace. His ideals and mine had gone down into the mud and into the furnace fires. I was surrounded by a friendly company. These professors came to me to talk about England and its heroism and its sufferings. One of them had just come back. He knew.

At the dinner table there was good food and good conversation. Always for me there was too much food in this land of abundance, and I never sat down to a meal without thinking of the meagre rations among my own folk. The conversation was led by Dr. Nicholas Murray Butler, to whom his professors listened with respect and attention. He continued it afterwards in his study. The president of Columbia University has known everybody worth knowing, including all the great scoundrels like Mussolini and Hitler and Ribbentrop.

He has been behind the scenes of history. Now and again he has helped to make history. A man like that has something to talk about, and we listened with an absorbed interest to his stories of famous statesmen and the crises of the past forty years. If his advice had been followed, the second World War would not have happened. But he had failed like the rest of us who in other ways had worked for peace by pen and word.

Dr. Nicholas Murray Butler presided over my first lecture in Columbia University, where I gave two. They were both, I fear, very bad. I was dreadfully nervous, as usual, and I was not in good form owing to the hang-over of the Lisbon microbe, and the very warm weather in New York, which made me feel as limp as a piece of chewing gum. Before each lecture I was stricken by stage fright but had to appear genial and bright to various members of the faculty to whom I was introduced. One of them who arranges these lectures—a continuous stream of talks, open to subscribers outside the university and a great source of intellectual education—was a very charming man named Dr. Potter. I was greatly attracted by him because of his long, sensitive face and thoughtful, humorous eyes. He tried to put me at my ease and told some amusing stories, one of which was a commentary on this mad world and that "idiots' delight" which is war:

A learned professor approached one of the leaders of the Lemmings—those strange creatures who commit mass suicide.

"I am a great student of your species," said the professor. "I may claim to be the greatest authority on your habits and way of life. But there is one thing I can never understand, and that is why at regular intervals you go down to the sea and drown yourselves."

"Sir," answered the Lemming, "I also am a student and

have studied the habits and customs of the human race. But there is one thing I utterly fail to understand, and that is—why you don't!"

I had many conversations in New York with men and women of varying degrees, and always there was some reference to the war in Europe, even if that subject did not dominate their minds. They were critical, now and then, of Great Britain for her unpreparedness, though always enthusiastic in praise of British courage and doggedness. They listened eagerly to Winston Churchill whenever he spoke, and found his words invigorating and the style of his oratory exciting. They thought we had made a poor show, with many mistakes, in our various attempts to help other nations— Norway, Greece, and now Russia. There were various interpretations of the letters B.E.F., the most popular being "Back every fortnight."

But there was no mention, I noticed, of Japan at that time, though Mr. Cordell Hull was busily exchanging notes with the Japanese Foreign Office. President Roosevelt's words conjuring up a menace to the United States did not freeze their blood or bring any shadow of fear over their minds. They could not conceive of any peril to the United States actually touching them from the Axis powers, though they agreed that it would be an uncomfortable world for their own country if Hitler were to win. The crowds streaming down Fifth Avenue and Broadway in sunny weather were far away from the war, it seemed, though in the measurement of time they were less than three months away from it. No one heard the hooves of the Four Horsemen riding down Fifth Avenue.

III

Life in New England

Before setting forth on my lecture tour in the middle of October in a year of destiny, I spent a few weeks in New England and had more than a glimpse of its life and tradition in an intimate way. My own family was there, at a little country place called Lakeville, some four miles from the small town of Middleboro, Massachusetts, and about eleven miles from Taunton. It was really to see them again after a year's absence that I had flown across the Atlantic and engaged myself for the desperate adventure of a lecture tour. My son Anthony was hard at work writing and lecturing on behalf of Britain and British relief, trying to put the British point of view by telling people about the war. They were avid for any sort of firsthand account. With him was his wife Maisie, once a bacteriologist in the Lister Institute of London, and their two children, Martin and Frances, who had been my playmates in an English garden. One of my literary brothers, Arthur Hamilton Gibbs, had given them a roof over their heads—which they needed badly, since many of my son's lectures were free—in a little New England house "across the street," as my sister-in-law calls it, from his own home. Neighbouring houses, beyond a private golf course, were filled with my brother's friends and friends of another brother of mine, Cosmo Hamilton, who remains as a romantic legend in Lakeville, where they tell many affectionate stories about his amazing personality. So I had come into a little society with a warmth of friendship which reached out to me instantly and generously and took me at once into the heart and mind of New England.

The two children, Martin aged eleven and Frances aged six, for whom I had yearned in England, had grown taller and had adopted the American ways of life and speech as ducks take to water. Martin had written to me from time to time with the news that America was marvellous. I could see why he thought it so. He was having a fine free life on the edge of a big lake called Long Pond, in which he went swimming and boating with little Frances and a group of American boys who were his buddies. When I asked him if he would like to go back to England he hesitated a moment and then said, "If I could take the lake with me—and if I could take Fitz." Fitz was a black cocker spaniel who dashed in and out of the house, generally with a pair of my socks in his mouth, and chased the children, biting their breeches, yelping at them on the bicycles on which they hurtled down to the waterside, and behaving almost as tempestuously as Frances herself, who has the restlessness and adventurous spirit of Boadicea. Cooees and red Indian cries hailed the coming, from time to time, of the village boys, who swarmed into the playroom for games with Martin's guns and English soldiers, aeroplanes and tanks, or called him out to join them on their "paper route"—the delivery of the evening papers to neighbouring houses, for which one of them had a contract. They were of the true type of Tom Sawyer and Huckleberry Finn, and my grandson, brought up in the more reserved manner of English school-boys, had adopted their ways and customs with hilarious delight. He could talk to them in their own vernacular, and Frances did not lag behind. But one thing I noticed quickly. The lads were very gentle and sweet with Frances and were never in the least degree rough with her, though she demanded equality of risk and roughness in all their games.

While in Lakeville I came to learn very quickly something of the daily setup of American life, from the hour before breakfast, when the radio heralded a new day from several bedrooms with blasts of music, song, studio laughter, drama-tised advertisements of Wrigley's Chewing Gum, Bosco, Postum, White Owl Cigars, Old Gold Cigarettes, and other American products—between short spasms of news about the European war, so far away, so infinitely remote, it seemed, from American life and safety—with the latest home news of more strikes and political labour troubles of more direct and urgent importance.

American home life, I found, is full of comings and goings in various types of automobile. American mothers and some fathers are always driving back and forth. The children have to be taken to school after the struggle to get them ready in time. Then they have to be fetched from school. There is the adventure of morning shopping in the nearest town, when the car has to be laden with a variety of food, beyond the range of English households even in peacetime, from the

A & P stores, where you grab what you want and wheel it to the cashier in steel perambulators made for that purpose, or from other chain stores stocked with the infinite assortment of goods essential, it seems, to American well-being, because the radio advertising insists upon the lifesaving and health-giving qualities of so many little things without which the English people seem to rub along fairly well in their primitive way. The family cars dash about over an area of forty miles or so on the daily round of social and domestic activity, and to the English mind it all seems very restless and dynamic.

I came to know American small-town life as it goes on in Middleboro, Massachusetts, and probably in thousands of others. My abiding impression is that these people are truly democratic in a way not yet known in England and very cheerful, kindly, neighbourly folk who find life good and get a lot out of it.

After brief acquaintance: "How do you do!" cries the small shopkeeper as one enters.

"How do you do!" says the man in the shoeshine shop.

"How do you do!" says the man behind the counter in the drugstores, the boot shop, the department stores, or the to-bacco store. This is followed by a friendly conversation about the weather—unusually mild up to the first week of Decem-ber—the world situation, the troubles of labour—an epidemic of strikes—and the unpleasant character of Mr. Hitler.

They have shrewd minds and very good manners, these small-town folk. The rough edges have been worn off since last I was in the United States. They are very courteous. The magnificent and free American education is beginning to reap its harvest in a higher standard of intelligence and social behaviour. The movies have had something to do with it, I am told, and the radio even more.

They are fond of dogs, I have noticed, and people who are fond of dogs are fond of children and have kindly souls.

Fitz of Lakeville had friendly greetings in Middleboro.

"You're a fine little cocker spaniel, ain't you!" said the man outside the A & P store. "And I know all about little dogs!"

So it was all down the street.

Hired help is hard to get in America, except among the coloured folks who do not come North in great numbers. The American housewife, on thirty-seven hundred dollars a year, does most of her own chores, and if she gets a maid or a middle-aged woman to lend a hand she has to treat her tenderly.

But in the larger country houses—in one of them to which I was invited many times with friendly warmth—I found life went on rather like that of an English country mansion. The tradition was the same in its continuity and habits, though perhaps rather more dynamic and active in variety of interests. The history of Hill-top Farm has been written by one of its daughters, and the story of its family by one of its aunts. I read both books and was touched by their charm. For they reveal the life of an American family of old English stock going back many generations, with a strong sense of family and a love for the old houses, the old furniture, the old traditions of loyalty and character which they have inherited. There is something fragrant and touching in Lydia's book about her childhood and young girlhood with her sisters and relatives. It was a pleasant life at Hill-top Farm. It is still a pleasant life, steeped in good memories of girls who had horses to ride and rode them fearlessly and well. Their father raised cows and ran this old homestead as a farm until he laid out a golf course and had other interests more important to his government and state. All his girls took a hand in this farming work, though they made time for riding. Lydia is a fine horsewoman and good to see as she comes riding across the grass or through the woods. But she is now a flying woman and keen on that adventure, and she has another passion which takes her into a studio as a sculptor of unusual talent. Her sister Katharine studied singing in Germany before Germany became an outlaw nation and has a flutelike voice, which one night I heard. The children of Hill-top Farm who laugh through the pages of Lydia's family book are now grown women, though the youngest, Phoebe, has only just "come out."

Their mother is a remarkable woman, and I owe her a debt for enlightening me on many points of American history and politics. She has a liberal and well-poised mind, taking broader views than the ladies of Boston—in the winter Hill-top Farm is abandoned for a big house in Boston—who regard her as rather "red," though in England she would belong to the old tradition of the Liberal party.

In this old house at Lakeville, beyond the lake and the golf course, I found New England life at its best. And this family—so cultured, so well planted on the soil, so steeped in their own family tradition, and yet so keenly alert to all that is happening in a war-stricken world—helped me to understand what was moving in the American mind at this time when the United States was, for the most part, unaware of the dark shadow creeping up to them from the East and the West.

I remember some words spoken by the father of the family and his liberal-minded wife, with Lydia their daughter close at hand.

"People over here aren't awake," said the father. "They are all sunk in self-complacency. They don't realize in the least that your war with Germany is our war, too, and that we have been too late and too long in getting busy about it."

"The President has had a difficult time," said the mother. "You must remember our diversity of races over here and our vast distances. He has had to lead public opinion step by step. Europe seems incredibly distant to the people of the Middle West. A lot of education is necessary before the whole people are ready to follow his leadership and support his foreign policy. The isolationists——"

"They make me mad," said Lydia. "I have no patience with them. They're just plain dumb."

She used that word in the American sense, from the German derivation of *dumm,* which means stupid.

Lydia was passionate and intense in her anxiety to give more help to Britain. Lydia was one of those few girls in the United States who did not shrink from the idea of sending an American Expeditionary Force to Europe. She had a secret ambition as a pilot. It was to take an American bomber across the Atlantic.

I had further introduction to New England life before setting out on my lecture tour through many American states. I went boating on the lake with young Martin and Frances, and it was there in the woods that fringe the lakeside that I heard of the ghost of the angry Indian. It was my son who told me about it.

"This whole country," he said one day, "is haunted by the

spirit of the angry Indian. Henry Beston was telling me the other day, and I think it's true. He's dispossessed, but you feel his presence still. Nature is hostile to the paleface. Poison ivy makes sores on him if he touches it, and it's everywhere in the undergrowth. The fierce changes in the climate—a drop of thirty degrees quite suddenly—are vengeful. It's a violent climate. It lashes out. One feels a kind of hostility in these woods."

It was a fanciful idea, but there was, I found, a constant reminder in New England of those redskins who were its first inhabitants, though almost all of them have gone and only a few poor souls survive in this state. Many times in the woods by the lake I had a sense of seeing a young Indian standing quite motionless with his body against a tree—quite motionless until he released an arrow from his bow. I saw him many times with the eye of imagination but with a sense of reality.

I saw him again along the Mohawk Trail. That was on a motor tour I made with my brother Arthur and his wife and a young girl named Jo who was a relative of the family at Hill-top Farm.

Looking back now upon that wonderful drive through New England, I am aware of something tragic which lay behind this beauty—a beauty of nature more wonderful than I had ever seen before in any country. This was in the American fall, as they call their autumn, and we went at the very chosen moment for its glory, when the mountains and valleys and steep ravines were wearing the flaming colours of an autumn foliage ranging in every tone from scarlet to russet gold. It was, though we knew it not, the last autumn in America before a war which maybe will last through many falls and will bring to the people of the United States, inevitably, great agony of soul, enormous tragedy, the death of youth, the tears of women, before victory comes. Here we drove through peace and loveliness, exquisite beyond words to describe, almost beyond the range of art to depict, for it would be a brave painter who attempted to put such colours upon his canvas. The maples had turned vivid red, their foliage hanging from the boughs like tattered tapestry woven into the colours of other trees by innumerable gradations of delicate tones which no mediaeval needlewoman ever worked upon her frame. There was a blue sky overhead, and the sun drenched this countryside, and white clouds like ships in full sail came over the foothills of the Berkshire Mountains as we ascended to their heights. With us was a representative of American youth, high spirited, elated, ecstatic. Jo, as we called Miss Josephine, was a stimulating companion on the road. The sight of the hills stirred in her such passionate joy because of all this beauty that she seemed almost to suffer anguish. She cried out constantly— cries of wonderment, joy, and pain.

"Oh! . . . Oh! . . . Oh! . . . I can't *believe* it! . . . Oh! . . . Isn't it absolutely *marvellous!* . . . I've never *seen* such glorious things! . . . Oh! . . . Oh! . . . *Look* at that! . . . It makes me want to *scream!*"

She did scream, and the joy of her enthusiasm, the ecstasy of her youth, accompanied us all the way to the Green Mountains with music and mirth.

We had picnic lunches by little rivers rushing over rocks and overhung by this flaming tapestry of foliage. We had driven through many hamlets of New England, with their white frame houses more than a century old, very prim and neat, and through New England towns with avenues of tall trees like those in France. Then we arrived at the town of

Manchester, more unlike the English city of that name than any place could be on earth. It was our goal because my brother and the ecstatic Jo had arranged to play a game there on a famous and beautiful golf course framed by the hills.

We put up at a guesthouse run by a lady who had lived for some time on the French Riviera and whose husband was a well-known writer. It was a pleasant and spotless place in which one felt at home. There were only a few other visitors, and they were interesting. One of them, who was a friend of our hostess, had a ranch in Canada and knew Florida and most of the beauty spots of this earth. She was elegant and witty but had her serious moments, one of which was when she took me to one side and told me how deeply she felt for the sufferings of England during the bombardment and how strongly she felt that American aid ought to be more speedy and effective.

That evening after dinner there was a conversation about the war.

It began when one of the ladies in the guesthouse, hearing a great deal about this American aid from some of the others, suddenly threw down a challenge.

"Is there anybody here who goes as far as saying that we ought to send an American Expeditionary Force to Europe?"

There was a silence.

The challenging lady developed her thesis.

"All my friends are anxious to send all possible help to Britain, but they stop short of that. They never get over that line. They begin to think of their own boys in high schools or colleges. They don't want them to be sent over to make an invasion on the Continent and get killed by German guns in a war for Britain, or, if you like to put it that way, in a war for liberty. I agree with them. But I'll put it to the vote in this room."

She asked each of the visitors in the guesthouse. Not one voted for an American Expeditionary Force, not even the elegant lady who had spoken so warmly of her friendship for England and so bitterly about the lag in American aid.

Our hostess, a very highly educated lady with a gift of words and an emotional quality, interpreted her own feelings.

"Theoretically I could bring myself to vote for sending American boys overseas. I believe that England is fighting our battles against an enemy who is our enemy. And there is nothing too good or too big to help England now. And yet when you ask me directly about sending our boys overseas I can't bring myself to say yes. Something in me, something in my very soul, stops short of that."

There was a soldierly looking fellow among the guests, a bronzed man with a great gift of silence. Suddenly he started talking.

"Let's keep out of this lousy war," he said. "It was made by a bunch of crooks on both sides—the so-called statesmen and politicians of Europe. Chamberlain and his crowd were double-crossers like Hitler and his gang. The men who have got to fight this war are just the same kind of dupes as they were in the last war. The poor bloody soldier will be the gun fodder, as usual, and asked to die for slogans as false as hell— war to end war, a world fit for democracy, homes for heroes, liberty, civilisation, and all that. We heard it all last time. And a beautiful bloody world they made of it when the job was done."

I guessed what was working in his mind and what was the motive of his speech. I sympathised with him almost to the full extent. I had an equal hatred of war. I had written millions of words denouncing its abominations. But somehow this war seemed to me a necessary war not to be dodged, because it was a straight conflict between civilised and uncivilised codes, literally between the spirit of all that is good in life and all that is evil. If Hitler were to win, evil would prevail and the light would go out of life. The human mind itself would be enslaved. Art would die; beauty would be killed. Those under the heel of Hitler would not have the right to think freely but would be put in the clamping irons of the Nazi code. I defended Chamberlain. He had tried his utmost for peace; he had gone beyond the limit almost of honour itself—so his critics said—to prevent this war. He had been humiliated and scorned, especially in the United States, where the word "appeasement" was heard with derision. Britain had no guilt in this war. It was not for Empire or possessions or power. Only when Hitler had broken all his pledges and trampled over other people's frontiers had we seen that Hitler menaced all liberty and was possessed by seven devils. We could not let him get away with it without abandoning our faith in the decencies of life and in the light of civilisation. It would be a surrender to the powers of darkness. In spite of all the horrors of war this conflict would have to be fought out.

So I argued in sincerity, and the other guests took up the argument, mostly on my side, though deeply moved by the other man's denunciation of war. The talk went on and on. Veils fell from people's eyes. They talked from their inner convictions, reaching down to the truth inside themselves. Jo, our fellow traveller, was first to rise and break the spell by a light laugh.

She turned to me with laughing eyes.

"You have much in common with President Roosevelt," she said. "You must go and see him in Washington. You speak the same language. You have the same ideals. I'm sure the President would be glad to have a chat with you."

It was midnight when we went to bed.

In that conversation about war, as now I remember, no word was said regarding Japan. We had been speaking and talking only of Hitler and his Germany. There seemed to the American mind no other threat to peace.

I went several times to the city of Boston, the most beautiful in New England and one of the most beautiful in the world. It still has an old-fashioned quality here and there, with many little streets of eighteenth-century houses as charming as Queen Anne's Gate in London, with steps leading up to front doorways with white porticoes and reminiscent, to the Englishman, of Kensington or the old streets in Westminster. But Boston now does not depend for its beauty on the eighteenth century. The modern apartment houses along the Fenway are very handsome in a fine setting, and there is a view of a noble city from the embankment along Charles River. The public parks and gardens are well laid out, and there is a spaciousness and dignity in Boston not found in many American cities which owe their growth to industry.

I spoke in the famous old Tavern Club in Boston, to which I had the honour of being invited. Its members are among the most notable and distinguished citizens—judges, lawyers, doctors, professors, architects, scientists, and the leaders of civic life. It has a clubhouse in which one feels instantly an atmosphere of tradition, dignity, and friendliness.

"You will be among friends here," I was told by my sponsor. "We are all admirers of England. Most of us know and love

England. You won't find any isolationists here. No one will heckle you when questions are asked. They will all want to make it easy for you."

There was a great gathering. I was introduced to the leading men, and I felt the real warmth of their welcome to me. There was no doubt about that, and I found the atmosphere comradely and kind.

I spoke about the war in Great Britain and described the ordeal through which we had passed. In the course of my remarks I paid a tribute to President Roosevelt as a great leader who had gained the admiration of my own folk. I was speaking before a great crowd of Republicans who have had their quarrels with President Roosevelt, but they had no qaurrel with his foreign policy, and they gave my words an applause which afterwards I recognised as generous. They listened with intense sympathy, and afterwards there was a lot of questioning by men who asked good questions. They wanted to know about Russia, about the possibility of a British attack across the Channel now that Germany was so heavily engaged. They asked me about the situation in Ireland and a score of other questions which I answered frankly to the best of my knowledge. There was one question asked that night which afterwards I expected and got in every hall and theatre and auditorium.

"What about Rudolf Hess?"

When I started on my lecture tour throughout the United States I had in my mind the background of New England, and it was a good foundation for further knowledge of what was moving in the minds of the American people.

IV

The Pacific Coast

AMERICAN LECTURE AGENTS are careless of geography, as it seems to those who talk for them. Their lecturers are not sent on a nice neat circuit from one city or state to another, according to the map, but travel hither and thither in an erratic course for hundreds or thousands of miles in the wildest way. It is not their fault. They have to fit in their engagements according to the dates open on the lists of those societies and groups who are making out their future schedules for the next lecture season. But it means endless railway travel to the speakers, in parlour cars and Pullman cars, in upper or lower bunks, by day and by night. Sleep is not always easy. American trains are the most luxurious in the world, but I have one grudge against them. There are no buffers between the coaches. In order to join up their couplings they just bang them together with jolts and jerks which shake one's teeth in one's head and the bones in one's body. These crashes in the night awaken one roughly or cause frightful dreams of earthquakes and cataclysms until one gets used to it, as the human brain and body can get used to almost anything.

But there is one advantage in this incessant railway travel that is well worth while to the student of life and character. One meets many interesting people and has, if one will, long talks with one's fellow travellers, with whom it is very easy to get into conversation. They are good conversationalists, these American travellers on long-distance trains, and always I have found them friendly, informative, and humorous men. Some of the best conversations in my life have been with American judges, lawyers, engineers, professors, doctors, and business-men sitting next to me in a parlour car or opposite at the dining table. On all these journeys I have never met one uncivil fellow or one who did not respond in the kindest way to my opening remarks or one who did not give me interesting information, generally told with wit, and good stories about American life and history. And often these men have spoken with a knowledge and wisdom and shrewdness and judgment about the world situation which has left me with the conviction that the average well-educated American is a fine type of civilised man in a world which has gone mad and bad over so many areas of insanity.

Now, this introduction is due to my having started my tour, after the lectures in New York and the speech in Boston, at Columbus, Ohio, to which state I had to return for other talks before flying to San Francisco.

I had a travelling companion who was to act as my A.D.C. on this and future journeys, apart from the trip to the Pacific coast. This was a very tall young man, just graduated from Brown University, by name of Robert Keedick, commonly

called Bob, and the son of Mr. Lee Keedick, the famous and
respected lecture agent of New York. It was a pleasure to
travel with Bob. The eyes of all ladies and many men went soft
at the sight of him. He was typical of American youth as pic-
tured in the *Saturday Evening Post* and as played by film stars
in Hollywood. He looked after me with vigilance and tender-
ness, though always he pretended that I was looking after him.
He received my telephone messages, guarded me from too
many social engagements, arranged transport and hotel ac-
commodations, and was liaison officer between myself and the
reporters and photographers, college girls who desired to interview me or get my autograph, and the societies who had
arranged my lectures, and the people in every city who were
good enough to invite me to their clubs, houses, and dinner
parties. Bob is not much of a conversationalist, which was rest-
ful, though when he talked there was always a laugh in it. We
beguiled many train journeys by playing chess and cards. We
fined each other a dime whenever either of us left something
behind in a hotel. We drank innumerable "cokes," coffees,
and ginger ales. We yawned in unison on railway platforms at
midnight and trod the streets of many cities. Without Bob
Keedick, now and then, I felt like a lost soul in a bewildering
world.

At Columbus, Ohio, the first man I met was an old acquaintance who took my thoughts back, twenty years or so, to
a strange and tragic chapter of history. We had last met in
Russia during a time of famine, when twenty-five million
people were starving on the Volga.

"Do you remember?" asked Mr. Clapp.

I remembered.

Now Russia was in the picture again, fighting with heroic

and amazing resistance against the full weight of the German mechanised armies. Nearly twenty years before, this genial man had worked under Hoover and Haskell on the American relief which, by a miracle of organization, had fed eleven million Russians for a year. My reports on the famine had helped to save four and a half million others—my one claim to a heavenly crown. It had been a great adventure in Russian villages where peasant families had lain down to die in verminous trains, through typhus-stricken crowds, in hospitals without medicines, where naked children huddled together for warmth, in a land laid waste by war and revolution, in Moscow and Leningrad and Kazan. Since then the Russians had pulled themselves together, built up a war machine, developed a technical skill which brought forth guns and tanks and rifles and ammunition.

"Russia is putting up a great fight," said Mr. Clapp. "It's a miracle."

Before my lecture that night I dined with him and his wife and a small group of people who were rather silent at first, until presently conversation went round the board, led by Mr. Clapp. I remember a very pleasant professor of English literature who was to be my chairman, and a little lady who was the wife of an American general. Inevitably the conversation came round to the war in Europe and to the ordeal in England. The little lady to my right became passionate about American apathy and complacency.

"We want waking up!" she said. "We are all asleep! One day we shall get a nasty shock. It will serve us damn well right!"

"What about Japan?" I asked.

Nobody seemed to think much about Japan.

After my lecture that night questions were asked by the audience. There was the usual enquiry about Rudolf Hess, and I remember two others.

"Why was Britain so unprepared and willing to let Germany rearm without doing anything about it?"

Not an easy question to answer. I said that we had clung onto the hope of peace. England had hated the idea of another war. We had made a religion of the League of Nations. It was an unsatisfactory answer.

"Why doesn't Britain attack Germany now that Russia is fighting so hard?"

I tried to explain our difficulties of transporting troops, owing to our heavy losses in ships, and the strain on our man power which prevented us from raising an army on the continental scale. Anyhow, we had to defend the British Isles from the threat of invasion and keep a big army at home for that purpose.

Something in my lecture, mostly about the war over England, must have touched my audience. Many people came up to express admiration for British courage and heroism.

"You have all been wonderful," they said. "We all want to help you as much as possible. Many of us are working for British War Relief."

"When you spoke of British man power, were you asking us to send an American Expeditionary Force?" asked one man.

"No," I told him, "I haven't come here to ask for anything. I am only here to tell you what is happening in England."

"We don't want to send our boys overseas," said the man. "I have a young son. I don't want to have him killed over in Europe."

"If I were an American father," I answered, "I should think as you do."

After the lecture some of my friends joined me in the hotel restaurant.

"I drink to England," said one of the ladies, touching my glass with hers. It seemed that my lecture had stirred her emotions. She had been a little stiff, I thought, at the dinner table, or a little reserved. Now I found her full of sympathy and very kind. She and her husband insisted on coming with us to the railway station, where we had to get a late train to Chicago, from which I was to fly to San Francisco. The wife of the man I had met in Russia took my arm and piloted me through the traffic.

"God bless dear England," she said when we parted.

I was very much touched.

Bob came with me to Chicago and saw me leave on the plane from the airport.

"A safe trip," he said. "I'll meet you in Fort Worth."

He was, I think, slightly apprehensive for my safety and a little doubtful whether I should ever get to Fort Worth after my visit to California.

I had a wonderful flight. No sense of nervousness was justified in this aircraft whose engines vibrated with a perfect rhythm and enormous power. I had faith in the two pilots whom I saw for a few moments before they went into the cockpit and locked the door behind them. I noticed that whenever one of them came out he was always careful to lock the door. There was a young woman who looked after us and handed us hot drinks and sandwiches from time to time. She was one of those aircraft hostesses who are specially selected for their good looks, their charm of manner, and their courage.

From time to time this lady came to sit by my side for a friendly conversation. I found her highly intelligent and well informed. We spoke about the war in Europe.

"It's a terrible world," she said. "Men won't learn sense. They just keep on destroying each other. I should have thought the last war would have taught them a lesson. Tell me more about England. How do your people stand up under all that bombardment?"

I told her more about England.

We flew through a cloudless sky into which presently there came the flaming feathers of a glorious sunset. Then dusk came, and, in a little while, darkness. We were flying through the night. We flew over high mountains, and the plane rocked and tossed a little, as though those mountains were trying to drag us down. Then it became quiet again and smooth, and our wings carried us quietly through the night sky over Salt Lake City and Denver and Sacramento and other cities. I have never seen anything so beautiful. I looked down upon cities of shining jewels sparkling like diamonds upon black velvet. All the lights were on and made geometrical patterns on the plain like strings of shining beads. They were cities of magic, fairy cities of a poet's dream.

We dropped down into Denver, and through the darkness a new passenger came on and took the only vacant space, which was next to me. He was an officer of the R.A.F. and we knew each other. He knew my son and my family; I had met him with intimate friends of his and mine. He had played tennis in an English garden I knew with a family of dark-eyed girls—Clarita and Anita and several others. The odds against our meeting at night in Denver city were some hundreds of millions to one.

"It's *very* odd we should meet like this," he said several times. He was on his way to India across the Pacific, and I envied him his trip.

"I don't know that I'm to be envied," he answered with a quiet laugh, "but it will certainly be interesting."

We flew on through the night, chatting about the war, which did not seem to be going in our favour, apart from the unexpected resistance of Russia. "Japan is playing a tricky game," he told me.

I was still entranced by the magic of American cities beneath our wings, and presently I saw something so exquisite, so enchanting, so otherworldly that I gave a little cry. It was San Francisco, spread out below us in lines of fairy light. We could see the whole sweep of it round the coast, all shining like a city of stars. There was a myriad of those stars down there as bright as the Koh-i-noor on black silk, marking out the streets, the avenues, the boulevards, the parks and gardens, the sea front of this great city of the Pacific.

"That looks rather marvellous," said the group captain of the R.A.F. in his quiet way of understatement.

"I have never seen anything so magical," I answered. "It's beyond belief. This is the most beautiful vision that one could see in the world. It's unreal. It's supernatural."

We flew down lower. Our wings slanted and the scene below us tilted. We were coming down. Beneath us we could see the aerodrome brightly lighted. Our great aircraft skimmed down like a swallow; its wheels skimmed the earth slightly. We taxied round a wide sweep and came to rest outside the white buildings of the airport.

"Happy landing," said my R.A.F. friend. "Beautifully done."

It was on the afternoon of the next day that I looked over the waters of the Pacific into a golden haze. No shadow crept across. No word was spoken by friends of mine about an island people out there thousands of miles away—little yellow men who at that very time when I was looking across the water, upon the Pacific Ocean, were busy with their maps and charts, with their little eyes straining at dots which marked the positions of Pearl Harbor, Wake Island, and Guam, and Luzon in the Philippines.

"There are many changes in San Francisco since last you were here," said my friend Henry Braden, who drove me from one point to another along the Pacific coast. "I must show you our two new bridges."

With the pride of all Californians in their own cities and state, he showed me two great bridges, higher, he told me, than any other bridges in the world, as far as he knew—280 feet high and very long. I looked at them and was duly impressed. But for some reason my mind travelled farther than the last span of the bridges and went on the quick wings of imagination to the other side of the ocean. I remembered a conversation with a naval friend of mine named Bernacchi, an explorer who had been to the Antarctic with Scott and Shackleton and lately had visited Borneo and Malaya, where he had interests in rubber.

"The Japanese," he told me, "have their eyes on Malaya and the Dutch East Indies. One day we shall have to fight for those possessions. As sure as fate the Japanese will make a grab for them."

I remembered, also, a number of speeches by Japanese generals and admirals which I had translated from German reports. They made no secret of their intention to seize the

Dutch East Indies and Malaya when destiny should decide the time—not far away. In an English garden not long before my coming to the United States I had had a long conversation with the Japanese Ambassador to the Court of St. James's and with his military attaché. They desired peace with Britain. They gave me little pamphlets presenting the Japanese case in China.

"The situation is very critical," said the Japanese Ambassador. "I am very much afraid that it is becoming very grave."

Looking out to the Pacific Ocean, I thought of those words and asked a question of my friend.

"Is there any danger from Japan?"

He did not seem to be worried by any thought of danger from that direction. He was more worried by the sea haze which hid some of the beauties of his coast when he drove me up to Telegraph Hill and showed me other views.

Mr. and Mrs. Braden, whom I had known in England, were my guardian angels in San Francisco and entertained me in their home, where I heard good talk about American politics and English ways and was asked many questions about the buildings which had been hit in London. But I met other friends and other angels who were very kind to me in California.

My lecture was under the auspices of the Town Hall Forum in San Francisco. This was organised by a man of dynamic energy, restless industry, and vivid personality—Dr. Rappaport. He had an office in the Clift Hotel where I was staying, and these rooms buzzed with great activities. Dr. Rappaport shook hands with me warmly, rushed to the telephone which rang every two seconds, introduced me to his colleagues and assistants, gave orders down the telephone for certain printed bills, summoned the press to interview me, called upon photographers to take me at all angles, and kept up a stream of conversation while doing six jobs at once. He spoke with good humour, with passion, with irony, with eloquence. I thought: This man ought to lecture instead of me. I can't compete with him.

He was a bit doubtful of me, I thought, after his first searching glance. He thought I lacked fire and was one of those theoretical idealists who would bore his audience by mild platitudes regarding the spirit of England, which was my subject.

"Don't be afraid of your audience," he told me. "Let them have something good and strong. I'm told that they don't want propaganda. That's all nonsense. Give them propaganda! They need a lot of it. Denounce the isolationists. Ridicule them! Tell these people the real facts. Don't be timid and evasive. They'll take anything if you speak with sincerity. Tell them that this is their war as well as England's. Don't spare your language about Hitler and all his demons."

He became inspired; he made a very fine speech; his eyes flashed fire. His hands were restless and dramatic. I became more and more convinced that I was no orator. I became more and more certain that I should disappoint him when I faced the enormous audience he had attracted to his Town Hall Forum.

Dr. Rappaport worked me hard. In his office I signed so many copies of my books that my wrist tired. In my room at the hotel I was interviewed and photographed from all angles. Twice in one day I was taken over to the radio stations to be interviewed on the air, first by a talented young man who did his job very well and then by a lady who took away my fright by her quiet, soothing, and sympathetic way. To me it is a terrifying thing to go on the air, and it is especially alarming when one has to face a microphone and answer questions never seen before with an immediate reply. My tongue fairly clove to the roof of my mouth before one of these ordeals. I had to suck, as secretly as possible, some of those tablets called Life Savers, in order to keep my saliva going. But in spite of my intense nervousness I acquitted myself successfully, at least as far as not dropping heavy bricks or drying up in my answers.

The Clift Hotel in San Francisco was, like most hotels in big American cities, a great palace with vast numbers of rooms piled up to a high altitude and everything that man desires, or ought to desire, in comfort, convenience, and abundance. On each floor was a lady who played the part of hostess, kept a sharp eye on the guests, and when they left said, "Come again," in a most gracious way. My floor lady was friendly and helpful. In private life she was a student of music and did this job at the Clift to provide herself with the necessary livelihood.

"How is it," she asked one evening, "that mankind is so incurably foolish, and yet the average of intelligence seems getting higher?"

That was a poser not easy to answer.

"The tragedy of the modern world," I said, "is the inability of the average intelligence to control its own destiny. In many countries the machinery of government is seized by groups of gunmen with their following of young thugs. The reasonable and intelligent crowd are powerless."

The floor lady sighed and glanced at two people waiting for the elevator.

"I can't make out," she told me, "why civilisation has allowed these things to happen. When you think of all the struggles we've had to make a civilised world and all the genius and wisdom of the ages, it seems queer that we should be in such a mess now."

"We've all made ghastly mistakes," I said.

She nodded.

"We've made a few in the United States. But I suppose you English people can take care of this war?"

"We would like some help," I told her. "We're rather overstrained."

"I'm devoted to music," she said. "But it doesn't seem to do any good to anyone."

"It's very important," I answered. "In this world of darkness the musicians and the poets and the painters keep the lamps burning. All will be lost if those go out."

"I'm glad to hear you say that," said the floor lady. "It's hard to keep one's faith nowadays in the spiritual side of life. In this hotel it's difficult sometimes."

One of the two people who had been waiting for the elevator gave a laugh.

"You two are having a grand time with each other!" he said. "You're getting down to fundamentals. Great stuff!"

The floor lady blushed at this irony.

"Didn't know you were listening, Mr. Schwarz," she said. "It was a private conversation anyhow."

"Oh, don't mind me," said Mr. Schwarz. "Keep going!"

He waved his hand as he entered the elevator.

My friends drove me round San Francisco. We went through Chinatown, and it looked different after my exploration of it twenty years before, when I had been guided through its labyrinths by an American detective who knew its underground passages leading from one house to another, like a rabbit warren. I went with him into rooms where Chinese were smoking opium or playing fan-tan. I came up into little Chinese temples with lamps and flowers, for ancestor worship. I touched the chubby hands of Chinese babies and saw women with their feet squeezed into tiny slippers.

"It's all cleaned up now," said one of my friends. "And these Chinese make very good citizens."

It was the middle of October in the year of grace 1941.

The population of San Francisco looked to me very cheerful as they went on their daily round. There was no look of anxiety in their eyes. They were unconscious of any approaching peril when their city would be blacked out and they would hear the howl of sirens for air-raid warnings. It was less than three months before black bats of death were to come out of a blue sky to Pearl Harbor in Hawaii, diving low upon American battleships and dropping tons of high explosives without a declaration of war. There was no foreboding. No word of anxious apprehension reached my ears. Mr. Cordell Hull was writing notes to the Japanese, stating the fundamental principles of American policy. Nobody was excited about that academic discussion. At least I met no such person, though there may have been men and women who saw the shadow creeping across the Pacific. In the sailors' hostels and low dives there may have been men who knew what was happening behind the scenes in Japan. I did not meet them.

In Dr. Rappaport's rooms a quiet, thoughtful-looking man, whom I guessed to be a Jew, lingered to get a few words with me.

duced many fine plays in this verdant setting. But next August they will not be there because there will be other things to do, less joyous. Their drama will be acted elsewhere, and it will be a grim affair in the heroic style. But no premonition of that came to my friend Langfield or to the pleasant fellow I met with him when I was there . . . though it was less than three months away from the scream of bombs over Pearl Harbor in Hawaii.

My time had come to leave San Francisco and to go farther down the Californian coast to Los Angeles.

"Come again," said the floor lady who studied music. "I have much enjoyed our conversation."

Before I left I had a visit from the organisers of my lecture, Dr. and Mrs. Rappaport. They brought me rich gifts—a bottle of California port, a bottle of sherry, and a bottle of sauterne. They said kind and generous things.

"God bless you and God bless England," said Mrs. Rappaport in a soft voice.

The journey to Los Angeles was through dramatic scenery between the ocean and the mountains. The train had observation cars, and at intervals the passengers were addressed by a voice through a loud-speaker calling their attention to the beauties of nature on either side of them. It rather spoiled the beauties of nature.

In Los Angeles I put up at a pleasant hotel where I soon became friendly with the staff. At the cash desk was a young woman with very dark hair and a look of suppressed impatience with life and coffee shops. When I handed up my check she read some words which had been written on it by the girl who had served me.

"Sir Philip Gibbs."

"That's right," I told her.

"Yes, but why?"

"Why, what?"

"Why Sir?"

"I was knighted by the King."

"Yes, but why?"

"I was a war correspondent in the last war. I suppose the King thought I had done my job fairly well."

"And had you?"

"I hope so."

"Well, you ought to know."

This direct questioning was rather embarrassing. At another time this girl told me something about herself and her views on life. She had been in the hotel business in California and Honolulu and other places. Her experience had been that women were more difficult than men. She would rather deal with three thousand men than three hundred women. On the whole she thought life a silly business anyhow.

The floor lady took a lot of trouble for me in finding the addresses of some film directors in Hollywood.

"I'm afraid they're not in the book," she told me. "They keep themselves out of the directory because they would be plagued to death by out-of-work or would-be film stars. I don't blame them. No, I don't think you will find Alexander Korda or Alfred Hitchcock."

After prolonged search she found Zoltan Korda, a friend of mine and the brother of Alexander and Vincent—those three Hungarian brothers who had made a big success in England and by their work at Denham in the London Film Studios, where first they produced *Henry VIII* with Charles Laughton in the star part. My son had worked for them a good deal.

"Well, that's a bit of luck," said the floor lady brightly. "I'm really glad that I was able to help you."

On the following morning I set out in an ordinary omnibus for Hollywood, which was a journey of half an hour or so. Thence I took a taxi to the centre of that headquarters of romance which finds its way into all the picture palaces in all the cities and towns of England and America and, before this war, into every country. My taxi driver asked me whether I had come from England recently, when he recognised my accent, and added with a laugh, when I replied, "Then you and I must be mortal enemies. I'm a Hungarian."

"Do you feel like that?" I asked.

He did not feel like that. From the viewpoint of the United States he thought the war in Europe looked a rotten business. Lousy. He hoped the American people wouldn't get into it. He was now an American citizen. All the same he hoped England would smash Hitler.

"That man is a monomaniac. He's drenching the world in blood because he's crazy for power."

I put up for a while in the Hotel Roosevelt in Hollywood, a very elegant place in a straggling town which surprised me because it was unlike Hollywood as I had imagined it. Down its main street were the usual lines of small shops and department stores, including the inevitable Woolworth, with movie houses and drugstores and hot-dog restaurants—by no means beautiful or romantic. The film studios were a long way off, and the houses of the film stars and directors were still further, on the Beverly Hills and overlooking the coast.

While I was sitting one evening in the Roosevelt an elderly man came in with his daughter. They both looked a little dejected, and I was startled when the father turned to the girl and said, "I guess you'll be shot tomorrow morning."

"Think so?" she asked with an air of indifference at this grim supposition.

It was a moment or two before I grasped the situation. This was one of the girls trying her luck in Hollywood. She was to be shot for the camera and not by a firing squad.

I met the Kordas in their studios. They were very busy but received me cordially. Alexander had grown rather grey since last I had seen him. Zoltan looked in better health and had not lost his very pleasing smile. Vincent spoke English more fluently. I saw part of a film they were making from Kipling's *Jungle Book* and lunched with Vincent and Zoli Korda in a Hollywood restaurant.

They spoke gravely about the war and were keen to know about familiar places in London and whether they still stood up after the air raids.

Vincent stared at me sombrely now and then.

"Hitler is the new Ghengis Khan," he said. "I don't see yet how he is to be stopped. The Germans are still very strong. How do you account for the continued resistance of Russia? That is a miracle."

He told me that he worked very hard but found work an anodyne to thought of all the world's agony.

That evening I dined with Zoltan Korda and his beautiful wife Joan. He drove me up to his house on the Appian Way. It was dark when we arrived, and he showed me the view from this mountaintop. It was quite marvellous. It was like the view I had seen from the aeroplane. There below lay Los Angeles with its myriad lights like shining jewels, a city of cut diamonds laid out on a black cloth.

Zoli Korda and his wife lived in an enchanting house on the top of a mountain. Its main room was like an old English barn, though very white and clean, with a high roof and gallery. There was a log fire on an open hearth, and it was charmingly furnished. Mrs. Korda, who was once Joan Gardner, had not changed since I had met her last in Paris or since she had played the chief part in a film story of Oxford —*Men of Tomorrow,* by my son Anthony. That is to say she looked a beautiful young English girl, very simple and very straight in her manner. But she was now the mother of David, with whom I fell in love. For David, aged four, was a fine and friendly fellow. He appeared first on the high gallery.

"Come down," said Mrs. Korda.

"Shall I throw myself over?" he asked.

"Better not."

He came trotting down the stairs and shook hands with me gravely. Afterwards we turned over the pages of a book by Munro Leaf—*Manners Can Be Fun.*

That night I dined with the Kordas down in Los Angeles at Murphy's restaurant, which was crowded with cheerful people eating prodigiously. The Americans are hearty eaters, and in this land of abundance the portions served out to them are always four times as much as I can face without blanching. I had come from a severely rationed nation where food is so scarce that everybody talks about it morning, noon, and night, and where the meat ration for a week is limited to eighteen pence, or twenty-six cents, for each person. Zoli Korda ordered a steak. It was a steak of prodigious proportions. I regarded it with stupefaction. Zoli regarded it with satis-faction. "It looks good," he said. But he left half of it, I noticed. What a waste, I thought. That would have fed an English

family for a week. But it was not wasted. Later in the evening
a neat parcel was put on our table. On it were the words,
"Murphy likes dogs too."

It was a noisy restaurant. Americans like their restaurants
noisy. They like life noisy. Quietude to them is death. They
like the radio blaring forth as soon as they open their eyes in the
morning, and all day long it blares in the American home while
the women work and the children play. It travels with them
in their motorcars fixed up with a radio set. It is turned on in
trains. In railway stations one waits to the music of military
bands and to dramatised advertisements of American products. It is only at midnight that tired hands reach out and
switch over that noise from the outer world telling of war and
death between tributes to Kreml Hair Tonic and White Owl
Cigars and filling the ether with the false laughter from radio
studios, the organised pep of heart-cheering talks, the wild
music of jazz bands, the mirth and frolic of studio parties,
the news of ships sunk and sailors drowned, and armies moving
in retreat, leaving their dead and dying in the snow, and the
wonderful virtues of peppermint chewing gum, Old Gold
Cigarettes, and artificial height makers for short men who
"now may be taller than she is."

Murphy's restaurant was full of noise. Mr. Murphy himself
made some of it. He had a fine baritone which almost lifted
the food off my plate. He was followed by a lady with a
contralto voice who sang with great emotion and real talent,
"There'll Always Be an England."

Zoli Korda looked across at me, and I saw his lips move.
With some difficulty I caught his words.

"They do not sing 'There'll always be a Germany,' " he
said, "or 'There'll always be a France.' There is a natural

alliance between the United States and England. It's very
significant."

Next day in Hollywood I took lunch at another house, very
much like an English farmhouse, on another hill above the
town. It belonged to Alfred Hitchcock and his wife. To me it
was like going home, because Mr. and Mrs. Hitchcock came
from my own village, from Shamley Green in Surrey, and
their maid Gladys came from Shamley Green, and their
chauffeur, an amusing fellow with a great gift for humorous
conversation, had driven Mr. Hitchcock's car through the
Surrey lanes. We talked of Shamley Green and the life there
during the air bombardment of England. I told them about
my évacués, mothers and children from London, who had
been parked in my billiard room for many months, with feuds
and vendettas between the two mothers and the children.

Alfred Hitchcock found these stories amusing. He saw a film
story in them. "You ought to write about all that," he said.
"It's great stuff."

I had another talk with Vincent Korda in his studio, where
he introduced me to a young Norwegian artist who had
escaped from his own country after its seizure by the enemy.

Vincent Korda spoke gravely about the war and the state of
the world, which was so terrible to his imagination that he was
glad of being overworked. He is a man with a sweet and
gentle nature—an artist with an artist's philosophy of life,
which has faith in beauty and form and style outraged and
killed by the war lords and the gunmen. I was glad to sit in his
studio for an hour and to get the warm grasp of his hand.
Here, I thought, is one of the fine rare souls of this cruel
world.

V

Texas with the Wide Horizon

In the parlour car of the train to Fort Worth in Texas, through the desert of Arizona, vast in its barren vista of brown earth and yellow grass, a little man crossed over and spoke to me.

"Say, you ought not to be so hard on your eyes. Forgive me, but I'm a doctor."

I had been straining in a poor light to read a book of small type.

I looked up and said, "Thanks," and put the book away. The doctor, a small-sized man, sturdily built and with genial brown eyes, sat down by my side.

"You're English, aren't you?"

I nodded and said that I hadn't been out very long.

"What part of England?" he asked.

I mentioned Surrey and saw his eyes light up.

"Surrey is a sweet county," he said. "Not that I've ever been

there. I only know England through its books and poetry. But
I know it pretty well. Its geography is in my heart. I know
the Tennyson country and the Wordsworth country. I know
where Meredith lived and the London of Dickens and Thackeray and Charles Lamb. I know Shakespeare's England and
all his characters. Try me out."

I tried him out with a few quotations which instantly he
capped. Through the long, roadless wastes of the Arizona
desert we recited Henry V's speech before the Battle of
Agincourt and met a fool together in the Forest of Arden.

"Do they read Tennyson nowadays?" he asked. "I love
the music of his lines.

> *"Tears, idle tears, I know not what they mean,*
> *Tears from the depths of some divine despair."*

He quoted lines from Shelley, Keats, Browning, and the
Elizabethan poets.

"I live in a little town in New Mexico," he told me. "There's
not much intellectual society there, but I dip into the old books
and don't feel alone."

He knew all the old books better than I did, though I had
read them as a boy. He loved George Eliot, who is now on the
back shelf. He loved Thackeray, whom I have loved. He was
a devotee of Dickens and, in his obscure little town in New
Mexico, consorted with Sam Weller and Mr. Pickwick and
David Copperfield and Tom Pinch. I found him an enchanting little man full of good humour and kindliness and love of
humanity.

"This war in Europe," he said, "is a dreadful setback. I
can't bear to think of all the old shrines of history which have
been destroyed in London. It's sad to think of Middle Temple

Hall and dear old Gray's Inn. Hitler is possessed by the devil or by seventy devils. He has declared war on civilisation and all human liberties. England took up the challenge first. We are following on, very slowly but very surely. We're already fighting an undeclared war. Our President is playing for time, but beyond a doubt we shall be in fully before long. The British people and the American people, who believe in the same ideals and have the same heritage of law, will defeat this beast which has come out of the old lairs. I'm sure of that. There's no alternative. This monstrous attack on all the decencies and all the beauty of life must be defeated, and we've got to take our share. To the American mind, especially to the semi-educated, it all seems a long way off, and they don't realise how it touches American interests or security. The President is educating them. Before long we shall be by your side."

We talked a long time, hour after hour, while night came over the desert and we travelled through darkness in a lighted car. Presently I left him to go to my little bedroom, but on the way there I jolted against a very tall, good-looking young man who was drinking some iced water from a tap and a paper cup.

"English, aren't you?" he asked with a smile. "I heard you talking."

"Yes, I can't help my English accent."

"How's the war over there? Not too good, eh?"

"Not too bad," I told him. "We're stronger now. And the Germans have given us a respite. They're busy in Russia and taking some hard knocks."

Presently this tall young man came and sat on the edge of my bed and smoked a cigarette with me. He had been brought up in France and was going to marry a girl who had been brought up in Biarritz. They were going to live in a place called Midland, in Texas, a little industrial town. He was a geologist and mineralogist. That would be his job there. It would be a bit of a contrast to the south of France and Biarritz.

"I'm against this war," he told me. "I dislike the idea of America getting into it. For purely personal and selfish reasons. It's such a great interference with what one wants to do. I want to marry and bring up a little family. I want to get on with my job. Why should I be drafted and drilled and made to waste all my good time and then be killed on some unpleasant battlefield? Most men of my age feel like that. We're not cowards. We're not abnormally afraid of death—though I prefer life—but we want to get on with our studies or with our jobs. All this interference is so annoying. The fellows in the army now don't see the object of it. Where are we going to fight? Who are we going to fight? It's not our war yet. It's all such waste of time, with a lot of messing about and demoralisation and boredom—without a definite purpose. My friends in the army are sick and tired of it already."

"Perhaps the purpose will come," I warned him. "Perhaps the United States will be drawn into this war by inevitable facts."

"Maybe that will happen," he answered lightly. "But I'm going to sleep and forget it. Good night, sir."

Above the Arizona desert through which we were still travelling the stars were shining in a clear sky. They were the same stars which looked down upon England and my little home there and all my friends talking or sleeping—yes, surely sleeping now—behind their blacked-out windows. The Germans were getting near to Moscow under those stars. Frightful agonies were happening in the snows of Russia. But it was quiet in the Pacific on this night of October 27 in the year 1941. The dark tragedy of December and Pearl Harbor lay behind the veil of fate where little yellow men were plotting.

I arrived in Fort Worth, Texas, and in a very short time made many friends there who, I believe, will remain my friends. They showed me something of Texas, a state larger than England and France, so that it needs a lifetime to know it all. They took me into their homes. I saw their cattle and horses. I met Miss Elizabeth Miller, who is worth a journey to Texas. I met the Stripling family, who mean a lot to Fort Worth. I fell in love with Texas, with the spirit of its people, with its friendliness to a lonely stranger, with its adventure of life and something in its air.

Fort Worth is not a beautiful city, but it is built high and built strong, and from one of its high windows which belonged to my bedroom in the Hotel Texas I looked across to its flat prairies stretching away, as it seemed, to infinity.

"Texas," said a man of Oklahoma, "has most rivers and and least water." The rivers run dry in summer.

"It has most cattle and least milk." They are cattle breeders and not cowmen.

"In Texas," said the man of Oklahoma, "the people look farthest and see least."

I stared down at the city of Fort Worth by night from my bedroom window, and I remember its painted picture now—painted in many colours on my brain. Below me were two long parallel lines of light—red, green, and yellow—and on either side of these lines were clumps of light shining brightly with red, green, and yellow splashes. They were the neon signs of the city, twinkling, sparkling, turning, writhing. Above the massive blocks of buildings, like mediæval fortresses in the night, black as ink, the clear sky was alight with the blaze of blast furnaces. Strange, fantastic sounds came up to my windows as I lay in bed trying to sleep but not sleeping. Bells were ringing—though heaven alone knows why, in the small hours. Police sirens wailed like air-raid warnings. There was the backfiring of motor vehicles and the honking of their horns. But the most startling and, to me, inexplicable noise was like the moaning of Brobdingnagian cows in agony. Because of the warmth of the weather in this amazing fall I had to keep my windows open, letting in this cacophony. Those cows disturbed me most until I discovered that they were the calling of the sirens from streamlined trains, shunting and moving down there on the railroad.

There was another reason why I could not sleep that first night in Fort Worth. I had met a realist, who faced facts fearlessly. He was an Englishman, long resident in Fort Worth and one of its pillars. He took a critical view about the war, about the lack of preparedness and the revolutionary elements in American labour, and the failure of statesmen and soldiers to do little sums in arithmetic before they made war, and the weakness of the Russians against the mechanised armies of Germany, and the slow lag of time in American factories and plants, and the complacency of the American mind, unaware of danger creeping near. Everything he said was a truthful analysis, by a keen mind, of the situation then. If one looked at the arithmetical side of things, the sum looked bad. If one looked back at all our ghastly mistakes, the future did not look bright. Russia was yielding and falling back. There was a pincers reaching out to Moscow. Russian losses must be prodigious. Great Britain, short of man power, was not attacking in Libya or elsewhere. An invasion of the Continent was out of the question for lack of shipping and many other reasons. I could not deny these things. When presented in array, grimly etched, the picture was exceedingly unpleasant, and I tossed on my bed listening to those unaccustomed noises of the night.

Young Robert Keedick had rejoined me in Fort Worth, and I was glad to see him again and have his friendly help in business and social affairs. He made a great success with the ladies of that city, who were charmed by his youth and sense of humour. He had a great time with me in Texas and was lucky in finding a companion of his own age, specially produced for him by my English-born friend Herbert Walker, who had grim forebodings about the war but a comradely understanding of young men. He introduced Bob Keedick to one of the prettiest girls in Texas and to one of the most intelligent. She was a dark-haired, merry-eyed damsel who had been educated at Smith College, and Bob Keedick spent pleasant hours with her when I was otherwise engaged. I remember how he made an appointment with her one night over the telephone. It was like a monologue by an American Noel Coward. No words were wasted.

"What's the setup for this evening?"

"That's fine."

"Do you think so?"

"Well, that's fine."

"I poked my nose out a bit too much last night."

"No?"

"Well, that's fine."

Everything seemed fine to American youth at that time. The war in Europe was a long way off. It needn't interfere too much with the fun of life in the United States. Anyhow, it was good to dance and laugh and talk intelligently to a nice girl. . . . At that time none of the Bob Keedicks of the United States thought that in less than two months they would all be called up for active service in a war which would be the greatest ordeal in American history. In less than two months Robert Keedick had been accepted for officers' training in the United States Navy.

Outside the Hotel Texas, one morning when I was strolling up and down to get some fresh air and sunshine, I heard two news vendors shouting out excitedly—some hot news to sell their papers.

"United States in naval war!"

"American ships cleared for action!"

"United States in naval war!"

"President orders instant action!"

I listened to this chant of grim tidings. Those two raucous voices were shouting news which would alter the history of their own people and of all mankind. But the citizens of Fort Worth did not seem to be interested. They hurried past without stopping to grab one of those newssheets. I was the only man who bought one at the corner of the hotel.

On that Tuesday, October 28, the President of the United States had declared that shooting had started after the sinking of United States ships by German submarines. He had given orders to shoot at sight. He had introduced a bill to arm merchant ships. "We are at battle stations," said the President. In a speech before the Navy League he advocated a revision of the Neutrality Act, not only as far as arming merchant ships, but permitting them also to carry American goods into the harbours of our friends. Merchant ships, he said, must be protected by the Navy.

This was a challenge, not only to Hitler, but to the isolationists in his own country who had already condemned him for pursuing a policy which inevitably would lead America into war.

Meanwhile the President was perturbed by the threat of strikes in the coal industry and on the railways. One of my friends in Fort Worth tried to enlighten me on this peril to the United States by describing in great detail the political conflict aroused by the A.F. of L. (the American Federation of Labor) and its rival power, the C.I.O. (Congress of Industrial Organizations), under the leadership of John L. Lewis. Critics of the President accused him of playing into the hands of revolutionary labour. They accused him of pandering to a system which demanded a kind of despotism for union men within the factories.

"We tell you what men you can employ."

"We tell you how much they must be paid."

"We tell you what men you can or cannot dismiss."

The power of the trade unions, said the critics of Mr. Roosevelt, had become a tyranny interfering with the free traditions of American industry. It shows the cloven hoof when it tries to force a strike in the coal mines when we are wanting to go full speed ahead on the production of armaments for Britain and Russia.

On this day of history the President had asked John L. Lewis for the third time to avert the strike which would paralyse the industrial effort of the nation.

The people of Texas were following these things with interest but without excitement. From one little lady who had invited me to the Women's Club of Fort Worth I heard some shrewd and witty comments about the political situation and human nature anywhere. This was Miss Elizabeth Miller, who looked like Jane Austen and spoke like that great humourist Sydney Smith. She is hard of hearing and, though she introduces lecturers to her club, doesn't stay for their lectures because she cannot hear them. That saves her a lot of wasted attention and puts her in a pleasing position. She has a great gift of epigram. I remember at random some of those pointed comments which kept me laughing.

Speaking of one American politician, she said, "He is one of those men who keep themselves in the public eye—like a cinder."

Speaking of an English statesman, she said, "His coat of arms should bear two double crosses on a yellow field."

Speaking of elderly folk, she said, "People become quieter when they get older. They've more to keep quiet about."

One little old lady who belonged to the Women's Club came up to me and spoke about the war. "If I had that man Hitler in my hands," she said, "I would twist his neck."

Miss Elizabeth Miller's brother, who drove me in his car from their house to my hotel, asked me why the Royal Air Force did not bomb Germany. That same question had been asked me by people in my audiences and always astonished me.

"They have been bombing Germany," I told him, "for more than a year. Surely you have read the news day by day in the British communiqués?"

"No," he answered. "I can't say that I have."

"They have bombed Berlin more than sixty times," I told him, "but more important than that is their bombing of German industrial centres like Mannheim and Düsseldorf and Essen. They have done fearful destruction in the Ruhr, which is the headquarters of German armaments. I have seen aerial photographs.showing all that. Then they have bombed Bremen and Hamburg time and time again, to say nothing of Kiel and Wilhelmshaven. And when our bombers make a raid now they go out in strong numbers—three hundred at a time."

"Well, I'm glad to hear it," said Mr. Miller. "But there must be something wrong with your news service. The American people don't get to hear that."

There must have been something wrong with our news service or something wrong with its presentation in the American press. Numbers of people told me they were perplexed and uneasy because they believed that we were not giving back to the Germans any punishment for their raids over England. It was hard to convince them that we had done fearful damage as far as our planes could reach.

It was with Miss Elizabeth Miller that I met Mrs. Tyrell, Mrs. Wilkinson, Mrs. Stripling, and other ladies of Texas, who showed me their state—or a tiny bit of it—their homes, their farms, and their way of life.

Mrs. Stripling seemed to me typical of all that is best in American family life and in the American tradition. She is an old lady who, as a child of six in the Southern states, saw the fires of the Civil War as Sherman attacked at Atlanta. "The South was ruined," she told me, "and my young husband and I came to Fort Worth and established the Stripling Stores. I am still very proud of them."

She has a large family of daughters. and grandchildren. Thirty-four of them sit down to her table on holidays and feast days. There was a selection of them when I had the privilege of sitting down at her table and listening to the reminiscences of an old lady whose mind is still alert and humorous and who has the manners of a *grande dame* of the old regime. She reminded me of the chief character in a play written by my son and Cosmo Hamilton, with some work of my own. *The Aunt in England,* it was called, and dealt with an old lady like Mrs. Stripling, though the imaginary character was an English duchess.

She and one of her married daughters had been to England and had made a pilgrimage to Meredith's house at Dorking and remembered going into an English rectory whose parson they had met by accident. To them this visit to England was like a fairy tale. They were lovers of England and English books and English ways of life. The old lady was reading again *The Mill on the Floss* by George Eliot—and I remember it was my mother's favourite book. "The young people only read trash nowadays," she told me. The hearts of the Stripling family bled at the thought of England under bombardment and of all the old shrines of history in London and other cities which had been destroyed.

I had a delightful dinner with this family, and over the long mahogany table, laden with good food, there was lively conversation. We discussed, I remember, the characters in *Gone with the Wind* and the quality of Scarlett, its vivacious and passionate and selfish little heroine.

One of Mrs. Stripling's daughters spoke about her small boy.

"When I told him I was going to meet an English knight he was very thrilled and asked if you would appear in armour, with a plume in your helm."

Another married daughter with dark, merry eyes was interested in the origin of words and challenged me when I said "drought" instead of "drouth." She wheeled in Webster's dictionary—that noble tome—and we turned up other words differently used by Americans and English.

There was a laugh from all the family when one of them saw a number of my books on a side table.

"I believe Mother wants you to autograph them but hasn't the courage to ask you."

"That is why I put them there," said the old lady calmly.

I felt very much at home with this American family and was exceedingly moved at their good wishes for England.

"We shall pray for your dear country," said Mrs. Stripling.

"Our prayers will be for England," said one of the daughters.

No one there in that drawing room guessed that before many weeks had passed their own country would be in the same war, beginning with dreadful tragedy. They thought only of Britain's ordeal by fire.

On the following day one of these laughing ladies drove me out of the city towards where I looked to the far horizon over an endless plain.

"Out there are the ranches," she told me. "Some of them are pretty big—thirty thousand acres or so."

I heard of one ranch in Texas of three hundred thousand acres with fifteen hundred head of cattle on it.

I went to one of the smaller ranches—not more than seven hundred and fifty acres or so. It belonged to a little lady named Mrs. Wilkinson, with whom I had tea at Miss Elizabeth Miller's, who in the course of it said, "I'm trying to be very English," and anyhow was very charming and humorous. It was not really very English, because in England we do not put the teacup on a plate, but the tea tasted just as well that way.

Mrs. Wilkinson manages her own ranch near Fort Worth and has, I understand, another in Tennessee, running to thousands of acres which she also looks after or "takes care of," as they would say. She is a small-sized lady but has the will power and spirit of small-sized men like Nelson and Napoleon. There is nothing she does not know about pedigreed cattle or Tennessee walking horses, which she breeds with great success. She showed me her prize bulls and her show cows. Being a city-bred man, I was a trifle nervous at first in getting close to her bulls, but they were tame and gentle creatures and built on majestic lines. Even I could see that they had noble blood and were kings of their race. They were handled by an earnest young man who looked like a college professor and who had made a deep study of cattle breeding.

He showed off his stock, and there were loud cries of admiration from his lady visitors. "Oh, isn't he glorious! . . . Oh, what a noble fellow!"

One of his cows was called Mae West and excited other screams of wonderment in her beauty and bulk.

What astonished me in this ranch and others was the small amount of labour with which they are run. Three men will look after a ranch of fifteen hundred acres and keep it in good shape.

"Come and look at my Tennessee walking horses," cried Mrs. Wilkinson presently. "I am sure you will fall in love with them."

I did. They were beautiful creatures as they were brought out for inspection, with a long, walking stride very easy and comfortable for gentlemen farmers riding round their estates, with two other gears, as motorists would say—the trot and the canter.

Mr. Wilkinson, the husband of the little lady who managed the ranches, was president of a bank in Fort Worth and a serious-minded man with a very gentle courtesy. He drove me over his estate and showed me the site of a new house where one day he hopes to make his home. It was on rising ground with a fair wide view over the countryside where there were clumps of mesquite trees and live oaks, or evergreen oaks, as we should call them.

On the way back to the city Mr. Wilkinson drove me in his car and we had a thoughtful talk. He pointed out an enormous bombing plant in the distance.

"When that is in full production it will be stupendous," he told me.

Then he spoke about labour conditions and the general welfare of the people.

"America has recovered from the depression," he said. "Every man can get a job if he wants one, and the wages are high. Of course there is strong feeling in certain sections against John L. Lewis, the Labour leader. He is accused of playing a revolutionary game."

Mr. Wilkinson spoke about the international situation as it bore down upon American finance.

"New York bankers," he said, "are apt to get scared. They are more steady in Chicago and the Middle West. Here in Texas we have the old business tradition. Sentiment and honour still go with business affairs. We're not so ruthless as in the East."

He hoped England would win.

"What will happen after the war?" he asked. We discussed postwar possibilities, and then he referred to President Roosevelt and praised his foreign policy. "He has made many mistakes in domestic affairs, and I was against him standing for a third term, but if this war goes, I should vote for him standing a fourth time."

I took tea with Mr. and Mrs. Wilkinson and had candied dates and smoked-turkey sandwiches with a little group of friends.

It was in the coffee shop of the Hotel Texas that I had the conviction, strongly impressed on my mind in other cities and states of America, that the educational system of the American people is bearing good fruit and is creating an educated democracy with good manners and good intelligence, widely spread and reaching to all sections of the social life, in a way not yet observable in England. The coffee shop itself, attached to most big hotels, is a remarkably good institution. Outsiders can come in as well as hotel guests, and these places provide a wide variety and abundance of food and refreshment, admirably served and spotlessly clean. The coffee-shop waitresses, as I frequently observed, were pleasant-looking young women, not without a claim to beauty here and there. They take a friendly interest in their customers, and they took a friendly interest in me as an Englishman newly arrived.

"Tell me about England," said Caroline of Fort Worth.

I told her something about England in wartime, and she followed it up by her own observations.

"Do you know," she said, "I think this war will be forced on the United States by that man Hitler. You see, it isn't an ordinary war such as one reads about in history. It's a war between two ideas of civilisation. We belong to one idea just as England does, and so it's going to be our war, too, before long. We ought not to keep out of it. We ought not to let England fight it out alone, when our own civilisation and everything we believe in is challenged by Hitler."

"Do you know," she said again, "I read a lot about this war, not only in the newspapers, but in books such as *Berlin Diary* by Shirer. It seems to me that Hitler is really doing the work of the devil. I believe he is possessed by the devil. I can't help thinking so."

"Do you know," she said again, "in my opinion we're going to be attacked by Japan. I have a kind of idea that they will attack us suddenly when we're not expecting it. I don't trust them at all. They are very crafty little people, and I'm sure they're preparing for a war against us, although they're talking peace just now."

"Do you know," she told me at another breakfast time, "our people aren't thinking about this war enough. They're taking it all too easily. They think everything will go on the same way. They don't realise exactly that Hitler is attempting to get world domination."

"Do you know," said Caroline when she served me with another cup of coffee, "I've been thinking a bit——"

Twenty-year-old Caroline had been thinking rather well, I thought. She was glad to talk about international affairs and lingered at my table with an eye on other customers. Many coffee-shop girls have been to American high schools and American colleges, and if they do not reach the standard of Newnham and Girton and Lady Margaret Hall, which they do not, they have at least acquired a fair background of simple education and a desire to know more. They speak nicely, without slang, or not too much of it, and they are bright and cheerful and kindly and humorous, which seems to me an advance along the road of average intelligence. After this journey of mine through the United States I have a really deep admiration for the American system of education. Its public schools are far and away beyond anything we have in England. Its colleges are built on noble lines, with a sense of beauty. "Superficial," is what American critics say of their own results, and that, no doubt, is true of the average standard of all those thousands, those millions of young people who have been "exposed to education," as one wit remarked. But superficiality of knowledge is better than ignorance and entire lack of education, which seems to be the result of our own elementary schools in the lowest common denominator. Anyhow, they are teaching better manners in the United States, and we have not caught up with them as a democracy, which is a comradeship of the people without a sense of social inferiority. In the American mind that is instinctive, apart from the very rich, who are now becoming less rich on account of a taxation approaching our own in ruthlessness.

Mr. Herbert Walker, a most hospitable man, was good enough to give a luncheon party for me in his club.

"We are all the old stagers," he told me when he introduced me to his friends.

One of them was a handsome elderly man with a whimsical sense of humour which made him greet his friends in German. *"Wie geht's Du?"*

"I had a German father," he said, "born in Hamburg, but I'm one of the old stagers of Fort Worth, and nobody holds it against me. My wife is very busy with British War Relief—always working."

I sat next to Mrs. Rymer. She had brought her knitting with her. Like many other American women—thousands and thousands of them—she was always knitting for England and the bombed-out people of London and other cities.

"We send over a mass of stuff," she told me. "We collect

disused clothes, and we have rummage sales for almost everything. People bring their old trinkets and treasures. I hardly
think England knows how American women are working for
them everywhere. I hope our gifts are properly distributed."

"I hope you get proper thanks," I told her. "On behalf of
England I thank you now with all my heart."

I had a frightful doubt that these American women, working so wonderfully and generously for British Relief, did not
get their full need of thanks. But they assured me first of all
that they were not working to get thanks and secondly that
they get them—thousands of letters from grateful people.

My lecture on the Spirit of Britain, which I varied as much
as I could by different anecdotes to prevent a parrotlike speech,
was, I am told, a success in Fort Worth. Anyhow, though I
count myself as a poor speaker, they said generous things
about it, and people came up to me afterwards and said, "God
bless your country." But I had one misfortune in that city of
Texas, similar to that of Charlie Chaplin in his film of *The
Gold Rush,* where he gave a party elaborately prepared, un-
attended by any guests. I threw a party in the Hotel Texas.
A private room of vast dimensions was engaged. The hotel
became interested. Two darky waiters put on white gloves
and carried up silver buckets of shining ice, and the table was
spread with many cookies. Only two people came, to the dis-
gust of my two dark waiters and to my own disappointment.
I had sent out the invitations too late for busy people. But
my two guests were tolerant and kind, and I had a pleasant
time with Mrs. Stripling and Miss Elizabeth Miller.

"You have been a success," said Miss Elizabeth Miller
generously when I took farewell of her.

In fact, Bob Keedick and I had had such a good time in

Texas that we were both disconsolate when we left that state.

"Let's go back," I suggested. "Let us forsake this lecture tour and stay in Texas where the people are so kind and so vital and you and I have friends."

"Great idea," said Bob, "but what would my father say?"

He had met a pretty girl in Texas who was also intelligent. That may have had something to do with his dejection when we left.

Texas is a great state. I had had only a glimpse of it, but I was really impressed by its atmosphere of simplicity and good will and friendliness.

VI

Oil and Indians

W<small>E TRAVELLED</small> to Oklahoma City in the state of oil and Indians.

Some years ago a famous friend of mine, who was one of the most humorous of men, with a gift of laughter and great genius, had arrived early one morning in that city before any of its people were about. Instead of going to bed he strolled about the streets and presently met a human being who crossed the street to greet him.

"Sure, now," said the stranger, "you must by G. K. Chesterton, the famous English author."

G. K. Chesterton modestly admitted his identity.

"Well, now," said the stranger, "it would give me very great pleasure, Mr. Chesterton, if I might show you some of the antiquities of this city."

Chesterton used to tell this story with laughter bubbling from his eyes, for the antiquities of Oklahoma City do not go farther back than 1889, when it was first founded in a great rush for oil and real estate. This fine city, as it now stands, with great hotels, banks, office buildings, picture palaces, and richly stored shops, is of such recent growth that, at dinner there one night, I sat next to a distinguished old gentleman named Dr. Scott who was there on that famous day in 1889 when it was open country, crowded only by covered wagons, horse buggies, and tents, and a swarm of eager, adventurous men who had just arrived to stake out claims offered to them by the Government.

I knew something of that story, and I knew more when I was driven around the city, and afterwards into the Indian Territory beyond, by one of its leading lawyers, Mr. Tolbert, who was a storehouse of knowledge and a good friend to me.

There is something very romantic still about this city of Oklahoma. In it, close to it, and all around it are the oil wells which create its wealth. The derricks above the oil wells are like spiders' webs against the sky, which was cloudlessly blue when I was there. Cloudless, until one afternoon there was a glory in the sky more wonderful than anything I have seen. It was such a sunset that only Turner could imagine in his painted dreams. The sky was garter blue, but above the horizon of the long, flat plain inhabited by Indians—more than a hundred thousand of them hereabouts—there was a sea of gold from which arose spreading scarlet wings rising until, above the city of Oklahoma, there was a pageantry of magnificent colour from flame red, orange, purple, and palest gold.

Mr. and Mrs. Tolbert, in whose car I had been driving, were moved as much as I was by this glory of the sky.

"I have never seen it like this before," said Mrs. Tolbert. "Perhaps it is an omen of something."

It seemed as though God, or nature, were sending some message to mankind over there in Oklahoma. I wondered if it were a message of war or peace to the people. But they were not worrying. They seemed infinitely remote from that war in Europe. Most of them were utterly assured in their minds that those fires in the Old World would not and could not reach out to them. Most of them, but not all of them, had that sense of assurance. It was curious that soon after my arrival in Oklahoma City at the Hotel Skirvin Tower—a great bastille of a place divided into two towers with an underground passage between them—I had a serious conversation about the war with a young girl whose mind was brooding on it, unlike so many of her fellow citizens. She was the girl behind the bookstall in this hotel. She had time, it seemed, to read some of the books she tried to sell and had read some of mine—*Blood Relations* and others. That is why she spoke to me.

"This war is terrible," she said.

I agreed.

"It's beyond thinking about—all its horrors and cruelties. Don't you think so?"

I did think so, having seen some of those horrors.

"Is Hitler insane?" she asked. "I think he must be half crazy and half a genius. Doesn't that happen sometimes? Don't they go together? Madness and genius?"

"There is an old saying about that," I answered.

"If one believes in a God," said this girl very simply, "Hitler can't win. But it seems that the devil has something to do with it. Don't you believe in the devil?"

I admitted my belief in many devils. It seemed that old Satan had his hand on the shoulder of Adolf Hitler.

"I believe it's coming closer to us," said the girl. "I don't believe we can keep out of it. I can't help thinking we're already in it. But I hope we don't have to send an expeditionary force to England. I hope our boys won't have to be killed in masses."

"I hope not," I said with great sympathy.

Dr. Scott, the oldest pioneer of Oklahoma City, was ill in bed when I arrived but very anxious to get up in time for my address, which was to take place at the club of which he was president. He did so, and I had the honour of sitting next to him—a distinguished-looking old man, delicately made, with very courtly and old-fashioned manners. While we dined he told me something of the old pioneer days and afterwards sent me a book he had written about them. He told me about that first day of the great rush, Monday, April 22, 1889. He was there. It is his most vivid remembrance, and in his book it stands recorded.

"Not a cloud flecked the sky all day long. Scarcely the whisper of a breeze could be noted, or the bending of a blade of grass. The wind of spring was in the air and the freshness of spring was evident to all the senses. A certain area upon which today stands a city of two hundred and twenty-five thousand people was, on the morning of that day, an unbroken prairie, low and level in the loop of the North Canadian River to the south, but rising and more rolling to the north. The land had been burned clear, and the soft new grass of spring, sprinkled with multitudinous wild flowers, made the view a peaceful and charming one. But this was in the morning and up to noon. By evening the grass and flowers were crushed beneath the feet of thousands of hurrying and excited men, and the deepest scars of horses' hooves and wheels of innumerable vehicles. In six hours the natural beauty of the scene was completely obliterated beyond recognition or hope of repair."

Dr. Scott told me of the early troubles before the rising of the city. Greed and jealousy and all human passions entered into this staking out of claims. There were moments when men looked into each other's eyes with intent to kill if their claims were taken from them by groups of greedy rivals. Dr. Scott himself was on the first committee set up to adjudicate on the claims and to establish some kind of law and order in that rough, excited community of men. Very soon the quietude of Oklahoma, where once only Indians had roamed—these Indian tribes now pushed further and further into the desolate lands and rounded up from other states to this territory—was broken by the sound of ax and saw and hammer. Wooden shacks arose, replacing the tents. In Dr. Scott's book there are many drawings of this pioneer camp with its tethered horses and the old buggies and covered wagons on the edge of the prairie. In less than sixty years after those days a big and not-unbeautiful city had arisen, with many streets and many fine buildings. I looked out upon it by night from my bedroom windows and by moonlight saw its towers gleaming like giants' castles touched by enchantment.

At dinner on the night of my lecture I met many of its leading citizens. It was a distinguished company there, with judges and lawyers and doctors and oil men and engineers. I remember some of them now as I write. One of the men opposite to me had Indian blood in his veins and was proud of it. Next to me was Dr. Brandt, the president of Oklahoma University and very young to hold such a position. Farther down

the table was Dr. Bizell, the past president. Opposite was
Judge Bond, a very distinguished-looking man with a vivid
way of speech. Most of the company there knew England
although so far away from it. I was questioned about the
ruins of London and other English cities. They paid me a
great honour by rising before my speech, and when I looked
at this big gathering of men, each of whom had made good in
this pioneer city, I was aware of the romance and the character and the quality of American life at its best.

Dr. Scott, first among the pioneers, oldest in this gathering,
gave me a handsome introduction and made a delightful
speech, interrupted four or five times by calls for doctors to
leave the room for urgent medical service. Dr. Scott did not
allow these interruptions to worry him at all or spoil his
oratory. I was subjected to a fire of questions after my address, and inevitably there was the question about the mystery
of Rudolf Hess, which haunts the American mind.

"Why was England so unprepared?"

"Why did not England attack Germany when the enemy
was heavily engaged in Russia?"

"Did England think victory was possible?"

"What were the food rations in England?"

"Does England want America to send an expeditionary
force?"

"Will the loss of Moscow be a deathblow to Russian resistance?"

"Is Britain strong enough to resist invasion?"

"Why doesn't the R.A.F. bomb Berlin?"

In private conversation at table I had heard many views.
These gentlemen of Oklahoma had been on visits to England

and still remembered them with pleasure. Some of them had seen the old cathedrals and the Oxford colleges. They were astounded by the courage of British civilians.

"We feel rather ashamed of ourselves, in this land of abundance," said one of them. "The waste of food must seem very shocking to you."

"We are in the naval war already," said another. "Our two fleets ought to sweep the enemy sharks out of the Atlantic."

There was no talk about Japan.

With Bob Keedick and Mr. and Mrs. Tolbert, in whose car we went, I was taken to the Indian Territory. On the outskirts of Oklahoma we could see the derricks of the oil wells as far as the eye could reach—two thousand five hundred of these spidery webs against the blue sky. The country was mostly flat, with here and there a few woods. We passed two noble rivers, the North Canadian and the South Canadian, and another with an Indian name which I have forgotten. For miles the soil was red, almost blood red in the rivulets and water pools. It was like the rich red soil of Devonshire. It seemed to me a very solitary land, but here and there we passed small farmsteads belonging to Indians.

"They do very well now," said Mr. Tolbert. "They own their own land and they don't pay any taxes. Most have cattle and horses and poultry. The Federal Government, after our old misdeeds and mishandling of the Indian tribes, takes a paternal interest in them and looks after their welfare. They still have grievances, but on the whole they are content and do not dwell on the tragedy of the past. Many tribes are increasing, and the birth rate is going up. Some of these people became very rich when oil was discovered on their land. They didn't know what to do with their wealth. They spent it on expensive automobiles and all sorts of foolish things. Now their money is put into a fund for the Indian peoples and administered by the Federal Government. It's much better for them."

We passed Indian farms where alfalfa was growing and others growing wheat and cotton. Here and there horses were grazing or cattle were moving on the sky line.

"See that house?" said Mr. Tolbert, pointing to one of the farmsteads. "It belonged to an English Jew named Johnston. He married an Indian woman and settled down here. I daresay he made a good life of it. His half-caste children all did well and revealed very good brains due to that mixture of Indian and Jewish blood."

Presently, as we drove deeper into the Indian country, our friend pointed to a little farmhouse not far from the road.

"A very nice Indian woman lives there," he said. "Would you care to have a talk with her?"

I was keen to have a talk with her, and we walked to her farmstead. Outside were the tall poles of a tepee or wigwam, and while we were looking at it an Indian woman came to meet us with a boy and girl and a small dog.

"Good morning," she said in good English. "What can I do for you?"

I was introduced to her as a visitor from far-off England, and she held my hand and caressed it with the other.

"I am sorry for England," she told me. "They have been having a bad time."

Her hair was raven black and beautifully combed. Her skin was nut brown, and she had large deerlike eyes. She was Mrs. Botone, and she told us that she had a son who had just reached manhood. On his last birthday a few days ago she had given a party, and many Indians had come for singing and dances. That was why she had put up the tepee. She liked the old Indian customs, but her children and the younger folk were not very fond of them any more.

I had a long talk with her, and she took me to one side and spoke about the war.

"I was frightened when I heard about it," she told me. "I thought they would take my boy away from me and get him killed. I cried for several days, but I didn't let anyone see. Then I felt better about it. The war is a long way from America. I don't think they will take my boy."

For a moment tears came into her eyes, but she smiled them away. It didn't seem likely then that her boy would be taken away to the war. It was more than a month before December 7 and Pearl Harbor.

We went back to the tepee, and she showed me how she had put seats made of leaves round the fire in the centre, with its crossed sticks.

"That is how it was done when the Indians were alone in this land," she told me.

Her youngest boy and girl spoke to me in their Indian tongue and laughed as though at a good joke.

"They don't like speaking Indian," said their mother, "but I try to make them."

She had a sister named Mrs. Smokey whose husband was descended from a white captive taken by the Choctaw tribe and brought up by them. He was a Spaniard and very handsome. Smokey, his descendant, was a fine-looking man.

I gave the boy half a dollar and asked him what he would buy with it.

"Candies," he said promptly.

The little girl was aloof and haughty.

Later in the day I was photographed with Mrs. Botone, who combed her hair very carefully before standing in front of the camera and put on a fine black shawl with a long fringe. She was a well-to-do woman, with two hundred acres of her own and some cattle on her land. Before we parted she gave me a present because I was a stranger who had come from a far land. It was a little bead doll of an Indian woman with two long plaits of hair, beautifully made by herself. I keep it as a souvenir of the original inhabitants of the United States, whose ghosts still haunt the woods and streams.

We drove through an Indian town called Anadarko. It was like any American small town, with drugstores and chain stores and a picture palace. The Indians, strolling about, were in American clothes and very unpicturesque. Farther away in this Indian territory, inhabited by a hundred thousand Indians of many tribes who had been driven up here from the Southern states, we came to a very remarkable institution known as the Riverside Indian Boarding School. It is a college for Indian youth under the jurisdiction of the Federal Government and has a large number of students. They are divided into houses of twenty—ten boys and ten girls—aged from about twelve to eighteen.

"Come and see my angels," said a very cheerful lady who is devoted heart and soul to this work.

We took lunch with her angels, who were Kiowas, Apaches, Caddos, Cheyennes, Choctaws, Sioux, and children of many tribes. They take turns in cooking and serving the meals, and in our honour they had made a banquet. I was introduced to Agnes Spotted Horse and Rachel Bosin, and Ruby Redbone and many others. Before our meal they sang grace sweetly, and afterwards we were waited on very nicely by Rachel Bosin, a Kiowa girl, and Ruby Redbone, an Apache, who interested me very much because of her tribe, about whom I had read so much as a boy in the thrilling stories of Captain Mayne Reid. She had the face of a young eagle, a black young eagle, and there was a flash in her eyes.

"I am proud of being an Apache," she told me later in the afternoon, when we had become good friends.

After lunch I sat with a crowd of them in a nicely furnished drawing room and tried to draw them out. At first they were very shy, but before long I got them talking in their own language—so that I could hear what it sounded like—and then in perfectly good English.

They knew a good deal about the war over in Europe and thought it must be bad.

"We hope it won't come over here," said a young Kiowa boy. "I'm just the age when they may want to take me."

"What will you do if America stays out of it?" I asked.

He shrugged his shoulders.

"I shall go back to my father's farm. What else is there to do?"

Rachel Bosin, the Kiowa girl, and Ruby Redbone, the Apache, took charge of me and led me about the building, which is very large and well appointed like all American schools. The walls were decorated with paintings of Indian life and customs, extremely well done by an Indian artist. He is likely to have a successor in his art, because upstairs, in one of the bedrooms, we found a young Indian youth busily engaged in painting a red Indian chief doing a war dance.

"It is very difficult," he said modestly.

But he was doing it with skill and talent, every feather and every detail, very delicately.

"Come and see our library," said Rachel Bosin. "We have many books."

I was interested to see what those young Indian people were reading. They were the books upon which I had been brought up and which I had devoured as a boy. *Little Men* and *Little Women, Robinson Crusoe, David Copperfield, A Tale of Two Cities, Treasure Island, Sherlock Holmes,* and all the old favourites. It seemed to me astonishing, or at least remarkable, that these children of the tribes should have as their mental background the works of Dickens and Scott and stories like *The Scarlet Pimpernel,* which I saw on their shelves. But they were Americanised in their minds and customs, and the legends of their own race were becoming dim and only like fairy tales. They could still speak their own languages but seldom spoke them. Soon they will die out, unless the American Government has the good sense to keep them alive in the schools.

We went into the gymnasium, very spacious and high. One of the young Indians put on his feathered headdress, and one of his comrades played the drum for him to do a war dance. The beat of the drum sent a little thrill down my spine. Its rhythm had called the Apaches on the warpath in dark forests. There was a wild, fierce note in it. The tall youth was joined in his dance by a tiny lad who did all the traditional steps of the war dance perfectly. The girls gathered round. The Indian brave shouted his war cries and brandished his tomahawk, and the girls uttered little screams of laughter. It was a joke now. Blood had gone out of it. It was like an English boy pretending to be a knight in armour.

I made good friends with those young Indian people. They were glad to have a visitor from England who took an interest in them, and they were proud of their school and all its splendour.

"It has been very nice having you here," said Rachel Bosin. "I would like you to stay three months."

Many of them lined up to say good-by, and I shook hands with Ruby Redbone, the Apache girl, and with Agnes Spotted Horse, the Kiowa, and with many of the others.

Afterwards, in Oklahoma City, I pursued my study of the original inhabitants of America by going to the Indian Museum, which has a splendid exhibition of Indian life and history. I had the best guide possible in Mrs. Czarina Conlan, the enthusiastic curator of the museum, who is equally proud of her Choctaw blood on one side and, on the other side, of her descent from the noble family of Colbert in France, whose coat of arms she has. Here were portraits, costumes, weapons, and personal belongings of many famous chiefs, belonging to the Five Nations and other tribes. I remember that Bacon Rind was a distinguished chief in recent times, and I saw his portrait and ceremonial clothes, with a fur cap which he always wore.

Mrs. Conlan took me to one case which certainly thrilled me when I looked at its exhibits. Here were many scalps with the hair and skin of the victims who had perished at the hands of Indian warriors in the days of conflict.

"Of course," said Mrs. Conlan when she took me into other rooms, "when my ancestors were here before the coming of the white men, they lived in the Stone Age period and made their weapons out of flints. Here are some beautiful spearheads and knives."

"Where do you think they came from before they were in America?" I asked her.

She had a theory—not upheld by historical evidence—that the red Indians belonged to the Egyptian people. It is remotely possible that their Mongolian ancestors were in touch with Egyptian civilisation—the first on earth—and that the pyramids in South America have some connection with those in Egypt.

I had a fascinating time in this historical museum, and Mrs. Conlan's knowledge and enthusiasm lit up the exhibits.

"You must go to see Mr. Ben Dwight," she told me. "He is governor of my tribe—the Choctaws—and a very interesting man."

I went to see Mr. Ben Dwight, and he was well worth meeting, a small-sized man with a big mind. I found him cordial, merry, and informative. He is a highly educated Choctaw, having been to more than one university and taken several degrees. Like all governors of the tribes, he was appointed directly by the President of the United States and has very important responsibilities to his people, representing them at state conferences, in which he puts forward their grievances and petitions.

"We still have some outstanding troubles," he told me. "The Government still has unsettled claims of ours for money which is due to us under solemn agreements, but I take a reasonable view of all that and do not want to claim billions of dollars. On the whole the Indian tribes are happy and contented, and we try to forget the tragedy of the past and all causes of ill will."

"What is the origin of the Indian races?" I asked, thinking of Mrs. Conlan's Egyptian theory.

Mr. Ben Dwight laughed.

"That is still being argued out. It's a very good subject for argument. But I lean to the conviction that we are Mongolians."

"How many are you now in the United States?"

The little Choctaw chief knew the exact numbers.

"Three hundred and seventy thousand, according to the last census. But we are increasing. Some of the tribes have a high birth rate, and better conditions of life and social wellbeing are reducing the death rate." He thought that there were about two to three million Indians in North America before the coming of the palefaces.

We had a talk about the war, which he thought terrible. All his sympathy was for England and those countries who were fighting for liberty.

"I'm afraid we shall be drawn in," he said. "We are already in the naval war."

This miniature man with the blood of the Choctaws was keen, alert, and highly intelligent. Highly efficient also, I am sure. I was very much impressed by him.

So I had an interesting time in Oklahoma, due very largely to the kindness of Mr. and Mrs. Tolbert, who put all their time at my disposal and showed me everything they could. I left with many pleasant memories, and since then I have had a charming letter from all the young people of the Riverside Indian Boarding School with whom I came in contact. Each one of them signed it with the name of the tribe to which each boy or girl belongs. There are the names of Rachel Bosin and Ruby Redbone and Agnes Spotted Horse, and other Kiowas and Caddos and Apaches and Wichitas who sent their love to me.

I was bound for Tulsa in the same state of Oklahoma, and in the train I read a copy of the Tulsa *Tribune*.

There was grave news in it. Oklahoma seemed incredibly remote from Europe, as remote as another planet, but certain incidents happening over there were touching the lives of American citizens and the destiny of the United States.

The United States Destroyer *Reuben James* had been torpedoed and sunk west of Iceland, with one hundred and twenty men aboard. It was the first American warship to be lost since the European war began. In an interview President Roosevelt stated that he saw no probability of severing diplomatic relations with Germany and thought there would be no change in American policy.

There was another big headline in the Tulsa *Tribune*.

"Reds in Crimea flee, Nazis say."

The Germans claimed sweeping victories against the Soviet Armies. Moscow was in peril.

I had been told that Tulsa was the richest city in the world, where there was so much wealth from oil that ladies had golden doorknobs and gold-plated baths. I regret that I did not see the doorknobs or the baths, but I did see a skyful of derricks above the oil wells and a finely built city in which I stayed at the Mayo Hotel without undue luxury. A gracious lady named Miss Clarkson had sent a basket of choice fruit to my room, but as I was suffering from internal disturbance, from which I thought I might die later on my lecture tour—I had a premonition of a little white gravestone in Omaha—I could only enjoy it visually.

Now I remember Tulsa chiefly by a conversation I had with a young fellow who sold me a packet of cigarettes in a small store.

"English, ain't you?" he asked.

I admitted that fact.

"Well, I've a grudge against England and the English," he said.

"How is that?" I asked.

"Do you want me to be honest?" said the young fellow.

"I'd like to know," I answered.

"All right, then. Why didn't England pay her debt to the United States? Didn't even say sorry. That don't seem right to me."

I put up some kind of defence, without conviction, because I have always maintained in written and spoken word that we ought to have paid that debt, in spite of all the New York bankers who didn't want us to pay it and in spite of the economic law that if the United States did not buy British goods because of high tariffs it was hard for us to pay when we had let off all our own debtors who owed us more than we owed America.

"Now see," said the young fellow. "If I hire a suit of clothes, that's a debt. And if I don't pay my instalment, I get an attachment. That means that I'm fired by my employer. See? And that's as it should be. A debt is a debt. All right. Then why did England revoke?"

I made another answer which did not satisfy this moral inquisitor.

"Now don't misunderstand me," he said. "I believe in giving all possible aid to England, because she's putting up a great fight against Germany. Right. But not by convoying ships. Now see here. Germany is perfectly right in sinking our ships, ain't she? Supposing you and me are having a quarrel—to the death—and I have a free hand and my wife puts a knife into it so that I can stick you in the back, wouldn't you take away the knife? I guess you would. Well, then, Germany is right in taking away the knife which we're sending over to England. See? Right. We ought to quit or get in—otherwise we'll get a headache. One thing or the other. People seem to think that we can go on convoying ships and not get into the war. That's dumb. Of course that question about the freedom of the seas wants an international lawyer to argue it out. It's beyond me. I just let it pass. But if we don't want to get into this war, and we don't, we had better quit that convoying racket. See? Now over here in these United States we can take care of Germany if she attacks. And I don't think she will. It's a hell of a long way off. What are the Germans going to do when they get here— which they won't? I mean to say, it's unreasonable. Mind you, I am not so dumb as to think it would be a comfortable world for us if England went down. It would be darned uncomfortable. The world is shrinking in time and space. We're all tied up together in an economic way. We want to trade with other people. We can't maintain our standard of life if we're isolated from the rest of the world. If England went down, Hitler would put an economic strangle hold on Europe. We're interested to that degree. But no more than that. Our lives ain't threatened. They're not going to send bombing aeroplanes over Tulsa, Oklahoma. See what I mean? Right!"

He softened later in his attitude toward England.

"Mind you, me and my friends want England to win. Don't mistake that."

"Do you meet many English people in Tulsa?" I asked.

"None," he said. "But I like the first Englishman I've met here."

"Meaning me?" I asked, feeling flattered.

"Meaning you," he said. "Shake."

We shook hands warmly.

He was an honest and friendly young man.

I was somewhat alarmed on my arrival in Tulsa by the fear that I was booked to speak in a church. This I dislike very much, and I remembered a painful moment when on a previous tour many years ago I was led towards a pulpit and told that I had to speak from it. I was put at ease, however, by the Rev. Mr. Eckel, who was to be my chairman. "It's a hall attached to the church," he told me. I found that he had been at Wadham College, Oxford, and was a contemporary of Philip Guedalla, the English writer. At first I thought he looked a trifle austere, but when he and his wife came to my table he told some humorous stories and I found him a very human and good-humoured man.

My audience in Tulsa was large and sympathetic. Before going onto the platform I smoked several cigarettes in the kitchen with Miss Clarkson, who had given me that basket of fruit, and with a remarkable lady named Mrs. Ferguson, who has been a columnist in the American press for many years.

"I daresay you will get some rather hot questions tonight," she warned me.

One of them was pretty hot.

"What do you think of Colonel Lindbergh?"

"I believe in free speech, as you do," I answered. "And if we believe in that, as we do, Colonel Lindbergh has a perfect right to express any ideas which may be in his head."

For some reason that answer aroused laughter and applause.

"Is Pastor Niemoeller dead?" asked a little lady.

I could not give her information on that point.

"What about Rudolf Hess?" shouted a voice.

"Why was England so unprepared?" asked another.

I had heard those two last questions before. I was to hear them many times again.

There was no question about Japan. There was nothing asked about the likelihood of a German declaration of war against the United States. Those questions were remote, it seemed, from the minds of the American people.

VII

Through Flood and Storm to Omaha

Bob KEEDICK and I had a long journey from Oklahoma to
Nebraska, that is to say from Oklahoma City to Omaha in the
Middle West. There were great floods covering vast areas of
territory. Round about Tulsa the turbulent Arkansas River
had been held within its banks only by the feverish toil of
many workers who battled for twenty-four hours without rest,
until suddenly they were rushed north to Bird Creek, where
there had been a break through which immense waters
swirled over many farmsteads. It was the worst flood in the
history of Oklahoma, and many families were fleeing from
their homes while others were caught and drowned.

Bob Keedick and I stared at the floods from our carriage
window. They were close below the railway track, and our
train moved slowly and cautiously over wooden bridges,
watched by labouring men on the line.

"Doesn't look too good," said Bob. "If those wooden piles
were to slip——"

As far as the eye could reach the countryside was flooded. There were great lakes, broken by the trunks of bare trees or the roofs of shacks.

We came to a halt in a small town called Parsons.

"I shouldn't like to get stranded here," said Bob.

We had breakfast at the buffet.

Our darky conductor, in an empty coach, was informed that we should be hours late. There was a train wreck ahead of us.

"Not my fault, gen'lemen!" said the darky. "I'm doin' the best I can for you."

Bob and I strolled through Parsons. It was not a beautiful place. There was nothing alluring about it.

"A good opportunity to buy a set of chessmen," I suggested.

"Hardly possible in Parsons," said Bob.

We went into several shops, but they laughed when we mentioned the game of chess. However, by good luck we found a set with a chessboard of the right size. Triumphant, we returned to the train.

"How's it going?" we asked our coloured friend.

"Well, it ain't goin'," he answered ruefully. "It just don't go."

We were held up for ten hours on that train between Parsons and Kansas City. We played innumerable games of chess. We became hungry. We smoked too many cigarettes. We discussed the chances of reaching Omaha in time for my lecture. They didn't seem bright. At last, having passed the train wreck, we reached Kansas City when it was nearly dark. We were met by agents who informed us that the organisers of the lecture in Omaha had hired a private plane for us to do the journey of two hundred and fifty miles.

"We want some food," said Bob. "We haven't eaten for many hours."

We went into the railway buffet, cold and hungry, but an anxious little man approached us.

"I'm your pilot," he said. "Tex Legrone. I think we ought to get going. The weather may get worse, and it'll be dark before we reach Omaha."

He had a birdlike face with little wrinkles about the eyes and mouth. He was a veteran of the air and led us out to an aeroplane which I confess did not inspire me with any confidence. It was a very small aeroplane with scarlet wings. It looked like a toy.

"Get in, gentlemen," said Mr. Tex Legrone.

He put on a pilot's cap with flaps over the ears, and without delay we taxied over a wet aerodrome and then rose and flew above the earth.

Bob Keedick looked at me and smiled.

"If my father knew about this, he would get anxious," he told me.

Down below us was the flooded country. Presently we saw the Missouri River curled across the countryside in a wide loop like a lariat flung across the plain.

I leaned forward and talked to Tex Legrone.

"What speed do you make?" I asked.

"Two hundred an hour."

We did the first fifty miles in fifteen minutes to the tick. It was a small machine, but it flew like a bird.

"Been flying long?" I asked.

Tex Legrone nodded.

"I was three years in the last war. I've been flying ever since."

I regretted my lack of confidence. We were in a brave little aeroplane with an ace flyer.

But we had some nervous moments. I began to think of that little white grave in Omaha. The sky darkened. Rain beating against our fuselage turned to sleet. Down there snow was lying white on the plain. Mr. Tex Legrone could see very little. His birdlike face peered from side to side. A stiff wind was blowing, and our machine shook and bumped a bit. It seemed to me that our pilot was not sure of his bearings.

Bob Keedick and I exchanged uneasy glances. I didn't like the look of things. I felt distinctly apprehensive.

Mr. Tex Legrone was circling round in a wide sweep, bearing north. There were no landmarks because of the darkness. Visibility was almost nil. The city of Omaha did not put in an appearance.

Very unpleasant, I thought.

Bob Keedick and I exchanged a few casual words. He saw that I was a bit nervous. I don't think he was altogether happy, but we gave a grin to each other.

Mr. Tex Legrone was an experienced pilot. He was also a happy pilot. Flying very low, he had found a river which seemed to cheer him up. He knew where he was in that flurry of sleet and in that darkness descending upon us. He found the aerodrome at Omaha. He made a perfect landing.

"You did that very well," I told him, with great gratitude in my heart for him.

"A bit tricky," he said. "It was a good thing we didn't wait while you had something to eat. The weather is getting worse. I don't think I shall fly back to Kansas City tonight."

Waiting for us at the aerodrome were three gentlemen of Omaha. They were Mr. Japp and two friends in the American

Legion. They were good enough to sit with us in the buffet while we drank hot coffee, which we much needed after a long day without food or drink. We were in plenty of time for the lecture after all, though the American Legion of Omaha, who were running it, had been anxious about it. They had got through to the train at Parsons by telephone and had learned, to their dismay, that we should be ten hours late. It was they who had arranged for the flight in Tex Legrone's plane.

Bob and I dressed at the Hotel Fontenelle and found that we had been invited to dinner before the lecture by Mr. and Mrs. Doorley. Mr. Doorley was the proprietor of the Omaha *Daily Herald* and had entertained me in his home twenty years before. Now, by bad chance, he had a sharp attack of influenza and was in bed.

"You won't remember me," said Mrs. Doorley as we came into her beautiful drawing room, "but it doesn't seem such an age ago when you lectured in Omaha after the last war."

It was pleasant to sit in her room and meet a party of charming people, among whom was a pretty daughter of the family. They were eager to get firsthand news of England, where they had many friends, and they questioned me about all the details of English life in time of bombardment. I was in the heart of the Middle West. I expected to meet isolationists who would heckle me and perhaps create a lively scene in the lecture hall. But these people among whom I sat were all pro-British, and they did not think I should have any trouble with isolationist groups.

After dinner I went up to Mr. Doorley's sickroom and found him lying on a couch reading the evening paper. His pretty daughter was there and said to her father, "For this birthday gift thanks a lot," before leaving us together.

There were many things we wanted to talk about, but young Keedick was anxious about lecture time, now approaching closely.

"Tell Winston Churchill," said Mr. Doorley as a parting message, "to get in touch with the President over American labour. The situation is becoming dangerous."

My lecture seemed to interest a large audience, among whom were many men of the American Legion. No one heckled me. In the heart of the Middle West there was no sign of a isolationist, so far as I was concerned. The questions were lively but not hostile, and afterwards people crowded up to speak to me. One pretty lady spoke to me with some passion in her voice. "There are a lot of bums in this country," she observed. "Why don't they send more food to England? I suppose every country has a lot of bums and crazy folk. It makes me mad."

There was an English Cockney there who came up and spoke about his old home in London. He was proud of being a real Cockney. He proved it by dropping his aitches.

"Your people are just too wonderful!" said another lady. "I don't think we should be quite so heroic if the Germans came and bombed us out of our homes. I know I shouldn't!"

I think it was Mr. Japp who took me round to the American Legion Club, where I understood him to say a free meal was provided for its members every day. He told me a lot of things about the American Legion, but some of them were blown away by a strong wind which threatened to cut my throat as we went round sharp corners.

"Here I get pneumonia," I thought. "Here I qualify for that little white gravestone in Omaha which I escaped narrowly this afternoon."

I was glad to get into the shelter of the club. There it was very warm and comforting, with groups of American Legionnaires and their wives sitting at small tables on which there were attractive-looking glasses. Some of the younger men and women were dancing to canned music which made quite a lot of noise. Conversation and laughter filled the room with racket of a cheerful kind.

"Come and meet some fellows," said Mr. Japp. "Omaha has a strong Legion Post, and we're all very keen on it. Don't forget that we men of the American Legion have voted for American intervention in this war, including an expeditionary force. You will find this crowd a hundred per cent anti-Hitler."

I found that crowd very warm in their welcome. At the table where I sat was an Englishman from Limpsfield, not enormously far from my own village in Surrey, and an American doctor and his wife who were glad to meet me, they said, and proved their gladness by offering me cordial liquids. Through the noise of the music and the dancing we had an exciting conversation about the war. Some of these new friends of mine were of the opinion that England needed American man power to win the war. But they admitted that this idea was far beyond the average American mind throughout the country.

The Englishman from Limpsfield was concerned about the shipping losses. Mr. Japp was greeting his brother members and then dragged me up from the table to speak a few words to the American Legion with the help of a microphone.

"That's going to spoil a pleasant evening," I told him. "These people don't want their dancing interrupted by any words from me."

"They'll love it," said Mr. Japp.

The Americans can stand almost any punishment from public speakers, and there was a round of applause when I stood in front of the microphone and addressed the company. Heaven knows what I said. I spoke like a man in a dream. But I seemed to speak the right words. There was thunderous applause before I returned to my table and resumed a drink which made the room go round and round very pleasantly.

I returned to my hotel some time after midnight. Bob was annoyed. He had been to the movies after leaving strict injunctions that I should be parked in the Hotel Fontenelle after the lecture. He considered these late hours as a danger to my health.

"What will my father say," he asked, "if I let you break down halfway through our schedule?"

"I shall break down," I told him. "I haven't the faintest hope of ever getting back to New York. An American lecture tourist needs the physical strength of a gladiator, and I am not a gladiator."

VIII

Way Down in Old Kentucky

WE WENT to Lexington in Kentucky and came in touch with the spirit of the South and the speech of the South, and its coloured folk, and its old plantations and love of horses, and gentlemen farmers, and free-spoken women.

There is a libel about Kentucky put about by the Yankees.

"They're a slow-moving folk. It's difficult to tell the difference between a man of Kentucky and a rock. One has to watch until one of them moves. . . . It's the rock that moves."

All that is ridiculous. Almost the first person I met in Kentucky was a lady named Cleo—Mrs. Cleo Smith—who was quick, dynamic, and vital, full of warm emotion, laughter, and dramatic intensity. She was a dark-haired, dark-eyed lady with merry eyes and the gift of humour. She became my fairy godmother in Lexington. It was she who introduced me to the dangerous enchantment of mint julep. It was she who took me to the house of the Mint Julep King and showered favours on me, all with the greatest sense of fun.

I met the gentlemen of Kentucky and found them genial, hospitable, and warm in welcome. My lecture was sponsored by the Lexington *Herald-Leader,* and the editor, Mr. Guthrie, and other members of the editorial staff laid themselves out to show me the beauty of Lexington and the glory of Kentucky. They gave me a grand time, and here I would like to pay a tribute to the American reporter and newspaperman. Everywhere I went on this tour through the United States I was met by newspapermen who interviewed me at great length. Never once did they let me down or make me say things which I had not said and did not want to say. They went to great trouble. However early I arrived in a city, and often it was at six-thirty or seven, American journalists would be there searching the train for me or waiting at the hotel to come up in my bedroom with staff photographers who wasted an incredible number of bulbs in taking my haggard features. They were kind and friendly, these newspapermen, to a brother journalist. They were well informed, well educated, and extremely courteous. Often after they had put their pencils away they lingered for informal conversation about world affairs and I turned the tables on them by interviewing them, receiving much information about the American mind and mood or about local history and the political or social setup in their own city and state. I found them to be realists, humourists, and friendly fellows. They gave me the low-down with great candour. America is well served by its newspapermen, most of whom have graduated at some university, and the old bad tradition of the American reporter as drawn by Dickens and other critics is a thing of the past. The editor and staff of the Lexington *Herald-Leader* were men of quality and they gave me a fine time.

The Kentucky folk are proud of their state, as well they

may be, and there is still in their minds a humorous hostility against the North, rather like the pretended feud between Scots and English. A Virginian, describing a group he had met at a race meeting, sorted them out in the following degrees of social merit:

"There was a noble and courteous gentleman from Virginia, and there was a gentleman from Kentucky, and a man from Indiana, and a feller from Nebraska, and a son-of-a-bitch from Boston."

Mrs. Cleo Smith—I hope she will pardon me if I call her Cleo, like all her friends—was good enough to take Robert Keedick and myself to the house of Judge Yantis and his wife for a mint-julep party. Now, Judge Yantis has the reputation of being one of the most knowledgeable men on the magic of mint julep in the state of Kentucky. It was Cleo who, with her gift for dramatising, described him as the Mint Julep King. But a sad thing had happened. Judge Yantis was on the water wagon by doctor's orders, strictly enforced, he told us, by his lady wife.

"I met a feller in the whiskey trade," said Judge Yantis, "and when I told him that I had been on the water wagon for three weeks he said, 'Yes, I noticed that my sales were falling off.'"

But with the spirit of hospitality which belongs to all Kentuckians, Judge Yantis had arranged a little party in my honour with mint julep as the reason thereof. Among the guests was a grand old gentleman named Colonel Donkin—there are many colonels in Kentucky—who never opened his mouth without saying something witty, gallant, or teasing, especially addressed to that lady Cleo. He has a brother who was a general in World War I and who was a friend of

Pershing, who put him in charge of a battle in France at a critical moment when other generals had said the action was impossible. General Donkin won the battle and smashed the German counterattack. "My brother belongs to Kentucky," said the colonel modestly.

Mrs. Yantis handed me a little napkin with a lace border which I took without knowing its significance. Now, mint julep is not only a drink. It is a ceremony and a tradition. It has to be served in silver mugs frosted with ice so that they have to be held in a napkin. The mint has to bunch out beautifully three inches, or thereabouts, above the mug.

"There are some terrible people," said Mrs. Yantis, "who cut the stalks of the mint. That is all wrong. Each sprig has to be pinched so as to extract the juice without hurting it."

"Put your nose well down!" cried the lady Cleo.

I put my nose well down into the sprigs of mint, breathing in its pungent scent and feeling apprehensive, having heard much about the potency of this drink which is made of pure bourbon and goes down like a zephyr, so softly and so sweetly that one does not know one's state of intoxication until one is past knowing. I had heard of the definition of mint julep by a coloured butler.

"One mint julep is good for any gen'leman.

"Two mint juleps are too much for any gen'leman.

"Three mint juleps are not enough for any gen'leman."

I had a lecture ahead of me, and I was timid and hesitating in my approach to the silver cup from which I took a few sips now and then. The taste was exquisite, the effect delectable. Bob Keedick was a braver man than I and might have been born in Kentucky. He swigged down his cup without turning a hair. Youth can take these risks.

I was taken round Lexington by Mr. Guthrie of the *Herald-Leader* and by Mr. Wachs of his editorial staff. It is an interesting old town with many fine old houses built before the Civil War and in the time of the slave trade, which was very profitable here.

"Round Cheapside was the biggest slave market in the Southern states," said Mr. Guthrie, and I stared at the site of that old market place and saw the ghosts of innumerable Negroes brought here and put up for public sale—men, women, and children clinging to each other with bewildered and frightened eyes as the slave dealers auctioned them like cattle to Southern gentlemen and farmers.

"That's Mary Todd's house," said Mr. Guthrie. "She was the wife of Abraham Lincoln. He came courting her here and used to look out of her window at that scene in the slave market. Maybe it was here that he took his decision to free the slaves."

I was shown another house, very historical.

"That was Colonel John Morgan's house," said Mr. Guthrie. "He was one of the heroes of the Confederate Army. He rode in at the front door there, kissed his wife and children, and rode out at the back door to escape the enemy."

There was the old Court House—quiet now, but only twenty years ago, in 1921, the scene of a fearful drama of lynch law when a vast crowd surged around yelling for the delivery of a trembling Negro accused of a bestial crime. Shots were fired after the reading of the riot act, and eleven people were killed and thirty wounded. Now the coloured folk are getting "uppish," I was told. Church people and Baptist missionaries go down to them and preach social equality and urge them to stand up for their political rights. Mrs. Roosevelt gives parties to coloured folk at the White House. Education has reached them. They are resenting their inferiority. They are forming their own unions. Up in Harlem, New York, white women go and dance with them, and they are getting race-conscious, to the fear of some people who view this coloured problem with apprehension and alarm. The promises that were made to them after the first World War have not been kept. I was there on a day when the darky division which had served in France marched through the city of New York to the cheers of the crowd. From a balcony Charles Hughes made a speech to them promising them full equality of rights after their fighting service for their country. Irving Cobb made a speech to the coloured officers which was very moving. . . . A few weeks later there were race riots in Springfield and other cities where coloured folk were chased from their homes by home-coming soldiers who could not find houseroom. It is all very difficult. . . .

I was taken out into the Bluegrass country, very pastoral and very lovely. With its little low hills and grassland it reminded me very much of my own county of Surrey, round about the village of Shamley Green, and the wonderful horse-breeding farms to which I was taken were like English parks as they were kept by the Duke of Norfolk and other great lords. The white-railed paddocks, the noble trees, the old houses, the stables and barns had an English look which made me homesick.

The lands of those domains, way down in Kentucky, belong to the Whitneys, the Wideners, and the Fishers, and other families who made their wealth out of big business or the mechanical progress of their country.

Mr. Guthrie and Mr. Wachs, my friendly guides, told me

the history of the Fisher family, who are among the greatest horse breeders in Kentucky—and therefore in the world.

"Old man Fisher was a blacksmith before he took to building coaches and then to the Fisher body for automobiles, which made his fortune. There's a good story about him which he tells himself. A young man went to him to raise a loan for some business project but was so timid that he could not get the words out when it came to the point. Old man Fisher was amused. 'My boy,' he said, 'I was like that myself when I went to a bank director to raise a loan for the Fisher body. I was so nervous that I kept on chewing a quid of tobacco, which filled my mouth with saliva. Suddenly the banker asked me a question. It was necessary to answer, but it was also necessary to· get rid of that saliva. I looked round wildly for a cuspidor, but there wasn't one. I saw a window near me. "I'm saved," I thought, and let go. But the window was shut! . . . However, I got the loan—ten thousand dollars.' "

The stables on these horse-breeding farms are marvellous. Inside they are as big as cathedrals and perfectly appointed, regardless of cost, which must amount to millions of dollars.

In one of them I saw the most famous race horse in the world—Man o' War, now twenty-five years of age, the son of Fair Play and the sire of many famous racers.

Man o' War was shown to us by a sturdy old Negro—Will —who has been in charge of him for many years and who is filled with pride, enthusiasm, and eloquence on the subject of that animal. He was truly a noble-looking horse, with an immense chest and a body formed for strength and speed.

Nigger Will did his stuff. In a long monologue, never ceasing while we stayed and listened, he narrated the glorious exploits of Man o' War, all the races he had won, all the money he had gained—millions of dollars—all the sons and daughters he had produced. It was a long saga of the royal family of horseflesh descended from English sires. Outside in the park was a statue of Fair Play by some sculptor who loved horses and knew them well—one of the best equestrian statues in the world, I should say.

We saw some of the other horse farms, equally wonderful, superbly kept, and we saw the houses of their owners—great mansions built like the country houses of English lords, who are now abandoning them under the strain of war taxation. As I write I wonder what will happen to the great establishments of the Fishers, the Wideners, and the Whitneys. For war taxation is touching them too—ruthlessly. And as I write I remember that when I drove round these parklands in Kentucky the war slipped from my mind. Here was peace. That European war was far away. What did it matter to Kentucky? What meaning did it have to these gentlemen of Kentucky or to the coloured folk who served them, no longer as slaves, or to gay, free-spoken ladies like the lady Cleo? The Four Horsemen of the Apocalypse were not riding through these paddocks or on the tan of the training schools. At least I did not hear the thunder of their hooves. And yet it was not much more than thirty days away from December 7. If I had listened more intently, I might have heard sinister vibrations, like the beating of drums, like the howling of air-raid sirens.

"What would you like to see now?" asked one of my guides.

"I would like to see an old Kentucky house," I told him.

"I can show you one," he answered. "It is where I live."

I am glad I made that request of Mr. Wachs of the Lexington *Herald-Leader,* for I spent an enchanting hour or so in an old Kentucky mansion crowded with the ghosts of other generations. It stood some distance outside Lexington and was built on noble lines in the seventeenth or eighteenth century. It was very tall, with high white pillars on each side of its portico and long, well-spaced windows. The rooms were large with high ceilings. It stood in a park of two hundred acres well wooded and stocked with cattle and sheep. Strange that its owner should be a journalist!

As we approached, a young man came down to the house with a gun under his arm and an Alsatian loping by his side. He wore a Robin Hood hat and a leather jerkin above his riding breeches and leggings.

"My son," said Mr. Wachs.

He looked like a young English squire, and his father told me that he wanted to be a farmer. It is likely that Adolf Hitler has interfered with that ambition as he has interfered with all our lives and spoiled many dreams.

I went upstairs to the bedrooms of that old Kentucky house. Every room was furnished in the eighteenth-century manner with beautiful four-poster beds and chairs like my own Chippendale and Hepplewhite at home. The walls were panelled with walnut wood cut down from trees on the estate, just as the bricks from which the house was built had been made from the clay on the same land.

"Come down and see the basement," said Mr. Wachs. "It's rather interesting."

We went down below into enormous basement rooms, cold and damp.

"Here the slaves used to be kept," said the owner of the house. "These were their sleeping quarters."

I touched the old brick walls. Surely some vibration would

come from them, giving me a vision of those crowds of Negroes herded down here at night with their women and children, singing, perhaps, some of the old plaintive melodies which are now sung by Paul Robeson and others for radio listeners. These walls had heard many groans, many whimperings, many tears. Perhaps, also, some laughter from Negro picka-ninnies and the wailing of newborn babes. All that had gone with the wind. We stood alone between those walls, in the great kitchens and storehouses of eighteenth-century Kentucky. Things are happier now in spite of a world war, except for men fighting in jungles and dying in deserts and dead in the snow.

The dining room and drawing room were very noble. After standing with admiration in them I sat in the study smoking and talking. We talked about the war—so far away. Mr. Wachs questioned me about England's strength and her will to win. He discussed postwar problems.

"Are you going to make a peace of vengeance?"

He wanted to know whether Britain was anxious for an American Expeditionary Force.

He spoke gravely about the chances of America being drawn into the war, and I was struck by the fact that this gentleman of Kentucky should find the war so close to his country, so close to his mind, when in its parklands and horse farms it had seemed to me in another planet.

That night I spoke about the war to a big audience in Lexington. Before I went onto the platform the lady Cleo with the merry black eyes told me that she was a Christian Scientist and believed in vibrations. She was going to send me pleasant and helpful vibrations which would put me at ease before my audience. I feel sure that they reached me, for

I felt at ease and was aware that these Kentucky folk had a friendly feeling towards me and great sympathy for England.

One lady afterwards spoke to me with emotion.

"We American women," she said, "are working for England. We spend our time knitting and sewing and packing for your poor people. But we are doing more than that. We are sending you our prayers. May God answer them."

One voice in the audience asked a question which haunted me.

"How is Britain going to win this war?"

I made the best answer I could. I told them that the British people had an unshaken faith in final victory—a kind of religious faith based on the belief that it was against the powers of darkness which could not prevail. In the long run Evil must be defeated. In the long run the evil spell would be lifted. But secretly I wondered how Britain could win against the enormous power of our highly organised enemy. One thing gave me renewed hope and confidence in final victory. Since I had been in the United States I had seen many munition plants rising beyond the cities. They covered many acres. When they started production—in nine months or twelve—there would be a tide of tanks, guns, aeroplanes, shells, and all weapons of war. I was to see much more of that in the United States before my tour was ended. As I travelled, the bigness of this thing being forged in America held my imagination and staggered it.

From Lexington we went on to Louisville, Kentucky.

In Brown's Hotel there was a great coming and going of American women. There were eight hundred of them, and the elevators were so crowded with these ladies that a mere man had to stand and wait while they went up or came down.

It was some convention for the furtherance of women's work and interests. They were not, in the mass, beautiful. There were no glamorous girls among them. They were middle-aged or elderly dames who had left their families for a few days on some mission of high idealism linked up with a bit of fun. They talked earnestly, vivaciously, and interminably in the lounge, in the dining rooms, in the elevators, in the corridors, and in their bedrooms.

From previous experience I knew this to be a phenomenon of American life, unknown to other countries. American women of middle age, and even of old age, like getting together in great numbers. I had encountered their hordes in Rome, Paris, Athens, and other capitals. I had marvelled at their indifference to fatigue—up and packed at 7 A.M.—their unflagging energy in museums and picture galleries, and their ceaseless curiosity about life in other lands. They establish a comradeship with other American women, write innumerable postcards to nephews and nieces, old college friends, and their own children or grandchildren. They are shrewd, humorous, and sentimental. Here in America they wield political influence and bring terrifying pressure to bear on congressmen in the lobbies and through the post. It was the power of the American women who put through Prohibition against the wishes of the nation, and but for Hitler, who declared war against the United States, I think it likely that the women would have brought equally great pressure against any possibility of an expeditionary force to Europe.

While waiting for a room to be vacated by some of these ladies I went down into the basement to the barbershop for a shave and haircut. Having been placed in a recumbent attitude in a swivel cair, a soft-handed darky gently took one of my feet and placed it on a steel rest, whereby I knew that he was about to give me a shoeshine. He did his job with loving care and then retired to a distant corner.

"Are these coloured folk contented?" I asked my barber.

He seemed surprised by the question, and I remember his answer.

"Why not? If I was to be borned again, I'd like to be borned a nigger or a Jew."

"How's that?" I asked, as though facing a conundrum.

"Becus the nigger don't need much money," said the barber, "and the Jew gets it."

He laughed very heartily at his own wit—fully justified—and informed me that a nigger is a happy-go-lucky kind of feller who is quite content if he gets enough to eat and has enough money to buy a few things for the fun of life as he sees it.

"They don't demand as much as the white man," he added. "I guess they're more simplehearted—like children."

When I went upstairs to my room the telephone rang. It was answered by Bob Keedick. He announced that two college girls wanted to interview me for their magazine.

"Shall I tell them to go away?"

"No, let them come up, poor dears."

Bob thought I was weak. I yielded too easily, he thought.

Those two girls seemed to have lost themselves. We waited ten minutes and still they did not come, but Bob thought he heard a scurrying outside the door. He went in search of them, and they confessed that at the sound of our voices they had fled. They had no courage, they said, to face an English author.

When they appeared they looked demure and self-composed and proceeded to ask me questions which they had written down beforehand.

"How do you think the war affects English authors?" asked one of them.

I answered that the war was killing most English authors by paper shortage, lack of royalties, and slow starvation.

"What do you think of American literature?"

I teased them a bit and then relented because they looked so shy and so anxious to get a real and serious interview. They were nice girls and had charming manners. They were two good specimens of a system of education which fills me with admiration, as I have already said, because it is so widespread and so admirable in its results on the great majority of the American people who have learned a new approach to life, a new and gentle behaviour, a keen desire for knowledge if it is not too hard to get. They thanked me very warmly when I left, and Bob laughed as he closed the door on them.

"You are too generous," he remarked. "You give out too much."

"One can't be too generous to young people," I told him. "I remember my own timidity as a boy. I was as shy as a fawn. In any case, I couldn't let them down. As an old journalist I'm on the side of the novices in journalism."

The telephone bell rang again. Bob answered it.

"There's a man downstairs who wants to talk to you. He says he's an old journalist. Shall I say you're busy?"

"Tell him I'll come down."

I went down and found a little man waiting for me.

"There are a thousand things I want to say," he told me. He said most of them, and he was a very remarkable little man, having been a press photographer in many countries of the world. Before the war he had been in Germany and had photographed Hitler and Goering and the other leaders.

"I saw the coming of German militarism," he told me. "I hung onto the end of a branch one day and photographed the march past of the new German Army. 'This is a great scoop,' I thought. 'The birth of German militarism. The menace of the world.' I sent the photographs to the London *Times*. 'They'll give a page to those pictures,' I thought. But when the London *Times* arrived there was one miserable little picture tucked away at the bottom of the page. They hadn't seen the importance of my stuff, or they decided to turn a blind eye to it. Everybody turned a blind eye to Hitler's growing strength."

This little photographer—a veteran of his profession—was gloomy about the war. He thought it ought never to have happened. He couldn't see how England could win. In his opinion it was time to make peace.

"The English people won't make peace," I told him. "They will refuse to make any kind of peace until Hitler has been crushed."

"But how can England do the job?" he asked. "Russia is bound to get whacked. The Germans are certain to get Moscow. Turkey looks like ratting. You are losing all your ships. The aeroplane has beaten the navy, and we over here are utterly unprepared. It will be a long time before we get going in full production. Can you hang out all that time?"

I assured him that we could, but he harked back to the possibility of peace.

"Would your people make peace if Hitler went?" he asked. I said that might make a difference if the German Army

news again, getting the big headlines in American newspapers for their terrific fight for life against the German invaders.

Meanwhile, in the midst of a world war inflicting agony, tortures, murder, and death upon millions of human beings, young Robert Keedick and I travelled in a superluxury train to Baltimore. It was streamlined and had two dining cars and lounge cars in which coloured waiters in white jackets served cocktails and highballs and other drinks to the endless music of the radio. All the picture magazines were on the tables. One had only to raise a little finger to get anything one wanted from one of these black attendants.

So we came to Baltimore in Maryland, a romantic city crowded with the ghosts of history who dwelt in old houses still left standing after revolution and civil war and devastating fire. I was impressed by those houses as I walked through old streets down to the docks. They were high and stately, with flights of stone steps leading to tall doorways and with brass railings on each side of the steps and eighteenth-century brick-work and decoration. I knew just enough about American history to guess at the lives of those who had dwelt here two centuries ago and later, after Captain John Smith had explored Chesapeake Bay and that inland harbour from Jamestown, Virginia. He it was who brought back the first Indian girl to London. They called her Princess Pocahontas, and the first job I had was in La Belle Sauvage Yard at Ludgate Hill, named after her. But he brought back more than an Indian squaw; he brought also that delectable weed called tobacco, which grew in Virginia and Maryland. Baltimore was one of the ports from which this precious cargo was carried to England. In these houses dwelt the merchants and traders of that plant for which all Europe was now greedy. Wheat also was grown in Maryland, and the Baltimore clippers, famous sailing ships, both fast and strong, were laden with this merchandise. Some of these houses, no doubt, were boardinghouses in those old days and gave lodging to English skippers who sailed across the Atlantic to carry those cargoes back to English ports.

A strange dramatic history passed through this city on Chesapeake Bay. Not trade alone brought English pioneers, but the desire for freedom of faith in time of persecution. Lord Baltimore founded a colony here for his fellow Catholics, and freedom of religion was established for all. It is still a Catholic stronghold, and it seemed to me and to my young friend who walked with me through Baltimore that we had never seen a city with so many churches of all denominations.

In those old houses we passed had dwelt traders of more valuable cargoes than tobacco, wheat, or maize. These dignified men who worshipped God on Sunday and brought up their families devoutly and sternly in the fear of the Lord did not find it against their conscience to deal profitably in human flesh and blood. Black ivory was their merchandise. In their ledgers, kept in the back parlours of those eighteenth-century mansions, were entries of so many slaves, at such and such a cost, sold for such and such a profit. They came in the slave ships to Baltimore, and the living were sorted from the dead or dying. It was more profitable to sell full-grown, able-bodied slaves than to rely on slave breeding. In Baltimore ladies in their fur-trimmed jackets and hooped skirts who went shopping down Charles Street or who attended chamber concerts in the Assembly rooms were the pretty flowers whose beauty was paid for by the black cargoes of the slave traders —their husbands and fathers—or by the owners of the slave ships who sailed from Africa to Baltimore and back again on voyages worth much gold at journey's end. From Baltimore much of this black ivory was transported to the slave market of Lexington, where it fetched good prices. So much for a buck nigger, so much for a woman with a newborn babe, so much for the souls and bodies of black humanity. No one felt the sting of conscience.

As I walked through Baltimore on a Sunday morning such history came back to me. Here was a tall and massive monument to George Washington. The society of Baltimore had been torn asunder by that revolution he made and led. There were loyalists to the English King who sailed away to the mother country and then came back again, trying to pick up their old trade in tobacco and wheat and slaves. I passed another statue. It was of Lafayette, who had been one of the leaders of the French Revolution and who is still an American hero. In 1917 the United States had paid back the debt by the lives of many American boys at Château Thierry.

In the Civil War Baltimore had been torn asunder again. Many were for the North, many for the South. The old slave-trading tradition had been very strong; why should they go against the South? But the North pulled them also, the Spirit of Liberty, the old belief in the freedom of faith which had helped to found their city. It was to Baltimore that many former slaves surged in after the defeat of the South and the liberation of the coloured folk, though many stayed with their old masters, who still employ their descendants in much the same conditions apart from freedom of service and wage earning.

We went into the Washington Monument below its tall column. It was a Sunday morning, as I have said, and the two attendants were listening intently to a sermon on selfishness by some eloquent clergyman. They took no notice of us, and I hope the sermon did them good.

That was the only sermon I heard that morning, but I was entertained at lunch by an ecclesiastical company who, as Catholics, were keeping up the old tradition of Baltimore as a Catholic stronghold. I was the guest of the Very Rev. Father Bunn and the faculty of Loyola College. They had another guest who was.Mr. Fleming, editor of the Baltimore *Sun,* born an Englishman, though he felt himself, he told me, to be an American.

After•chatting for some time about world affairs in Father Bunn's spacious study I was introduced to various members of the faculty and had an interesting time with them. One of them was a young Belgian priest—a refugee from his own land—with whom I spoke in French.

"I am disgusted with Vichy," he. said. "They are playing into the hands of the enemy."

He thought his own King Leopold had been greatly maligned, though not in England. He was glad that Winston Churchill had asked the English people to suspend judgment. Now, he said, further evidence had gone far to prove that this young man had acted with honour and had not betrayed his allies.

A young English priest, ascetic and dark-eyed, though with a keen sense of humour, surprised me by telling me that he had done a broadcast based on my journalistic affair with Dr. Cook—the bogus discoverer of the North Pole as told in my book *Adventures in Journalism.*

We sat down to a good luncheon at a long table with these

priests on either side, and after a Latin grace there was general conversation. My host had been to a German university. He knew the German people—their qualities and defects. He thought, as I do, that Latin civilisation had failed to penetrate the German forests. The Nazi code was a hark back to the old paganism.

That evening I lectured at the Lyric Theatre in Baltimore, a charming theatre famous for its concerts and musical productions. It was a very fine affair with all the people in evening dress. The governor of Maryland—O'Connor—was going to attend my lecture. For some time I sat in one of the boxes with a company of friends, watching the audience come in—a nervous ordeal for any lecturer. The stage looked very large and very empty. There was nothing on it but a microphone and a gold-tipped standard bearing the Stars and Stripes. I knew I should feel as small as a mouse when I stood there alone.

"Why isn't the Union Jack there as well as the Stars and Stripes?" I asked my host chafflingly.

He laughed at my audacity.

"Not at this stage of the war," he answered. "We're supposed to be neutral."

It was all very impressive and beautifully done. When the governor entered the whole audience rose and a choir sang "Maryland, My Maryland" followed by "The Star-Spangled Banner." Father Bunn and I retired to the back of the stage and smoked several cigarettes while waiting to go on.

"This cigarette smoking is just a nervous habit," said Father Bunn, lighting another. He felt as nervous as I did, I think, but, as my chairman, made an excellent speech before I stood in front of the microphone and did my best to interest that distinguished audience whose faces I could dimly see beyond the footlights.

No questions were asked that night. After the lecture there was a crowded reception at Loyola College. Father Bunn was in good form and had a merry word for everyone and made jokes about their names—good English names of Smith, Brown, and Robinson, but mostly, I think, good Irish names like O'Connor, Macdermott, Fitzgerald, with a considerable number of Scots. As the custom is in the United States, everyone said something kind about my address. I might have thought myself a heaven-sent orator if I had let this wine of praise go to my head. They were sincere, but they were also kind. These ladies and gentlemen of Baltimore, mostly Catholics, and hundreds of them, had an old-fashioned courtesy lit up by good humour. They had the gift, cultivated in the United States, for saying in a few words something rather good and something rather witty. English ladies and their American husbands held me for a moment or two to ask after some place in England particularly dear to them. The Irish contingent, chaffed by Father Bunn, was pleased to hear that I had had an Irish grandfather on my mother's side.

"That makes us feel more at ease," said one of them. "Ireland is not very helpful to England. just now. Her neutrality is not very wise and not very sound."

These Irish gentlefolk of Baltimore had heard a lot about England in my hour-long speech. They had not resented it, I found, and if they were isolationists, I saw no sign of it nor heard a word of it. They had charming manners and the Irish sense of humour. Among them were old acquaintances I had met in London. They reminded me of our meetings and were full of sympathy for all that London had suffered and for all its ruins.

"Are you going to make the Germans pay for all that?" one of them asked. It was a pretty lady.

She said it made her mad to think of that wanton bombing of women and children.

"We American women are trying to help," said another. "But there is so little we can do to share your burdens and suffering."

No one in that assembly guessed that within a month they would be under heavy attack by the combined forces of aggression and that many American soldiers and sailors would have already proved their heroism to the death.

Before I went to bed I found a letter on my table. It was not a love letter. It was a hate letter and read as follows:

THERE WILL ALWAYS BE AN ENGLAND
OF COURSE!!
AS LONG AS ONE HUNDRED AND
THIRTY MILLION AMERICANS ARE
WILLING TO BE SACRIFICED.

Next morning I sat in the lounge of the hotel while waiting for a train to Detroit and had a long talk with a young businessman who took a gloomy view of labour and social conditions in the United States.

"If we get into this war," he said, "everything will happen as it did last time. That is to say, Labour will force up wages by political pressure. During the last war people earned so much they didn't know what to do with their money. Men who had never worn anything but cotton or wool next to their skins bought silk shirts—ten at a time. They bought high-powered cars. They bought every darned thing that was mostly useless. It's all happening again because of this munitions work. Wages go rocketing up in the munition plants. One hundred and fifty dollars a month for half-skilled men. An intelligent typist used to get forty-eight dollars a month in the city offices. Now one can't get one. They're all being tempted away by the wages in the new plants. One hundred and forty-five dollars a month—more than a university professor is likely to get. And of course they're all living in the hire-purchase system. That's the American habit. High-school girls marry, and their young husbands hire a house for three hundred dollars as first instalment—a house built for three years before it falls down. Masses of 'em are now being built outside this city for the munition workers. Everybody spends too much. Everybody buys everything on the hire-purchase system and lives beyond his means. It's the American way of life. They throw their money about in having a good time and don't think of the future. Take these football crowds. There were sixty thousand in Baltimore last week. Some of them paid twenty-five bucks for a seat."

This young businessman was giving me the low-down on the darker aspects of American life. He was enjoying himself.

"Of course everybody knows that our President played into the hands of John Lewis, the Labour leader of the C.I.O. (Congress of Industrial Organizations), before he broke with him. Now he is giving all contracts to the A.F. of L. (American Federation of Labour). Labour rules. They know their power and use it. Even Henry Ford capitulated and adopted the closed-shop system. Couldn't stand out against it any longer. So Labour is never satisfied. Look at all these strikes. There's no loyalty. They strike for more wages and more power. Even the President will have to do something about it. The Santiago plant is in the hands of the military."

He was speaking without the knowledge that in a month's time Labour would call off all strikes for the duration of a war not then declared.

A casual remark by this young man aroused my interest on another subject less gloomy and indeed full of light.

"Have you seen the Enoch Pratt Library?" he asked. "It's the most wonderful thing in Baltimore."

"I would like to see it," I told him.

It was worth seeing—the most astonishing public library in any American city of this size, beautifully done, admirably organised, for the masses of the ordinary reading public and young students.

It has a magnificent building with its main hall and rooms opening direct from the street, with a kind of public welcome to the passers-by.

"We want to make it easy of access," said the lady librarian. "We don't want to frighten people by too many obstacles. They come straight in and walk to the books they want."

They have eight hundred thousand books, all finely classified on a simple system which enables any young student to go direct to the shelf where he finds the book he wishes to read. The vast, spacious rooms are full of light and air. Flowers are blooming on the tables, provided free by Baltimore florists. A talented artist whose name I forget has painted an immense fresco on one of the walls, and it is a good job of work in the style, I thought, of Puvis de Chavannes.

"Does the public make good use of this?" I asked.

The lady librarian laughed.

"We can hardly keep pace with their demands. We are

rather understaffed really. There is a steady rise in the reading appetite. Then we have branches in other parts of the city, all going strong. All the young people are reading—not too badly, and of course we have many serious students specialising in every kind of subject, including art."

I was led round the library and shown some of its treasures. Many lads and lasses were deep in big books and did not raise their eyes as we entered their reading rooms. Here there was an answer to that other picture of life about the hire-purchase system and the squandering of wages. American youth was reading—"not too badly." That is a promise for the future. The standard of intelligence is rising, and I am not a pessimist about the postwar years. Surely to God human intelligence will be good enough to make a decent peace next time. Surely to God the democratic peoples will get some control over their own destiny to prevent new massacres of youth in new wars. Eternal hope and eternal argument! Friends of mine jeer at me for such rosy optimism. "Man is a lousy animal," says one of them. "Haven't you read the history of mankind? Have you learned nothing about the unending conflict of the human species?"

I have! But in the Enoch Pratt Library in Baltimore I renewed my belief in human intelligence. Here is one of the lamps of civilisation. Not even Hitler can put it out. Here, as elsewhere, are the blueprints for a better world, now being studied by a younger generation who are reading "not too badly."

X

The City of Power

I ARRIVED IN DETROIT early in the morning. It was Armistice Day, 1941. Fifteen hundred American troops from Fort Custer marched in parade, wearing steel hats and overcoats. A hundred thousand people of Detroit watched them march past. Among them were veterans of World War I. They had lain under the crash of shells beyond the Chemin des Dames, in the woods beyond Verdun. They had flung themselves into the barrage fire at Château-Thierry. They had left many comrades behind, lying quiet under rows of white headstones in the fields of France. At the beginning of World War II I had stood bareheaded among them, strangled by the thought that all this sacrifice had not prevented another war worse than the last, more murderous because it killed women and children, without mercy, and because the sky was more crowded with bombing planes. Something had gone wrong with the last peace. The world's statesmen had made ghastly

mistakes. Youth in Germany had marched under the leadership of a man possessed by a demon. Britain had wanted peace
and a civilised way of life. It had disarmed below the safety
limit, while Hitler armed. Its government had tried to prevent
that war by a policy of appeasement which failed. All the
idealists of the world—the peace lovers—had refused to believe
that Hitler, that demoniacal man, would perjure himself so
deeply and break his solemn pledges. "I have no further
territorial ambitions in Europe." That liar had let us all down.
But today in Detroit the American troops from Fort Custer
celebrated the Armistice again and the memory of those who
had fallen.

Over the radio to Detroit and all American cities came a
fine, clear voice speaking in remembrance and in warning. It
was the voice of the American President:

*Our observance of this anniversary has a particular signifi-
cance in the year 1941. For we are now able today, as we
were not always able in the past, to measure our indebtedness
to those who died.*

*A few years ago, even a few months, we questioned, some
of us, the sacrifice they had made. Standing near to the Tomb
of the Unknown Soldier, Sergeant York of Tennessee, on a
recent day, spoke to such questioners. "There are those in
this country today," said Sergeant York, "who ask me and
other veterans of World War I, 'What did it get you?' "*

*Today we know the answer—all of us. All who search their
hearts in honesty and candour know it.*

*We know that those men died to save their country from
a terrible danger of that day. We know because we face that
danger once again, on this day.*

"What did it get you?"

People who asked that question of Sergeant York and his comrades forgot one essential fact which every man who looks can see today.

They forgot that the danger which threatened this country in 1917 was real—and that the sacrifice of those who died averted that danger. Because the danger was overcome they were unable to remember that the danger had been present.

Because our armies were victorious they demanded why our armies had fought.

Because our freedom was secure they took the security of our freedom for granted and asked why those who died to save it should have died at all.

"What did it get you?"

"What was there in it for you?"

If our armies of 1917 and 1918 had lost, there would not have been a man or woman in America who would have wondered why the war was fought. The reasons would have faced us everywhere. We would have known why liberty is worth defending as those alone whose liberty is lost can know it. We would have known why tyranny is worth defeating as only those whom tyrants rule can know.

But because the war had been won we forgot, some of us, that the war might have been lost. Whatever we knew or thought a few years or months ago, we know now that the danger of brutality and tyranny and slavery to freedom-loving peoples can be real and terrible.

We know why these men fought to keep our freedom—and why the wars that save a people's liberties are wars worth fighting and worth winning—and at any price.

"What did it get you?"

The men of France, prisoners in their cities, victims of searches and of seizures without law, hostages for the safety of their masters' lives, robbed of their harvests, murdered in their prisons—the men of France would know the answer to that question. They know now what a former victory of freedom against tyranny was worth.

The Czechs, too, know the answer. The Poles. The Danes. The Dutch. The Serbs. The Belgians. The Norwegians. The Greeks.

We know it now.

We know that it was, in literal truth, to make the world safe for democracy that we took up arms in 1917. It was, in simple truth and in literal fact, to make the world habitable for decent and self-respecting men that those whom we now remember gave their lives. They died to prevent then the very thing that now, a quarter century later, has happened from one end of Europe to the other.

Now that it has happened we know in full the reason why they died.

We know also what obligation and duty their sacrifice imposes upon us. They did not die to make the world safe for decency and self-respect for five years or ten or maybe twenty. They died to make it safe. And if, by some fault of ours who lived beyond the war, its safety has again been threatened, then the obligation and the duty are ours. It is in our charge now, as it was America's charge after the Civil War, to see to it "that these dead shall not have died in vain." Sergeant York spoke thus of the cynics and doubters: "The thing they forget is that liberty and freedom and democracy are so very precious that you do not fight to win them once and stop. Liberty and freedom and democracy are prizes awarded only to those

*peoples who fight to win them and then keep fighting eternally
to hold them."*

*The people of America agree with that. They believe that
liberty is worth fighting for. And if they are obliged to fight
they will fight eternally to hold it.*

*This duty we owe, not to ourselves alone, but to the many
dead who died to gain our freedom for us—and to make
the world a place where freedom can live and grow into
the ages.*

Those words are memorable. It was the last Armistice
spoken by a President of the United States before another
and more terrible war would demand the utmost sacrifice of
the nation. President Roosevelt had uttered a grave and
solemn warning, but it did not reach the imagination of the
great mass of his fellow countrymen. They did not and could
not see that their own safety and liberty were threatened by
that war over in Europe. They were so far away. Every one
was so secure. . . . Japan? . . . That was all bluff. The Japanese
were just trying to find a way to save face.

In the Detroit papers that day more news of strikes was
printed. The welders in West Coast shipyards threatened to
walk out. Two Mine Union chiefs resigned from the Medi-
ation Board. Trouble was brewing in many labour strongholds.

At the Hotel Statler I was met by several newspapermen
who plied me with questions about the war and were amused
when I retaliated by questions about the United States and
the minds of its people. One of them was a Canadian, and I
was surprised—a confession of ignorance—to find that Canada
was only ten minutes away by suspension bridge to Windsor.
This Canadian had been in the last war and had fought at

Cambrai. He was interested in the morale of the Canadian soldiers in England. He had heard that they were getting very bored and homesick because the invasion had not happened and they were getting no fighting. He resented American criticism of Canada because they had not introduced conscription.

"The Government fears a split with Quebec," he told me, and added that in his opinion the fears were quite unjustified.

Two ladies named Mrs. Stringer and Miss Snow were my fairy godmothers in Detroit and arranged a full programme during my visit. It included inevitably a visit to the Ford Works, and I saw the whole astounding show of that stupendous plant which is now turned over to war production. It covers eighteen hundred acres and employs ninety thousand men. Up to date it has produced twenty-nine million cars, but now it is beginning the production of tanks and other weapons of war which will pour out from the assembly lines by mass production methods when all is ready.

It all begins on the River Rouge alongside the plant where barges come up with raw material to be converted into steel from the iron ore. We passed enormous coke ovens and then went into a great hall like the forge of Vulcan, in time to see the dramatic moment when one hundred and eighty tons of molten steel are poured into tubs and carried away overhead on travelling cranes.

We stood on a high platform awaiting the tide of metal to be loosed. A friendly guide handed us black mirrors to save our eyes from the burning light of the furnaces. Only a few workmen were visible. They were cased in asbestos to protect them from the sparks. The furnace doors were opened; a river of metal ran out and poured into the vast vats below. I was afraid of my eyes and looked at this spectacle in the dark mirror, where even in this image it was intensely bright.

I do not feel at home in foundries or in the near neighbourhood of blast furnaces. They always make me feel that man is remarkably like a devil when he works with fire and the fury of molten metal. Here in the Ford Works the scene was rather terrifying in its control of elemental forces. The men were flinging sacks into the tubs—the alloys which go to make hard steel. Great showers of sparks were flung into the air, and each spark was like a shooting star, intensely bright, intensely hot. These showers of sparks fell near us—too dangerously near, I thought, though I had faith in our guides, who moved us back a pace or two. The liquid steel gushed out, and as I watched it I thought of the fighting men in Libya, in Russia, in China, in England, waiting for this metal to come to them in the form of tanks, aeroplanes, guns. Henry Ford, the man of peace, the man who sailed a peace ship in the first World War, is now the master blacksmith of the democracies, fighting for life and liberty against devilish forces. I did not accuse him of inconsistency. He is forging the sword to slay the dragon of cruelty devouring women and children and all life's beauty. Here in the Ford factories was the potentiality of that weapon which no nation under evil leadership will withstand when it is ready to strike.

He is an extraordinary little man is Henry Ford, whom I met years ago for a minute or two when he came to one of my lectures in this city of Detroit. I remember that he wore a big fur collar on his overcoat and looked very delicate and ascetic. He is not a hard-faced materialist piling up wealth for its own sake, driving men hard to get the best out of them before they are thrown to the scrap heap. He is a simple idealist as well as an ironmaster. He is a sentimentalist as well as the founder of mass production. He believes in beauty, in holy shrines, in the spirit of men and women, and in human kindness.

All that is revealed in Greenfield Village, Dearborn, which he has built around his old home. I went there very early one morning, rising at six-thirty, in the hope of seeing him at his children's service in his little Martha-Mary Chapel dedicated to his mother and his wife's mother. By bad luck he was not there that morning, but I sat in the gallery looking down on the children while they were singing their hymns. It was very simple and very touching. I had to speak to the children, and some of them giggled because of my English accent, but soon I had them listening intently when I told them about the children of England under air bombardment and asked them to think now and then of those small people far away in the war zone.

Greenfield Village is a memorial to the early life of the American people and to their progress up to the recent history. Henry Ford searched the country for a typical little homestead, post office, and store of the early nineteenth century, which he could buy and remove to this spot. There they now stand, as though always there, a post office of 1805 with its handmade nails and shutters, an old-time gristmill, a general store, a shoemaker's shop, a cooper's shop, a blacksmith's forge. The real old articles sold more than one hundred years ago were brought to the general store. To bring back the life of the American people before the Pilgrim Fathers set forth Henry Ford transported an old cottage from the Cotswolds. Sheep were brought from England to start a flock, pigeons to coo on the roof, old English flowers to grow in its garden.

At one end of the village stands one of the old windmills from Cape Cod, and there is an old pioneer log cabin with all the domestic utensils used by the early settlers. Edison's laboratory is there with all its instruments as he used and left them. There is the cycle shop of the Wright brothers, pioneers of aviation, and, most moving of all, the little workshop in which Henry Ford himself made his first motorcar and then had to break down a wall to get it out. In the museum is a marvellous collection, showing the evolution of engines and a thousand other things during the past century or two. It is all well thought out, beautifully arranged, and stimulating to the imagination. Henry Ford knew what he was about. It was not a hobby but a big idea.

"When we are through," he said once, "we shall reproduce American life as lived, and that, I think, is the best way of preserving at least a part of our American history and tradition. For by looking at things which people used, and which show the way they lived, a better and truer impression can be gained than could be had in a month of reading."

In this village on the banks of the River Rouge, whose tide brings up the raw material for his vast plant, Henry Ford has revealed the dream in his mind and the vision which is bigger than his mass production. He wants people to be happy. He wants a cleaner and better world. In his simple, unliterary way he tries to express his belief in human progress towards something finer and better than the squalour of a half civilisation with its dirt and its sediment of misery. He gives the children of his workers good schools. He gives their parents gardens and allotments. He looks after their health and well-being. He pays them the highest rate of wage. If they complain of the strain on the assembly line, he moves them to lighter works. It is a pity that this devotee of peace has had to turn his machine tools to the production of war weapons—a pity but a grim and terrible necessity.

I saw these things in Greenfield Village, near Dearborn, by the favour of a good guide named William Adams Simonds, who has written a book about it all called *Henry Ford and Greenfield Village*. It is charmingly written.

One other fact about Henry Ford is worth recording because it has some bearing on the present war. For the past year or so he has thrown open his workshops to two thousand young naval men who have received a very good course of technical training in engineering. It was a *beau geste* to the Government of the United States, who had not been generous or wise in refusing Henry Ford's offer to provide innumerable tanks long before they now are called for in all desperate haste.

I had one amusing experience in Detroit, somewhat painful at the time, or at least embarrassing. As in other cities, I was taken round to a broadcasting station to be interviewed "on the air" and on the spur of the moment. I had enjoyed this form of broadcast talks demanding an alert mind and quick answers without the tedious and censored preparations demanded by the B.B.C. But my interviewer had got firmly into his head the idea that I was a dramatic critic. He questioned me on my opinion of various American actors and actresses of whom, I am ashamed to say, I had never heard. Vainly did I try to switch him off that line of thought. Always he returned to it, and I was at my wit's end to invent plausible answers.

I lectured in the Fisher Hall, a marvellous building put up by the Fishers of Lexington, of whom I have written. In addition to its theatre it has shops, offices, and restaurants and is a great hive of activity. I remember one incident which excited the secret laughter of young Robert Keedick, though I found it very charming. After my lecture, and in the presence of the theatre audience, I was embraced by a very gracious lady who kissed me on both cheeks. It was Lady Ashfield, who had been doing splendid and arduous work for Britain and British War Relief. I had the pleasure of sitting next to her at luncheon that day when I had to make another speech and answer many questions. It was all very exciting.

In the hotel a young waiter came up to me and made a friendly suggestion.

"There's a movie going on which you might like to see. It wouldn't take you ten minutes."

I went into a picture theatre provided by the hotel. They were showing a film of the making of American bombers, from the first step to the last. The pictures were good, but what startled me was the text of the commentary which went with them. It was astonishingly impressive. Its phrases were like hammer blows. The man who wrote them could use words of power, grim, strong, startling. They had the rhythm of an anvil.

"One bomber . . . Hundreds more . . . Thousands to come."

"Strong wings . . . Strong in flight . . . Strong in action."

It was a kind of prose poem on the coming might of the American war machine, terrible and avenging and liberating. I listened with a queer feeling down the spine.

"Who wrote those words?" I asked.

Someone answered, "Carl Sandburg."

They were very kind to me in Detroit, though they worked me hard. And when I departed I had more optimism than earlier in my travels. For I had seen mighty plants preparing to turn out vast numbers of war machines for our use and for Russia and for China. I had seen a tide of molten metal turning into steel. I had seen Henry Ford's plans and plant for defending us from the demons and the dragons who are ravaging the world.

But one thing was very queer in this experience of mine in Detroit. I was in one of the strongholds of the isolationists, according to information received. It was in Detroit that Lord Halifax was "egged," as they say in America. But no isolationist had come my way. In that theatre audience no one had risen to ask a hostile question or make a demonstration against intervention. It would have been a good opportunity. They did not take advantage of it. Something seemed to be happening to isolationism in the Middle West. Was it, by any chance, fading out?

I confess I was surprised to hear that a city called Lansing, my next port of call, was the capital of the state of Michigan, whereas I had always thought that Detroit was the more important city. In any case, I can recall very little of Lansing as I arrived late and had to dress hurriedly at the Hotel Olds before my lecture, having been transported there by a gentleman who might have been the original of Mr. Cheeryble, by name of Mr. Clarke. Later I was introduced to Mr. and Mrs. Maclean, the former being my chairman at the highschool auditorium—a big hall holding a fine audience.

Now my recollection of Lansing will be forever associated with poached eggs, for after the lecture I was invited by Mr. and Mrs. Clarke to their pleasant home on the Grand River ravine and, being received by the most informal and pleasing hospitality, found myself in the kitchen with Bob Keedick watching a demonstration by Mrs. Clarke of the only true way of poaching eggs which afterwards would strengthen us at that late hour.

Mrs. Clarke poaches eggs with art and craft. First of all she took a slice of bread and very deftly cut out a triangular piece before putting it into a frying pan with melted butter. Into that hole she poured a new-laid egg which immediately began to sizzle with the most pleasing sound. At the precise nick of time when the bread was browned and the egg at perfection she took a silver instrument and whisked the poached egg onto a hot plate. It was all done daintily and with great skill while that genial man, Mr. Clarke, was preparing certain liquids which had a most cheering effect. After dinners and luncheons and receptions, crowded with people whose names I had to memorize, this glimpse of American informality was very agreeable.

"One of these days we shall get bombed," said Mrs. Clarke quite cheerfully. "We are an excellent target."

"In what way?" I asked, lingering over my poached eggs and feeling very happy in a drawing room furnished in a somewhat old-fashioned style and very cosy on a cold night, with a cheerful fire on the hearth.

"Not far from here is a big Oldsmobile plant," she told me. "They're making aeroplanes, guns, shell casings, and all the beautiful new toys for the game of war. Well, it's no use worrying."

It was curious that she should even have thought of worrying at that time, which was November 12, 1941. It was still some weeks away from December 7, when the American people started worrying.

XI

Streamline Train

WE WENT from Lansing to Chicago by way of a local train to Jackson in which there were only four or five passengers. These local trains could not keep up with the competition of the roads now that almost everybody has his own car and uses it for short-distance journeys. But a severe rationing of tires after the burning of rubber forests in Malaya will crowd them again.

At Jackson we changed into a superluxury streamline train, sank into the deep comfort of chairs in the parlour car, ate too much in the splendour of the restaurant car, and spent many hours observing human nature in the lounge car, which was generously provided with a cocktail bar for liquid refreshment at any time. The train was lively on its way to Chicago. The passengers were well-to-do people, including many young women smartly dressed and familiar with the art of cosmetics. They had been on their journey for some time when we joined them at Jackson. They had started as strangers but, with the warm influence of old-fashioneds and other attractive forms of alcohol, were getting together very nicely.

It was a Sunday. Somewhere in the world was a murderous war. The enormous headlines in the Sunday papers recorded its history, its murderous fighting, its blood and death. The Russians were still resisting at Moscow, where two pincer movements of the enemy were closing in, thirty miles or so from the capital. The Russians claimed to be inflicting enormous casualties but were losing ground. Heaps of German dead, they said, lay in the snow. In Libya the British were smashing their way past Tobruk, but strong forces of German tanks were trying to break out of the trap into which they had been forced. It was all very confused—this desert fighting. There were isolated tank battles. Groups of men on both sides were cut off and captured. Some of the British and American correspondents had been taken prisoner. The desert was littered with battered tanks, broken trucks, the dying and the dead. Men were crying out for water with blistered tongues. Young British soldiers, young German soldiers, were being killed, wounded, blinded, burned, and parched by this bloody struggle in the sand. The war in the air went on. Ships were being sunk in the Atlantic and in the Mediterranean. Merchant seamen were being drowned. Hostages were being shot in Paris. There were hunted men in the mountains of Yugoslavia. Agony and despair covered many lands. Hunger and disease were stalking through many cities. Women and children were starving in thousands of villages. There was no happiness in Europe and laughter was forgotten.

But here in the superluxury streamline train on its way to Chicago we were all very jolly. As the train rushed on through space at a great speed we became more and more jolly. Laughter rose in gusts. Everybody was getting together. Groups of them were singing—jolly little songs, funny little songs.

A group of eight men—prosperous businessmen of young middle age—were enjoying themselves and emitting deep stomach laughs at the absurdity of one of them—a tall, lanky, lean fellow—who was undoubtedly drunk but very amusing.

He was backing a friend of his to outwalk any of the others for any distance.

"How much do you bet, buddy?"

"Fifty bucks. And I'll win it. I'll make it a hundred. Ted can walk you all dead. He has a fine physique. Look at him now. Look at his limbs. Look at his chest. An athlete. All you fellows are potbellied. You all eat too much. You all drink too much. . . . Have another drink, boys."

The young man who was being backed gave vent to explosions of laughter at these descriptions of his physical fitness. The others were convulsed with mirth at these descriptions of their degenerate conditions.

"I'm a bit of a walker," said one of them. "I walk a hell of a lot round a golf course. I'll take on Ted at any time if you'll put up a hundred and fifty bucks."

"You will? Then it's a bet. A hundred and fifty bucks."

"Any conditions about footwear?" asked one of the men.

"If you will all take it on, I'll join you," said a stout, square-shouldered man with a big jowl and blue eyes. "I haven't walked a yard for months, but I'm a man of spirit."

"You're soaked in spirit," said another. "If I put a match to you, you would burn."

They chaffed each other, insulted each other, and roared with laughter.

The tall, lean, lanky man who was backing his friend against the rest kept up a ceaseless monologue. He was standing all the time and swaying as the train travelled fast. He was undoubtedly drunk, but in a gentlemanly way, solemn, eloquent, courteous, and absurd.

"Gentlemen," he said, "this is a historic day. This walk will live in our annals. If any of you would like to increase the stakes, I am prepared to go as far as two hundred bucks."

He called to one of the white-jacketed waiters to bring another set of drinks. It was the sixth round, as far as I could reckon.

Farther down the car was a little grey-haired man who was standing drinks to two young soldiers. In return for his drinks they were willing to listen to his flow of words. It never ceased for two hours or more. He was passionate about the political situation in the United States. He was denunciatory, expostulatory, and vituperative. I never discovered whether he was for or against President Roosevelt or whether he believed in isolationism or intervention, but could catch only passing phrases, disconnected and meaningless.

"How is this country of ours going to get through all this?"

"I ask you young fellows whether you are willing to fight or die for dirty political bastards or for the sacred cause of Liberty?"

"What I want to know is just this. Now I'm putting it to you. I ask for your attention. I want your well-considered answers. I am not trying to thrust anything down your throats, my boys. This is a free discussion. Have another beer, sonny."

He was like a jack-in-the-box. Over and over again he rose a few inches above his seat with his forefinger thrust out and his eyes lit with the fire of intellectual passion.

One of the young soldiers was utterly silent. He never made any attempt at an answer but just sat there sipping his beer and smoking cigarettes with a look of intense boredom. The other young man spoke a few half-finished sentences, instantly interrupted by the little jack-in-the-box.

"Yes, but——"

"No sir, there is no 'but.' This is a clear-cut argument. As I was saying——"

He said a lot more.

"Well, I can't help thinking," said the young soldier.

"But haven't I just explained? Haven't I been making my point clear that——"

He made his point clear by tapping on the little table with his stiff forefinger.

Farther back in the car was a choral group. The young women were singing in shrill voices. Middle-aged women joined in. Six or seven men were providing the deeper notes. A pretty dark-haired woman was doing a little dance between the chords, with a glass in one hand and a sandwich in the other.

"Way down on the Suwanee River."

"Poor old Joe."

"Polly-wolly-doodle."

They were singing rather well, in harmony. Between each song they clapped and laughed at their own efforts. The little dancing lady with merry eyes broke a glass. Other glasses were brought by the white-jacketed waiters, who were grave and businesslike in this high-spirited company.

"I once came face to face with a ghost," said one of the girls who was standing up clutching the back of a chair to steady herself. She turned as I tried to pass her and was quite startled.

"God, here he is again!" she cried. There was a loud chorus of laughter.

"Pardon me," I said, making my way to my own place to fetch some cigarettes.

Hours later we slowed down. We were slipping into Chicago. A crescendo of noise had filled the last hour. Almost everybody was singing. Almost everybody was shouting. Then suddenly it all quieted down. It was time to pull themselves together to meet husbands and wives and mothers and aunts.

In the lavatory the tall, lean, lanky man was putting water on his head. He looked very, very ill, with a dead-white face.

"We shall never meet again," said one of the ladies to the girl who had danced with a glass in her hand, "but it has been great fun, my dear."

It was the girl who had danced with a glass in her hand who caught my eyes and smiled as I passed her on the platform in Chicago. She had been very lit up.

"Hullo, Mother!" she cried as a white-haired lady rushed up to her.

XII

The City of Chicago

A TAXICAB DRIVER in Chicago, hearing my English accent, turned slightly in his seat and asked me how long it was since I had been in America.

"Nearly twenty years," I told him. "Too long!"

"See any changes?" he asked, speaking over his shoulder as he steered round the edge of a lorry and plunged into a tide of traffic.

I told him I saw many changes in Chicago. New hotels and high blocks along Lake Shore Drive. And I found the American people changed—better educated, more genial in their courtesy, very well informed.

"You're wrong," he said. "They're all dumb."

I laughed at him and rebuked his pessimism.

"I'm telling you," he said. "They get dumber and dumber. Why, if I talk to them about history or economics, they don't understand the words I'm using."

Bob Keedick gave a big guffaw. He was enjoying this point of view.

"I ought to know," said the taxicab driver. "I meet thousands of them. They get into my cab. They have no use for intelligent conversation. They're all morons and half-wits. It's terrible."

"I don't agree with you," I told him. "I've been talking to people in all sections, and I'm certain that the American educational system is bearing good fruit."

"You've been lucky," he murmured dryly. "I can't find any sense in them. It's terrible. Can't speak proper English. Don't read. Never think. Something ought to be done about it. They ought to be taught birth control so that they don't go on reproducing their kind. When I look at all these crowds I get gloomy. What's the use of 'em? What are they making of life? How can we get civilised with all these dumbbells walking about? Not a single idea in their heads above that of animal life. What do they know about international affairs? Just nothing at all. How are they trying to shape their destiny? They don't try. They don't know what destiny means. They're just crazy."

I took an optimistic view, but he wouldn't listen.

Presently I asked him if there was any news. He was held up in a block of traffic and he turned on his radio.

A voice spoke to us. It was the voice of an announcer.

"The House, in accord with last-minute appeal by the President, approved today the Administration's bill authorising American ships to sail anywhere in the world under the protection of their own flag and guns.

"The vote was announced as 212 to 194, a margin of

eighteen votes in a hard-fought victory for the Administration."

"That's that," said our taxicab driver. "It means we're in the Battle of the Atlantic. It means that the isolationists have taken the K.O."

The news of the world was interrupted, as it is always interrupted on the American radio, by a dramatised advertisement of some popular product. Someone was describing a particular brand of nut chocolate, soft, luscious, creamy, full of health-giving vitamins, delicious to the taste. Yum-yum!

"Muck!" said the taxicab driver. "One can't get any news without having to listen to that advertising stuff. There's too much of it. It makes me mad."

We had further conversation about life, the city of Chicago, and human destiny. When we had come to our destination the taxicab driver shook hands with me heartily.

"I like a bit of conversation," he said. "I'm glad to meet an Englishman. I'm Roumanian-Irish."

We laughed at his own strange mixture of blood.

I was in the city of Chicago, and I explored it by day and night, having some time to spare before the date of my lecture.

"See the City Beautiful" was the slogan on the Chicago motor coaches.

I saw it.

I saw it after dark with all its lights. They were red, green, and yellow lights, outside all the big stores and small shops, high up, as high as the stars they looked, on tall towers and vast blocks. They were winking and blinking, twisting and writhing, going out, lighting up, spiralling, below a sky of blue velvet. There were lighted signs drawing pictures in endless repetition—pictures in fire of derby hats, boots, bottles, silk

stockings. There were stars of light, wings of light, all advertising American products. The tall skyscrapers under the sky
of blue velvet were floodlit and touched by enchantment. The
Wrigley Tower, built out of the profits of chewing gum, was
magical like a fairy tower.

I heard the noise of Chicago, with its ceaseless roar of
motor traffic like muffled drums. The overhead railway thun-
dered by, whistling, hooting, grinding, rumbling as one walked
beneath it. Police sirens wailed, motorcars honked. Bells rang.
Chicago is never quiet, unless one goes beyond the streets to
the long promenade by Lake Michigan—miles long—with only
the murmur of the city in one's ears like the beating of the
sea against rocks. There it is quiet and beautiful, with the
whole sky line of skyscrapers and blocks of white offices im-
mensely high, and towers and turrets, as fantastic as a dream.

I walked up and down there one day to get the sun and
then sat by the side of an old man on a seat facing the lake.

"This is a great city," I said by way of introduction.

"No," he said, "it's a rotten city."

I raised my eyebrows and laughed.

"How's that?"

"Rotten with politics. Rotten with graft. It wants clearing
up. One has to pay ten cents for a bus which hasn't been renewed for twenty years. And there's no connection with the
elevated, where one pays another ten cents. So the people get
robbed. In New York one can travel anywhere for a nickel
on the subways."

He took a pipe from his mouth and spat between his feet.
He was a tall old man with blue eyes and a little beard.

"I know England," he told me. "There's nothing you can
teach me about Liverpool or Grimsby or Hull or the London

docks. Been there scores of times. Now they've all been bombed."

"A sailor?" I asked.

He nodded.

"Since I was a boy of fourteen. I was mostly in sailing ships and never could get used to steam. I've been most places. The Pacific coast, South America, Hamburg, the Baltic. Now I'm retired. I sit here and watch the lake and do a bit of thinking. I've been thinking about this war and the world. My God! And they call it a Christian world!"

He laughed harshly and spat again between his feet.

"This war is going to be a tough business. When America gets going, it's going big."

He stared at the great grey water of Lake Michigan and then spoke with a kind of quiet passion.

"They'll have to get it—those dirty Germans. We've got to bomb them mercilessly because they had no mercy on other folk—machine-gunning women and children on the roads, dropping high explosives on civilian populations, bombing hospital ships and ambulances. That's not going to be forgotten or forgiven. People say it's the German leaders. I say it's the German race. I say it's the German nature. I know them. I speak a bit of their tongue. Thousands of men ought to be lined up all over Germany and shot like mad dogs. I'd leave a hundred, maybe, out of each thousand."

He spoke with a cold ruthlessness while relighting a black old pipe.

"The people in the captured countries ought to be helped to rise," he said. "You ought to see that they have weapons in their hands when the time comes for the rising. If you can't send them by sea, send them by air. Drop them down at night.

Smuggle them in. There's always a way. Those barstards must
be beaten or life won't be worth living in any country."

"Certainly they must be beaten," I agreed. "But some of
them are decent people. They didn't want this war."

"You're wrong," he told me. "I know those Germans. They
all think they're better than other folk—a superior race. I live
in a lodging house where there are Germans. They don't know
I understand their way of speech. They're always talking about
Hitler and Germany. They're certain sure that Hitler's going
to win. They want him to win. They talk about the invincible
German Army. They get glad every time he smashes through
another country. If America ever enters this war, some of those
people will find themselves in concentration camps. They're all
fixed. It's not like last time, when they did all their dirty
sabotage. I wouldn't trust any of 'em. If Roosevelt hadn't
taken action, South America would have gone to Hitler without a shot being fired. It's lousy with them."

He gave a heavy groan ending with a laugh.

"And they call this a Christian world. . . . My God!"

Young Keedick and I took walks in Chicago. We walked
the whole length of Michigan Avenue as far as the Drake
Hotel, where I had stayed twenty years ago. It was then newly
opened and lonely out there. Now it is surrounded by vast
blocks of buildings. But it still remains a hotel with the last
word in luxury. Bob Keedick and I took a little refreshment
there after our long walk and sank for a little while into its
richness.

Everything is on a vast scale in Chicago. It exhibits, in a
thundering way, the abundance of American mass production. In London there are big stores—Harrod's, Selfridge's,
Barker's—but here in Chicago there are bigger stores and

more of them, so that they seem endless and innumerable. Here are the Marshall Field stores, biggest of all in the world, and enormous chain stores and tremendous shops with long vistas of the goods they sell. In Paris before the war a boot shop exhibited a pair of golden shoes on a velvet pedestal. Here in a boot shop there are thousands of boots and shoes. There are hosiery shops with millions of silk stockings shown through the plate-glass windows. The names over the stores, I noticed, were mostly foreign and mostly Jewish—Goldsmidt, Schyder, Schultke. Food, diamonds, furs, candies, clothes are heaped up for show in this bazaar of the Middle West, and it is all symbolised in a fruit shop I saw with a golden horn of plenty from which poured out thousands of oranges.

Dense and endless crowds surged down the streets. When they halted at the crossings I mingled with them and heard snatches of conversation, mostly about the price of things—so many dollars, so many cents. Here and there were coloured folk. Standing in a doorway was a young coloured girl who looked alien and solitary in this crowded street, as though standing there in a dream.

I stayed at a hotel which would have excited the soul of Arnold Bennett because of its bigness. He would have gone into the kitchens to see the service behind the scenes for thousands of guests. He would have counted the hundreds of forks, the thousands of towels, the millions of lumps of sugar.

The Palmer House, Chicago, is more than a hotel. It is a small city with a theatre, shops, offices, ballrooms, dining rooms, reception rooms, concert rooms, restaurants, and drawing rooms. I explored all this as a study of American life in the hotel world. I lunched in the Victoria Room. I dined in the Empire Room. I took breakfast in the coffee shop, where hundreds of people were beginning their day at the long stool counters. I lectured in the Grand Ball Room. I went into the shops. I watched the crowds in the Reception Hall, always arriving, always going, as in the Grand Central Station of New York. I sipped pleasant liquids in the Petit Café, where smart people came for cocktails, highballs, and private conversation as the lights changed from blue to red, from red to yellow, or left them in a dim religious light, but not, as I heard, in a dim religious mood. Here in this great block was an exhibition of American life in its most prosperous aspects and a rendezvous of dancing, laughing, love-making, dollar-making, people of all ages, of all types—realists, idealists, pleasure seekers, money seekers, time killers.

Some big brain must be behind all this, watching everything, organising everything. It was Potter Palmer's brain who began it all in 1852. He was one of the founders of Chicago, then a city of forty-eight thousand. He worked on bold and original lines in the store which created enough wealth to give him the chance of bigger enterprises when he sold it to Marshall Field. He travelled to Europe, with a keen eye for all its new ideas and ancient splendour. "What's good for Europe is good for Chicago," he thought. "I'll show them." He came back and bought up great tracts of land in Chicago and put up great buildings on it, twenty-two of them, all destroyed by a devastating fire in 1871. The Old Palmer House was the finest hotel even seen in the Middle West. It was filled lavishly with marble from Europe. Its great ballroom was a wonder of the time. The New Palmer House is to the old like a modern battleship is to the first ironclad.

"Building as of temples and palaces," writes the author of a book about the Palmer House, sent to me by the management, "is a royal game, and upon it man has spent his worthiest and mightiest efforts throughout history. To build for beauty and worship, whether Parthenon or cathedral, is a quest for the immortality of the soul, as to build pyramid or mausoleum is an attempt to make the fame of earthly power everlasting." Old Potter Palmer has built his own memorial in this hotel, and if his ghost haunts it he will be satisfied by the number of its guests and its crowded business.

I sat one evening in the Petit Café reading the Chicago *Daily Tribune.* The news from the outer world was very grim.

The British Admiralty announces today that the aircraft carrier Ark Royal *has been sunk by a torpedo.*

The carrier was sunk while being towed, after being torpedoed by a U-boat. The casualties were not heavy as a large number of the ship's crew had been taken off.

So the *Ark Royal* had gone at last, after the Germans had announced its sinking several times before. I thought of a young officer I knew in England who was with it and hoped he was safe.

I glanced at other headlines.

HOUSE PASSES NEUTRALITY ACT
REPEAL 212–194

LEWIS TO FACE
SHOWDOWN IN COAL STRIKES
CALLED TO SEE F.D.R.
IN MINES CRISIS

U.S. STEPPING
CLOSER TO WAR
LONDON TOLD

I read that column about the United States coming closer to war and then looked round the Petit Café in Chicago. These people were not worrying. That news did not seem to interest them at all.

At the table next to me were four girls, smartly dressed. They were talking in quiet tones over their highballs of whiskey and soda. One of the girls ordered a second round.

"She has been married mentally for quite a long time·now," I heard her say.

The lights changed and dimmed so that I could see only the silhouettes of people about me. Out of this semidarkness, and in the confusion of voices, I heard a man telling a story to his friends.

"They only served one kind of cocktail—brandy and benedictine. They served sixteen hundred guests. Can you visualise it? Sixteen hundred glasses!"

Near me a little man was celebrating a government contract he had obtained through a purchasing agent who was his friend.

"I said to him: We fully understand your trouble about priority. Yes sir! Sure we'll do our best with that contract. Don't you worry. America first is our slogan. Yes sir!"

One of the girls at the table next to mine questioned her friend opposite.

"Are you raising little Catholics or just a family?"

A young man spoke over his cocktail.

"Oh boy! She's a lovely gal. I'm just telling you."

I had noticed a good-looking pair not far from where I sat. The man was about thirty-five, the girl much younger. They talked quietly and seriously.

"You're looking very pretty tonight," said the man.

The girl did not answer that remark but questioned him about his plans.

"What are you going to do, Teddy? How are we going to live? We can't grub along on nothing at all. My mother——"

"I propose to make a success of myself in a year," said the man. "One can do it in a year. It's easy!"

It was the evening of November 14. It was three weeks away from December 7 and Pearl Harbor. I had heard no comment on the war from these people in the Petit Café. It was far from their minds. There was no talk about Japan. Why should there be? Japan was far away, and in a shocking bad state, on the other side of the Pacific. This was Chicago, mightily prosperous, bursting with abundance, big, progressive, dynamic. And Chicago was against the war. They were isolationists. The Chicago *Tribune* was in the hands of Colonel McCormick, called by one of his critics "One of the foremost minds of the fourteenth century." He was against intervention. He was against the war. He had millions of readers who followed him.

No isolationists showed up at my lecture, which was under the auspices of the Charles Caroll Forum. My chairman was a very charming and distinguished priest, full of humour, and a live wire. He was very careful to point out to the audience that the Forum had no political purpose but was for the open discussion of all subjects in which American people should be interested. They could not isolate themselves from the rest of humanity, and they should be able to listen to speakers who might express views contrary to their own but who came to tell of things they knew. In introducing me, very generously, he said I had not come as a propagandist but as a literary man, journalist, and war correspondent, and therefore a recorder of world events.

"Here," thought I, "do I meet the isolationists?"

But they did not appear. In the open discussion the questions were not hostile, except from one man.

"How," he asked, "do you reconcile your present attitude towards the war with all your books advocating peace? I cannot see how you reconcile those opposite points of view."

"That's a mean one," said my chairman, smiling at me.

But I thought it a fair question and one that could be answered without embarrassment.

I admitted, with no sense of guilt or regret, that ever since the last war my pen had been busy denouncing war and praising peace. I was not ashamed of having worked for peace. It was the purpose behind all my novels and books on contemporary history. I had tried to keep a bridge between Germany and Great Britain to the last possible moment, knowing and dreading the horrors that would follow if the bridge broke down. It broke down when Hitler proved himself to be a liar and a perjurer, when he broke all his solemnly made pledges, when he crossed the Czech frontier and marched into other people's territory. War was then inevitable. This war had to be fought because Hitler had challenged all that we had been struggling for through many centuries: freedom of ideas, freedom of faith, the decent code of civilised human beings. It was the Spirit of Evil which had come out of the slime.

This answer did not satisfy my questioner. I had a letter from him afterwards saying that he was disillusioned and disgusted with me. I had preached peace and then ratted into the camp of the warmongers. I received that letter after December 7. My answer was simple.

"Do you wish to surrender to the Japanese?"

On my last evening in Chicago I dined in the odour of sanctity, not obtrusive above the bouquet of good wine and the aroma of good food. My host was the handsome priest who had been my chairman. Among the guests was a bishop who was as humorous as he was scholarly. Years ago he had served in a church at Bayswater in London, and he asked after the old places. He had been a friend of Cardinal Gasquet, whom I knew in Rome, and of Cardinal Bourne in London.

"How do they address a bishop in the United States?" I asked him. "Do they say 'My Lord' in this democratic country?"

His eyes twinkled.

"Generally they address me as 'Hey, Bishop!' "

We had ladies at our table and good conversation. There was no hint of isolationism. These people were convinced that America could not keep out of a war which England was fighting against diabolical forces with the Sword of the Spirit and even with American aeroplanes, all too few as yet. But the great mass of the multitude in Chicago were, I am convinced, untouched as yet by the knowledge that this was their war as well as Britain's and that very soon now they would be stabbed in the back by Japan. Those vast crowds walking the streets of Chicago, surging into the Palmer House, sipping little liquids in its Petit Café, taking the overhead railway to back streets, did not believe that the United States was in danger and that they would be called upon for sacrifice and suffering. They were one thousand miles from New York.

They were four thousand miles from Europe. Who could touch them?

One voice had warned them at that time, but they paid no heed to it. It was the voice of a man named Winston Churchill.

If the United States should become involved in a war with Japan [he said], *a British declaration would follow within an hour.*

"A mighty big 'If,' " was the comment I heard. "Japan has sent a fellow to talk peace. They're out for saving face. They're rotten all through, and they know it."

But Winston Churchill harped upon that theme of a possible Japanese war:

We now feel strong enough to provide powerful naval forces of heavy ships with the necessary auxiliary vessels, for service, if need be, in the Indian and Pacific Oceans.

In the Pacific [he went on] *we stretch out the long arm of brotherhood and motherhood to the Australian and New Zealand people.*

Churchill said that he was making this statement regarding Britain's intentions in the Pacific because "we do not know that the efforts of the United States to preserve peace in the Pacific will be successful."

It was a clear warning from a man who had all the facts before him. But his words, coming across the Atlantic, did not give any electric shock to American public opinion. Those words did not awaken them from their calm confidence that they were "untouchables." No one stirred uneasily in his sleep, I imagine, after reading this message.

They were three weeks away from December 7.

XIII

The Gardens of Cleveland

I HAD A BUSY TIME in Cleveland, Ohio.

"They have made you do everything except stand on your head," said Robert Keedick.

I might even have stood on my head, if my foot had slipped at one little ceremony in which I was chief actor, wielding a golden shovel tied up with ribbons. But that was the pleasantest thing I did in Cleveland and one of the best memories of this tour in the United States. It was when I planted an English oak in the Cultural Gardens of that city. The idea behind those gardens on the outskirts of the city is, to my mind, a beautiful one and an object lesson to the world of peace and good will among different nationalities. For here in Cleveland there are twenty-six different nationalities—Germans, Italians, Poles, Swedes, Irish, Czechs, Portuguese, and so on through all the range of races in Europe. They came to the great melting pot but kept the memory of their homeland while adopting a loyalty to their American citizenship. They do not want to kill each other. They live in peace among the different groups, and each nationality has its garden, symbolical of the country of its blood and spirit. There is an Italian garden with tall cypresses and clipped hedges, as one sees in Rome or Florence. There is a French garden, like a little corner of Versailles. There is a Czech garden, as one sees in Prague. There is an Irish garden with trees and flowers from the Emerald Isle. They have their statues and inscriptions cut in marble. Those trees, those plants, are from the soil of their own lands. And once a year or so, or when a new garden is opened, or when famous visitors arrive from foreign lands to any national group, the others come to lend a hand and to express good will. Surely this is a noble idea, especially now in a warring world with so many of these nations tearing each other to pieces, blasting each other's cities, bombing each other's women and children. It is an old Jewish gentleman named Weidenthal who had that idea and has devoted himself to its realization in living beauty. I was glad to stand by his side and to follow him through a Shakespeare garden where very tree has a history or a meaning.

It all began with this Shakespeare garden in which I planted a little oak. It was opened on Shakespeare's birthday in 1916 when the first World War was raging. The garden was ready for its dedication. Here was a cutting, now full grown, from the very mulberry tree which Shakespeare had planted in his own garden of New Place, Stratford-on-Avon. Here was a bust of the poet on a tall pedestal looking down the central path. There were flowers from Juliet's tomb in Verona. There were cuttings from Burnam Wood. It was laid out as an Elizabethan garden, with clipped hedges and all the flowers which Shakespeare loved and wove into all his plays. Later trees and flowers and plants were sent from England and Scotland and, by some magic, have grown and flourished in American soil. Many trees have been planted by famous men and women, the last being Lord Halifax, Ambassador from the Court of St. James's. And here in this lovely garden great actors and actresses have played Shakespeare's drama and recited his deathless words while the leaves of the old mulberry tree have quivered in the breeze and the flowers from England have drenched the air with their scent. I was aware of the spirit of this place. I walked in it with delight.

For my tree planting there was an escort of mounted police at the gate and a company of men and women associated with these Cultural Gardens assembled on the lawns. One of them, assistant vice-consul in the British Consulate, made an eloquent and moving speech before it was my turn to express thanks for the honour that was being given to me. I felt it to be a real honour to plant that little oak, which I did well and truly, stamping down the earth after my spadework, as often I have done in English gardens. Bob Keedick took a snapshot of this, and it struck his youthful sense of humour as being highly comical. But to me there was a symbolism in that little tree planted in American soil during wartime. It will grow in peacetime. When this tragic war is over it will go on growing until it becomes a sturdy and spreading oak. Under its branches, perhaps, young children will play and young lovers sit hand in hand, and Shakespearean players will flit about it as *A Midsummer Night's Dream* is acted once again—in a world from which the menace of war has been forever lifted. I wonder and I hope. Or will this garden be trampled down by new warfare because humanity is incapable of peace, and will my tree, when it is full grown, be a hiding place for men waiting to kill other human beings, yellow or black or brown? Who knows?

On the outskirts of Cleveland, in an old house left standing, I saw another scene which was very pleasant and touching to an English visitor. It was the headquarters of British War Relief in Cleveland. Seventy-five hundred American women have been working, since the bombardment over England, to supply garments for English women and children blasted out of their homes. They have spent their days in knitting, sewing, collecting, packing, with untiring zeal. I was touched by so much effort on our behalf and hoped they were getting thanks from England.

"We are not working for thanks," said one of the ladies. "But we get them, all right. We receive many letters from English mothers and boys and girls. Some of them are very touching."

I was led through the building and shown all the work. I have forgotten how many tons of stuff they have sent to Britain. A vast amount.

Now British War Relief is sharing up with American Relief for soldiers and sailors and the work of the American Red Cross. We shan't get so much. Perhaps we shan't need so much. In any case, American women must now think of their own lads first.

I met old friends in Cleveland, a lady who once lunched with me and a brother of mine, then a gunner, under the trees of an outdoor restaurant in Paris during the first World War. She was a young girl. Now she is a married woman. I met also a lady by name of Veronica Hutchinson, who once came to a country house of mine in Surrey which still lives in her memory as a little idyll. She is a hard worker in the Hallé Stores, running the book department with, I should say, great competence. I was given a seat at a table and faced with a pile of my own books to sign while a number of ladies arrived to buy them like hot cakes and have a few words with me. I found it embarrassing to sit there at the receipt of custom like a cheap jack exhibiting his wares. But it is an American custom and accepted as a natural thing. One lady asked me if I had read an article, reprinted in the *Reader's Digest,* entitled "Stalin's American Line." I had read it.

"That is a very real danger to this country," she told me. "The Communists are working underground. They are capturing the young people by their propaganda, and they are getting hold of labour. What are you doing about Communism in England?"

"There's not much of it," I told her. "English labour is very conservative. They refuse any kind of alliance with Communism."

She did not believe me. She was alarmed by this bogey.

"Supposing Russia wins," she said. "I can see Bolshevism spreading over Europe—and farther than that. This country is in danger. The Communists have their cells everywhere. They deceive well-meaning people by expressing liberal ideas while they pull the strings which are worked in Russia and attached to Stalin's Godless creed."

I had heard these ideas before. I heard them again. There is an uneasy feeling in many American minds that the Russian alliance may bring with it the microbes of Bolshevism to infect the labour unions, the intellectuals, and the revolutionary elements in American life.

I rose from my table to be presented to a remarkable old gentleman. This was Mr. Hallé, the founder of the great stores. I call him an old gentleman, but he would resent such a description, and justly, because he keeps younger than most men half his age. He was over sixty when he learned to fly. Ten years or more have gone by since then and he is still flying— or was until private flying was prohibited in wartime. He is a friend of Winston Churchill, who stayed with him when he was on a lecture tour in the United States. Now and again he receives a letter from that great man, who always cautions him not to take too many risks with that hobby of his.

Mr. Hallé laughed.

"It is amusing," he said, "to be cautioned against taking risks by Mr. Churchill, who has always risked everything and has never thought of danger for himself."

He spoke gravely about the war and thought the United States would be in it before long.

"All civilisation is challenged by Nazi Germany. We can't leave it to England, who is overburdened."

I was led round to a microphone in the broadcasting station of Cleveland, where I was received by a very pretty lady who proposed to interview me on the air. She did it with skill and charm, and I felt easy in her hands. She liked her job as announcer but confessed that the advertising side of it was getting too much.

"It has reached its peak," she told me. "If it gets any further——"

She suggested that if it went any further there would be a public revolt against it.

"I would like to hear your lecture," she said.

I warned her against any such idea and never thought I should see her again, but she came to the lecture and said nice things about it, which I thought was very sporting of her as she spends her days listening to too much oratory and too many speakers.

XIV

Washington on the Eve of War

I HAD BEEN READING a historical masterpiece called *Reveille in Washington,* and it helped me to see many ghosts in the city of Washington, D.C. They were ghosts of whiskered men, and ladies with little jackets and hooped skirts, down Pennsylvania Avenue; ghosts of gentlemen, bearded and whiskered, speaking with a Southern drawl, dressed in evening clothes, in the old Willard Hotel, with dark-eyed women whose white sloping shoulders showed above their bodices; ghosts of buggies and barouches outside the White House; ghosts of generals and colonels, congressmen and senators before the Civil War when all was confusion, intrigue, treachery, inefficiency, and muddled thought in Washington; ghosts of Negro slaves, planters, builders, and contractors in a half-finished city with rubbish heaps around it; ghosts of Virginians, threatening to break up the union of the United States; the wild ghost of an actor named John Wilkes Booth and the ghost of an angular,

hatchet-faced, sunken-eyed, bearded man named Abraham
Lincoln.

Washington then was on the eve of Civil War. Washington
now, when I went there on November 23 of 1941, was on the
eve of a world war. There were lights in the windows of the
White House. Somewhere behind those windows was a man
who knew the war was coming, though not yet when and how.
It was President Roosevelt who had seen the war coming—its
inevitability—long before the American people were ready
to follow his reasoning or his policy. They were not ready yet.
Step by step he had led them up to the Lease-Lend Act, the
arming of merchant ships, the convoying of American munitions of war, the shooting-on-sight order, and they had followed reluctantly, with one extreme reluctance in their minds
—never again to send an expeditionary force to Europe. There
they halted and would not budge. Cordell Hull, Secretary of
State, in full agreement with the President, had sent a stiff
note to Japan, reaffirming American principles, American demands for the withdrawal from China, American refusal to
admit to Japanese arguments. It was almost an ultimatum,
but if Japan challenged it or refused it to the point of war
it would be so much the worse for Japan. The Navy was
supremely confident.

In some of the private rooms in Washington with closed
doors there were a few anxious souls asking disquietening
questions.

"Are we ready for a war in the Pacific?"

"Will it be easy to defend the Philippines?"

"Is our Navy overconfident?"

"Hasn't the bombing aeroplane put the capital ship out of
action?"

"Weren't we fools to sell our scrap iron to the Japs for making munitions which will kill our men?"

"How is the President going to fight a two-ocean war?"

"Supposing Japan risks it—what then?"

They were the critics, the pessimists, the realists, and the analysts whose opinions were heard only behind closed doors.

A member of the British Purchasing Board sat on the side of my bed in the Willard Hotel. I had known him as a small boy in a suburb of London. He could talk freely.

"How are things going here?" I asked.

He laughed and seemed to think that they were not going brilliantly.

"We are, of course, strangled in red tape. It's not a purely British monopoly. But things do move—very slowly."

He drew a satirical picture, rather scathingly, but laughed again. He enjoyed the comedy. He regretted the delays.

I heard from him and from others that the British Purchasing Board was under the fire of a ceaseless and hostile criticism. Newspaper correspondents, especially of isolationist papers, invented or built up the most sinister charges against the members of the Board, against the British administration of the Lease-Lend Act, against the honour of the British Government and all its officials.

"We're accused of riotous extravagance," said one of them. "The isolationist newspapers carry stories, with great circumstantial detail, of our social orgies, our prodigal expenditure, all at the expense of Lease-Lend. The fact is, of course, that we find it hard to live on our salaries and don't get a penny from Lease-Lend. Every item is checked by American officials. They wouldn't pass a dollar not properly accounted for."

We were having luncheon in a foreign restaurant frequented by British officials.

My friend looked round the room and smiled.

"This restaurant is supposed to be one of our haunts of riotous living. It doesn't look like it, does it? We get very modest meals here."

It did not look like a place for bacchanalian orgies or wild extravagance. It was a quiet, respectable, and middle-class place.

"They tell the most fantastic stories," said my friend. "But it's no use for a Britisher to deny them. Our denials are not believed. It's only the American officials who can deny them with any effect, and the story always runs swifter and farther than any denial. The American public believes every word of these fairy tales, which are circulated not so much to hurt us as to discredit the American administration and government. Our friends, the isolationists, find it a useful weapon in their political campaign."

I heard some of the charges and was amused by them, though they aroused sore feelings among those maligned.

"Sir Louis Beale occupies a luxurious suite at the British Staff House—the converted mansion of the late Chauncey Depew—while British Purchasing Commission stenographers earning one hundred and five dollars a month pay twenty dollars a month to live on the unheated fifth floor which was formerly the servants' quarters."

A grand story to excite the democratic feelings of American readers against the selfishness and arrogance of the British aristocracy!

Sir Louis Beale was hurt and desired instant apology—

which he failed to get. So far from occupying a luxurious suite, he was living in one room in the British Staff House for which he paid one hundred and forty dollars a month. He shares a bath with several others. The fifth floor was not inhabited by stenographers or anybody else. There is a storage place above the fourth floor where linen, china, and junk are kept. The fourth floor is used by a number of women secretaries of British missions and is heated like all the other rooms.

Miss Helen Essary, in her column "Dear Washington," published in the *Times-Herald,* has the following tidbit.

"When the British Government took over an apartment house recently the check for its three years' rental came in the next day from the United States Treasury."

Another case of spending public money in the greedy British officialdom! What a scandal!

But the plain fact is that all expenses of British missions are paid out of British-owned dollars. The actual check is on the British Purchasing Commission's account in New York. Rentals are paid for one year in advance. An official denial was sent by the United States Treasury saying that no such check had ever been written.

Paragraphs of that kind, circulating all across the United States in newspaper services, are constantly appearing, poisoning public opinion and prejudicing it against their British visitors. Even if denials are made, they do not see them, and the old adage that there is no smoke without fire covers any kind of denial.

All that is unfortunate, because it builds up an entirely false picture which may never be smudged on. Even as far away from Washington as New England a lady said to me:

"I cannot understand why your Government allows its officials to wallow in extravagance and spend Lease-Lend money on their own pleasures."

Even more deplorable than that is the belief that the British Government and British manufacturers and merchants have been exporting goods received from the United States under Lease-Lend. One of the most frequent charges is that Britain is exporting commercial and military aeroplanes while begging for further deliveries of American planes.

If that were true, it would be a horrible scandal and disgrace. The real truth is that Britain exports no commercial planes to any country and that a very small number of obsolete military planes were exported some time ago to neutral countries in fulfillment of prewar contracts. They were useless to the R.A.F., and at the present time all British planes are used and desperately needed for the war in the air, and none are available for export.

"But what about wool?" ask the critics, deeply suspicious of British methods. "Wool is being exported in increasing quantities to the United States and underselling the American product to such an extent that wool factories are having to close doors."

The answer to that is that British woollen products have to pay a heavy tariff in the United States amounting to about 60 per cent of the cost to the customer. The increase in exports is largely due to a demand for woollen cloth for American uniforms.

"British merchant ships are carrying on their normal trade under the protection of American battleships."

That is another story put about and "proved" by naming certain ships.

But all British merchant ships are under naval orders for

essential war purposes. Whatever cargoes they carry are not for trade but for maintaining supplies from one part of the British Empire to another.

One by one these charges appear. One by one they are refuted. But the charge sticks, and the refutation does not carry weight.

"All the same there is something in it," says the American sceptic who reads such things constantly in his own newspapers and believes what he reads.

Among friends of mine in Washington I heard those grievances, recited with a laugh, but all the same it was vexatious to them and a slur on Britain. It was before the United States had been attacked by Japan and had war declared by Germany and Italy. Now we are together in that struggle, with all our resources pooled. The isolationists have withdrawn. Perhaps the time has gone by for those fairy tales, invented or cooked up for sinister purposes of besmirching not only British officials but the American administration.

There was none of this criticism from my audience in the Grand Ball Room of the Willard Hotel which was packed with people. One of my answers to questions led me into trouble afterwards.

"What does England feel about Ireland?" asked a voice.

"England feels a bit sore about Ireland," I answered. "We don't like the idea of a German Ambassador in Dublin, with a German Staff who are all spies communicating the comings and goings of our ships."

I softened this statement by saying that many young Irish Catholics were crossing over to England and Scotland and joining British regiments.

A few days later I received a letter from the Embassy of Eire at Washington protesting against this reference to German spies, asking me for authentic evidence, and assuring me that no such espionage had taken place. I still feel convinced that in the nature of things, and in the nature of the Nazi code, the Germans in Dublin are very efficient and active spies for Hitler and his Intelligence Bureau.

That evening I had dinner in the Mayflower Hotel, where in the hall was a fine model of that famous ship. In the company at table was a monsignor who referred to the Irish question.

"The Irish in the United States," he said, "would be split in half if De Valera went in with England and abandoned neutrality. They can't forget the ancient grudge, and, having obtained independence after centuries of struggle, they don't want Ireland to return to allegiance with England."

At the end of the last war he had been out with the American troops, and shortly after the Armistice he went up to a young American captain—a handsome fellow—and asked what he thought of things.

"We've finished the job with Germany," said the captain, who was an Irish-American. "Now I would like to knock hell out of England."

This story of the monsignor was received with laughter, as an amusing anecdote. But things have changed since it was told. There are many Irish now in the United States who are not very happy about the neutrality of Eire in a war which has flamed right round the world, overwhelming most of the little countries who also desired to keep their neutrality and believed that it would be respected.

I drove through Washington, getting a glimpse of its beauty, with some of its buildings floodlit by night. It is now, perhaps, the most beautiful city in the United States, and the most fascinating because of its international society and its position as the capital of the United States.

"Here," I thought, "the destiny of the world will be decided. What is happening behind these lighted windows, in that old White House, in rooms where secretaries are deciphering secret codes or copying secret reports from all the countries of the world, will decide, very largely, for good or evil, the shape of things to come."

It was November 23, two weeks away from the attack on Pearl Harbor. In Washington that night all was quiet.

XV

In Worcester, Massachusetts

I<small>N A PULLMAN CAR</small> on the way to Springfield I exchanged cards with a little man who had consulted a railway timetable in my behalf. We were alone together in that coach, the train being very empty. I found that my travelling companion was a judge of the Supreme Court in one of the states through which I had passed.

He looked up from his paper and remarked that Russia was still resisting.

"They're putting up an amazing fight," I replied.

"Amazing is right," he said. "I was over in Russia in 1936, just taking a look round. A man who was with me taught me a word which was new to me. 'Kaput.' Broken down. Everything in Russia was 'Kaput.' That's how it looked. Of course we only had glimpses and there must have been a lot hidden. I thought the Red Army looked in bad shape. I wasn't impressed by their soldiers, who looked weedy and undernour-

ished. I am astonished by their resistance to the Germans. I
never thought it possible. But I suppose Moscow is bound to
fall. The Germans are getting round it with a pincer movement."

"It doesn't look good," I admitted.

The little judge offered me a cigarette.

"Germany is a hard nut to crack," he said. "How does
England think she is going to win?"

"We're getting stronger," I told him.

He nodded.

"Yes, I suppose so. But British man power is not very great,
and your shipping losses have been serious. I don't see how
you can smash Germany unless American man power comes to
your aid, and our people are not ready for that. The one thing
they detest is the idea of sending an expeditionary force."

"So I have found out," I answered.

We went on chatting. He was a thoughtful, courteous little
man and had a twinkle in his eye now and then.

"The rank of corporal ought to be abolished," he said
presently. "Napoleon was a corporal. Hitler was a corporal.
Mussolini was a corporal. Those stripes on the arm seem to go
to people's heads."

He thought Hitler was an apoplectic.

"He has all the symptoms. Those sudden rages. Those brain
storms. And yet he must be a genius as well."

He asked me what were my impressions of the United States
and I told him that I was most struck by the spread of education in all sections.

He agreed.

"I am glad you think that. I believe our system is beginning
to show fair results. Some improvement must take place when

factory hands have been to high schools and some of them even to universities. It improves their manners, anyhow. It opens their minds. It raises them up. As a judge I am not a pessimist about our social progress. There is a long way to go, but we are on the right road. Taking it all in all, we are shaping out a rather good type of democracy, don't you think?"

He spoke of England with affection and admiration.

"You have a fine tradition," he said. "You go deeper and rise higher than we do, perhaps. I mean in education and culture and balanced way of life. In this war England has been wonderful. We marvel at English courage and will power and spirit. We ought to help more. We have been very slow. Our President has had to move cautiously, one step at a time, not too far ahead of public opinion. In the end we shall be with you. . . . Well, here I get out. I've enjoyed this conversation."

I had another conversation while waiting for a train to Worcester.

It was not with anyone so important as a judge of the Supreme Court but with a middle-aged Negro, one of the redcaps, who was taking care of my bags. I found him an intelligent fellow who expressed himself very well. We chatted while he stood by my bags and kept a watchful eye on other clients seated on the wooden benches of the great waiting room with its high roof and iron pillars.

"That war over in Europe," he said, "is terrible. It don't bear thinking about. Sometimes I keep awake at night and keep on brooding over the sufferings of those poor people which the war has hit—starving, no doubt—homeless, many of them, and not a hope. Frenchmen, Poles, Jews, and all sorts. More cruelty than the world has ever seen, maybe. No human mercy. The Jews have been murdered and ill-treated even before the war began."

He said, "Excuse me," and strode away to answer some questions from an anxious woman on one of the benches.

"Yes, madam. Twenty minutes late. I'll look after you, ma'am, I surely will."

He came back and stood clasping one of the wooden pillars supporting the benches.

"We was talking about Jews," he said. "I feel for them because I, too, belong to an oppressed race."

"Still oppressed?" I asked.

"Yes sir! We ain't allowed to vote like, ordinary citizens. There's discrimination against the coloured folk. We have not been given our full rights under the Constitution, which grants equality to all men whatever race or creed."

"I had an idea the coloured folk were happy," I said, to draw him out.

"Things are better," he admitted. "We redcaps now have our own union. Formerly we weren't on the railway staff. We were just outsiders, picking up a living as best we could. Maybe we earned more money. Now we have more security: we belong to the staff. We get fixed rates of twenty cents a package, all checked up by the railway officials. I'm one of their servants now."

He said, "Excuse me," again and strode away to carry the bag of a young girl.

"You'll be all right, missy. I'll tell you when that train comes in."

He stood by my side again.

"We coloured folk," he said, "have much to be thankful about. I went to a high school. I received a good education under coloured teachers. The younger generation don't know the hardships of their grandparents before the Civil War when they were slaves. The Civil War liberated the Negro race. We were on the level of poor whites after that. We had the same freedom and opportunity—in theory, that is."

This tall, middle-aged redcap looked at his watch.

"That train is mighty late this morning," he said. "I guess something's happened down the line."

He resumed his information about the coloured race.

"This is the land of opportunity," he said. "And I'm not now talking about coloured folk alone, but about the American way of life. It's on a high level. Almost every feller has a car, a radio, and a fair wage if he wants it. The foreign races do well here. They make good—Italians, Germans, Portuguese, Poles, and more especially the Jews, who are clever in money matters. Opportunity for everyone—up to a limit. The coloured folk are kept out of some of it. White folk don't mix with us much. Keep themselves aloof, as you may have noticed."

"Didn't the last war do something for you?" I asked. "Your men fought in France with the others."

"That last war didn't help much," said the redcap. "Afterwards there were race riots because coloured folk had houses which returning soldiers couldn't get. But we forgive, if we don't forget. We're not haters. We try to be happy and maybe have a gift that way. Coloured folk are kindly and patient. And though we have our grievances, we don't let them poison us."

He went off to attend to another client, and I missed him for two minutes. When he came back he made a kind of apology for having talked too much.

"It's not often I get the chance of talking to a gentleman. Now I'd like to ask you something."

"What's that?"

"How do you think that war is going? What surprises me is the fact that Hitler keeps winning. He seems to have God on his side, though it can't be."

"He'll be beaten in the end," I assured him.

"I surely hope that," said the redcap. "And I surely hope that England will have the victory she deserves. I listen to a lot about England over the radio. It's a fine country with a fine people. Mighty brave. Terrible how they've suffered—women and children in English cities. My heart melts for them when I hear of all them bombings. Terrible! And I'm glad to be talking like this with an English gentleman. It's a pleasure."

Our conversation was interrupted by the arrival of the train. My friend the redcap seized my bags and those of the anxious woman and the young girl. At the door of the Pullman car I gave him the usual quarter and shook hands with him.

"Good journey!" he said, "and God be with you."

The other passengers looked surprised at this friendly farewell between a passenger and a redcap.

When I arrived at Worcester there was no one to meet me, and after a quick glance round for reporters, photographers, and lecture organisers I took a cab to the Bancroft Hotel and, having seen the baggage into my bedroom, went down to the coffee shop to get some food. I was reading the paper quietly over a cup of coffee when I was aware of three men standing by my table.

"Sir Philip?" asked one of them.

I looked up and saw a square-shouldered, youngish man with a fresh-complexioned, clean-cut face.

"That's me," I said, regardless of grammar.

"Good God!" exclaimed the fresh-complexioned gentleman, bursting out into a laugh. "We went down to the station to meet you with reporters and photographers. I can't think how we missed you!"

"Sorry to have given you the slip!" I answered. "It was not intentional."

"I'm Judge Wahlstrom," said the fresh-complexioned man. "Here are Mr. Ayres and Mr. Turner. We were getting nervous about you. When I called up the hotel they said you were not in your room. I was quite alarmed. There's a big gathering coming to hear you at the Economic Club tonight."

"Join me over the luncheon table," I suggested.

Judge Wahlstrom, Mr. Ayres, and Mr. Turner took seats at the table and ordered some food. They were friendly souls, I found. Judge Wahlstrom, very young for a judge, had the gift of laughter. His voice rang out heartily at some of my remarks and some of his own. Mr. Ayres announced that he was going to drive me around. Noticing that I was smoking Old Gold cigarettes, he ordered, very quietly, another packet for me.

"Yes, don't you lose sight of Mr. Ayres," said Judge Wahlstrom. "He's going to be your chauffeur."

"I'm rather shortsighted," I told him. "You will have to keep an eye on me. Sometimes I don't recognise people who have been kind to me."

I told them about an evening party in New York when I became confused by meeting too many people. A man in evening dress came up to me and said in a friendly and familiar way, "Hullo, Gibbs." "Hullo," I answered, and then hesitated and said, "I can't quite remember——"

The man in evening clothes grinned at me.

"I'm the guy," he said quietly, "who took tea with you this afternoon and talked to you for two and a half hours."

Mr. Ayres of Worcester seemed to enjoy this story. During my stay in his city, when he drove me from one place to another with untiring generosity, he came up to me now and then and said, "I'm the feller who drives you about."

Worcester is a fine city, and its inhabitants are justly proud of it. From the Bancroft Tower there is a magnificent view which I saw at dusk when lights were beginning to twinkle in all its windows. It has many good buildings, and in some of them are housed great treasures of art and history. These cities in the United States, of which Worcester is a good example, have ransacked the old world for its masterpieces and historical relics. But they have also built their own memorials, not without modern genius here and there.

In company with Judge Wahlstrom and Mr. Ayres I visited the Worcester War Memorial. Here is a noble hall, simple and solemn in its architecture, with three tall bronze crosses. On one of the walls are the mural paintings by Leon Kroll. They are remarkable and beautiful in design and colour, covering an immense wall space. The artist painted them on canvas, and the main canvas, made of flax on an English loom, is thirty-three yards long and more than thirty feet high. The theme of this main painting is best described in the artist's own words:

"The idea was to honour the memory of the soldiers who died in defence of our country. I used the theme of resurrection, which is eternal, not only from the religious angle, but also because it means rebirth and, in a measure, the renewal of a pledge. People of all classes and races, who compose the modern American cities, gather in peace and harmony under

one flag and all that it implies. The gesture of the soldier seen
rising from his tomb symbolises the spirit of sacrifice in defence of our way of life."

On the side walls are long panels done with realism as well
as symbolism and representing defence on sea and land and in
the air. Their landscapes, with jagged tree stumps in shell-
blasted earth, with guns and gunners in the foreground, were
sharply reminiscent to me of the battlefields of Flanders in the
first World War.

I stood silently studying these murals. Their spirit and idea
reached out to me, but in my mind was the thought, inevitably, that all that sacrifice symbolised here had not been
followed by the peace and harmony also depicted. The men
who had died in "a war to end war" had not been upheld by
the statesmen and politicians who made use of their victory.
They had been betrayed. All pledges had been broken.
Ghastly errors had been made. We had all been stricken blind.
And now, as I stood there, millions of other men were being
hurled into another world war worse than the last, and this
memorial to American dead was not the end of death by war.
New shrines would have to be built for new dead.

"Every figure on that canvas," said Judge Wahlstrom, "was
painted from someone living in Worcester. We recognise our
fellow citizens. One is standing by your side."

With these new friends of mine I went into the Art Museum
and went round its galleries. Here in this city of Worcester, in
a country inhabited by red Indians long after the death of
many civilisations in the Old World, was the whole story of
mankind told in stone and pottery and painting brought from
the old temples and palaces and shrines. The children of
Worcester, Massachusetts, stare at Roman pavements from

Antioch, freshly coloured as though laid down yesterday. Here is Greek, Roman, and Etruscan pottery less broken than the shards of the modern garbage pail and with eternal beauty. Here are the paintings of the old masters of Italy, Holland, Spain, and France, keeping their quality of tone and colour. Here is a twelfth-century doorway from some old monastery. High-school boys and girls swarm in each day to see these things, to sketch them, and hear lectures on them. Something of what it all means must get into their minds. But that day we were alone there.

"I notice," said Judge Wahlstrom, "that one never comes to see these treasures unless a visitor arrives. I must say I'm enjoying myself!"

His laugh rang out again. He was keen to show me a lot more in Worcester.

He showed me a lot more.

Among other things we saw a wonderful collection of armour—one of the best in the world outside the Tower of London and Windsor Castle. Its collector, Mr. Higgins, is the director of a pressed-steel company in Worcester, and he had the idea that it would be a good thing to show how men had worked in steel from early times, worked with love and skill and to attain perfection of purpose for the use intended, thereby attaining beauty of line and craftsmanship. Mr. Higgins is a modernist. He thinks that a streamlined engine is beautiful. He wants to inspire his generation with an idea that beauty comes from perfect adaptation of material to the use of any mechanism. But he believes also in the spirit revealing the mind and soul of men. He is also an enthusiast with a great gift of words, which gave life and drama to all that armoury. He had suits of chain mail from oriental countries and the whole range of European armour from the thirteenth to seventeenth centuries, some of them miracles of the armourers' art and craft, wonderfully inlaid.

"It's interesting," said Mr. Higgins, "that all these suits were made for small men, according to our standard. Husky Americans couldn't get into them."

"Like those in the Tower of London," I told him. "The Guards tried to wear them, but the armour was all too small."

Mr. Higgins has searched Europe for that collection and has spent great sums of money on it. He has bought from Spanish grandees, French aristocrats, and other collectors who relinquished their treasure for a certain number of dollars in time of penury.

"Well, we've had a grand time," said Judge Wahlstrom, who had enjoyed himself quite a lot, as I had.

The judge had to get back to dress before our dinner at the Economic Club, but Mr. Ayres drove me on to a hill near his own home from which we looked down over the city of Worcester, a noble view of a fine city.

There were six hundred guests at the dinner, held in the Grand Ball Room of the Bancroft Hotel. They were the leading men of Worcester—lawyers, doctors, manufacturers, directors of companies, and worthy citizens all. As I faced them from the high table where I sat next to Judge Wahlstrom it seemed to me that those men represented all that is best in American life, its tradition, its integrity, its progressive spirit, and—its boyishness. For American business and professional men, "hard-boiled" as we think them, and as some of them may be, retain a boyishness far beyond middle age, especially when they get together. They are shrewd but simple. They enjoy a joke and are quick with their laughter. They keep a schoolboy sense of fun. The American businessman at his best does not despise the arts. On the contrary, many of them are patrons of art and ardent collectors. They have their hobbies, as important to them as their business when that is secure. I sat next to a man whose hobby is gardening, like that of Francis Bacon. He was very knowledgeable about trees and flowers. The men about me had done the grand tour in Europe like the eighteenth-century milord in England. They knew London, Paris, Rome, and had brought back treasures.

"I hate to hear that Middle Temple Hall is gone," said one of them.

"What does Pall Mall look like?" asked another. "Did you say the Carlton Club is a ruin?"

"I can't bear to think of Paris occupied by the enemy," said another. "I remember good times in Paris as a young man. The collapse of France was tragic and seems now inexplicable."

Judge Wahlstrom introduced me before my lecture with extreme generosity. As I told the audience afterwards, he knew more about my life than I did myself. He had even read my latest novel and woven its plot into his speech. "You need not bother to read it now," I said before getting on with my talk. "Judge Wahlstrom has told you all about it." I could hear the judge laugh behind me. He did not mind a little chaff. He enjoyed it.

They listened to me for an hour with great patience and good humour, and then, not having enough, it seemed, a group of them led me into a private room and made a half circle round me and fired questions at me for an hour more. These Americans are keen to know. They want to get at the facts.

"Do you think the British Government is justified in preventing food going to the Belgians and other occupied countries, on the lines of Hoover's American Relief during the last war?"

It was a middle-aged clergyman who asked that question, and I could see that there was emotion behind it.

"The British Government," I answered, "takes the view that the Belgians and the Danes and all the others are half starved because the Germans took all their food, killed their cattle, pigs, and poultry, and are likely to steal any more food that gets to them."

"It could all be organised," said the clergyman. "The people would be fed in soup kitchens."

I told him that personally I was in favour of getting food to these people if possible. I thought our main policy ought to be to keep them friendly to us, so that when the time for invasion comes they will rise and aid us. But that is regarded as a sentimental point of view. People who take the other side do not see why Germany should be relieved of its responsibility.

"What do you think of the British Intelligence Service in this war?" asked one of them who had sat with me at table, a legal-looking man with a hatchet face.

We were speaking behind closed doors. I had to confess that I thought our Intelligence Service had not lived up to its reputation in the last war, when it was marvellous. "Perhaps its reports were not acted on," I added.

A young Jewish lawyer asked a question.

"Wouldn't it help a good deal if the people of India were given their freedom? Wouldn't you get the fighting services of four hundred million people?"

"Not of fighting quality," I said, answering the last point. "One cannot put soft-eyed Hindus under German barrage fire. It would be like putting children in the firing line. As for the political side of things, India has given tremendous proofs of loyalty, pouring out its wealth and sending its best troops to fight in Libya and other places. Apart from complete independence, India is self-governing and puts up tariffs against British goods."

I don't think he was satisfied by that answer. He had in his head the firm conviction, shared by most Americans, that India is exploited by Britain for its own profit and that Gandhi is very near to Jesus Christ—both convictions being totally wrong, as far as my own knowledge goes.

A thoughtful-looking man with glasses raised a difficult problem.

"How are we going to deal with peace when it comes?" he asked. "How are we going to prevent a postwar slump and shape out a better kind of life for people and nations now deep in misery?"

The discussion became general. I raised the possibility of free trade in a zone covering the United States, the British Empire, the Scandinavian nations, and other countries who cared to join. There would be no chance of prosperity if the tariff walls remained as barriers, blocking the interchange of goods.

"I agree," said one of these Worcester men. "I remember the London Conference, which said that war would come, as sure as fate, unless the tariff barriers were removed."

"That conference was killed by F.D.R.," said another man quickly. "He wanted to keep the dollar from being stabilised with other exchanges. It sabotaged the whole basis of the conference."

"Cordell Hull has worked quietly and effectively for something like free trade," said one of the company.

Another man saw immense difficulties ahead.

"I can't see the United States opening its doors wide for competition from countries with underpaid labour and low social conditions, enabling them to undercut our manufactured goods. Our manufacturers would put up a stiff fight against any such policy."

"Wages and social conditions might be raised in other nations," I suggested.

"Take Japan," said the sceptic about free trade. "They turn out goods which are sold in the world markets at prices which are just ridiculous."

The discussion went on. Many other questions were raised, until one broke up the party.

"What do you know about Rudolf Hess?"

There was a general laugh. Judge Wahlstrom came to my rescue.

"Sir Philip has had a hard day," he said. "It's time he went to bed."

"I've had a grand day," I told him.

XVI

The City of Glass

Oɴ ɴᴏᴠᴇᴍʙᴇʀ 30, a week before December 7 and Pearl Harbor, I sat in a long-distance train on the way from Boston to Toledo. The coach was littered with the heavy supplements of Sunday newspapers, vastly wasteful of paper and pulp. I read the news from my chair in the lounge car.

Berlin admitted the loss of Rostov.

German forces at the northern gate to the Caucasus have fallen back from the principal sections of Rostov on the Don.

At the same time the enemy has made a sweeping drive on Moscow to the northwest, bringing the Germans within thirty-one miles of the capital.

There were other items of news set out in heavy headlines:

AXIS SMASHING HARD
AGAINST LIBYAN TRAP

SECOND MAJOR TANK BATTLE
GOES ALL DAY WITH
NEITHER SIDE ADVANCING

German and Italian forces trapped east of Tobruk have reassembled their remaining tanks and, in a mighty effort to escape their encirclement, have smashed head on into a British wall and become deadlocked in a new major tank battle, as the British announced today. The battle began yesterday morning southeast of Reozegh and continued fiercely throughout the day and into the evening without either side having given or gained ground.

That Libyan battle still seemed to be very sticky. The first hopes of a quick and decisive victory had been disappointed. It was not like Wavell's brilliant dash through to Benghazi, with only small forces under his command, against immense numbers of Italians. The Germans were making things very hard.

Those items of news took the biggest headlines. But there was a good deal about Japan which looked important. The Japanese were considering their answer to Mr. Cordell Hull's last note in which he had reaffirmed American principles, rather stiffly, and without making any concessions which would be a form of appeasement—that fatal word—according to newspaper correspondents, who seem to know all the secrets of Washington.

The Japanese Cabinet was considering the Washington negotiations for the second day in succession and there were all the signs of an acute crisis.

From Singapore came the news that the British had cancelled all leave for the troops, "as a normal precaution."

In Hongkong there were realistic war manœuvres in blacked-out streets.

In Chungking, the capital of Chiang Kai-shek's forces, the Chinese expected war soon and believed that the Japanese might attack Thailand.

In Washington Secretary of State Hull was conferring with Lord Halifax.

In New York it was reported that the Japanese would regard as a "provocation" any American or British air patrol of the Burma Road.

In Manila it was reported that Germans were fostering a Japanese-Chinese peace move.

Sitting next to me in the lounge car was a tall, rather impressive-looking man of middle age with a square-cut face and blue eyes. He looked up at me and entered into conversation. I had an idea that he might be a naval man in civilian clothes, but I discovered later that he was an American Army officer in high command.

"The American people don't seem nervous of war with Japan," I said presently, after some remarks about the weather.

He smiled across at me and gave a little shrug of his square shoulders.

"Not so nervous as they were two years ago. Then we had no army and no air force. Now they feel that we are preparing something very big in the way of defence and that we are two years further along the road, with tremendous potentialities ahead of us. That gives them a sense of confidence."

He beckoned to the coloured waiter and ordered a ginger ale. I lit up another cigarette and wondered how many thousands I had smoked since my arrival in the United States.

Really, I must cut down on them. It was becoming quite a vice.

"I don't believe the Japs will attack," said the American officer. "They are like a small boy screaming for something he wants to the last moment before subsiding."

"I am told they're not in good shape," I said.

"They're in a sticky mess. They can't draw out of China without losing face, and meanwhile their economic position is hopeless. I don't think they dare risk a war with us. It would be like committing hara-kiri."

"That's what I've heard," I agreed. "All Americans seem to think like that."

This Army officer nodded and was silent for a few minutes. Presently he spoke again.

"I believe the President wants a showdown. He wants to clear up this trouble in the Pacific. It has been going on too long. It's best to wipe the Japanese Navy straight out and have done with it."

"A war with Japan would not be helpful to Great Britain or Russia," I remarked. "It would stop the tide of munitions flowing in our direction. Besides, we have enough on our hands already, as far as the British Navy is concerned."

He didn't agree with me.

"On the contrary," he said. "It would liberate the Russian Siberian Army for action against Germany. And it wouldn't stop the flow of munitions to England. Sure there will be enough for both of us!"

He told me something about the enormous munitions plants he had seen.

He laughed at his reminiscence of all this—stupendous beyond words.

"I have just been visiting one factory," he said, "which is turning out bombs like hamburgers from a sausage machine. Never saw anything like it! The production is bigger than that of Germany and Russia combined. It's just staggering."

He was frank in his information. Supposing I had been a German spy or agent, I could have learned a good deal. But I don't think I look like a German spy. He regarded me out of his blue eyes as a very good Englishman.

He made one remark which I could not quite understand.

"As soon as we have got the bugs out of the fire-power problem——"

"American airplanes didn't have enough fire power at first," he explained. "Nor were they sufficiently well armoured. These defects are now being remedied. American observers in Egypt and other places are watching these things."

We talked about the problem of defeating Germany, and he was optimistic about the inevitable downfall of Hitler with American aid.

"We shall raise a big army," he said. "Three million men. Can any nation stand up against these potentialities? Will Germany stick it out when the sky overhead is black with bombing airplanes? I doubt it!"

We discussed many aspects of the European war, and I found this blue-eyed soldier was not conservative in his ideas.

"Any generals who fought in the last war," he said, "ought to be scrapped in this one. They're all too old. We want the younger men not tied up in tradition. That is why the German Army has done well up to date. The best thing that could have happened to them was when the Treaty of Versailles limited their army to one hundred thousand men. They were all young and picked men. They became the cadre of the new army."

I agreed with this and asked him a question about the American Army and its morale.

The American officer laughed.

"Not too good at the moment! The poor lads are very bored and very restless. They don't see the use of all this training—mostly without equipment. That European war seems a long way off to them and doesn't seem to threaten them. They're always on the move. That's to keep them quiet. They find it all very futile."

He smoked silently for a few minutes and then asked me a question which surprised me after all his previous words about the Japanese.

"Do you think the Japs will attack?"

"I don't know," I answered. "You know more than I do about that."

He had a lot of information about food supplies being sent to Britain. He had seen a lot of figures. Two hundred and fifty million pounds of cheese. Vast quantities of powdered milk.

This conversation in a railway train gave me renewed confidence. Here is a man who knows, I thought. I felt more optimistic about the future and its certain victory when I reached the city of Toledo.

There were people waiting for me in that big, noisy manufacturing city which bases its wealth on glass, I was told. Glass had saved it after the period of depression in 1929 and onwards. It makes more glass than any city in the world. It is the city of glass.

Two ladies and a dog were among those who greeted me. The two ladies were Mrs. Hineline, Sr., and Mrs. Hineline, Jr. The dog was a golden cocker spaniel of great distinction.

Mrs. Hineline, Sr., was one of those fairy godmothers who look after lecturers on tour, keep them interested but not too excited, see that they rest enough and sleep enough to stand up straight on the lecture platform, arrange interviews with the press, arrange social entertainment with the best people, and lead the lecturer by the hand to his place of doom in the kindest possible way. Mrs. Hineline, Sr., did all that for me, very tenderly. Mrs. Hineline, Jr., was accompanied everywhere by the cocker spaniel which has a special seat in her car, a tethering place in the Commodore Perry Hotel (he is the old sea dog who gave the British a whopping on Lake Erie), and receives the remains of roasted meats from the plates of his mistress's guests. His mistress is a humorous young lady who made me laugh very much. She speaks with the greatest candour of any woman I have met, except one. Her first words to me were candid.

"I have never read any of your books. I hope you don't mind—but I can't help it if you do."

"On the contrary," I assured her, "I am delighted that you have never read any of my books. Never do."

"I have had a lot of experience with lecturers," she told me. "Some of them are quite amusing and others are not."

She drove me about the city of Toledo and left her car standing outside various buildings—too long for the patience of the police. When she returned to the car a tag was tied round the handle.

"That means a dollar fine," she remarked. "If it weren't that I am good friends with the police—they all know me and my dog—I should find myself in the hoosegow."

"Where's that?" I asked.

She was astonished at my ignorance.

"Good heavens! Don't you know what a hoosegow is?"

It meant what the English call "the jug."

From Mrs. Hineline, Sr., and Mrs. Hineline, Jr., I heard some very good stories about previous lecturers in Toledo. Winston Churchill, they said, always had a heavy meal before his lecture. He washed it down with champagne. Probably that is why he had a heavy meal.

H. G. Wells had more sex appeal than most men half his age. One young lady wanted to kiss him but didn't dare make this request. His secretary heard of it and passed the word along. H. G. Wells presented his cheek to the young lady. "It wasn't too bad," she heard him remark.

When Thomas Mann arrived he was sensitive and distressed with regard to his foreign accent. A little old lady came up to him with great humility and said, "Mr. Mann, I understood your words, but my mentality is not equal to understanding their meaning."

Christopher Morley met a lot of people in Toledo and invited everyone to a party that evening—shop girls, social ladies, all sorts and conditions.

"My word, this is going to cost you a lot of money!" said one of his friends.

"Oh, that's all right," said Christopher Morley. "My manager will pay for all this."

J. B. Priestley had fallen into trouble with the American press. He was distressed about it and didn't think he would get an audience. He was surprised when he found a packed hall waiting for him.

"I don't know enough about art to be intelligent on the subject," said Mrs. Hineline, Jr., when she drove me to the

Art Museum. "I know more about dogs, so I'll leave you to it."

She left me in the hands of the directors, who took me round one of the finest museums in the United States where they have many treasures, as I saw in Worcester.

We started with a fine collection of Egyptian. mummies just as a school was leaving after a morning visit. I noticed little black boys walking among the white children, and they all looked happy.

One of the black boys asked the director whether the mummy cases were ever opened.

"Oh yes," said the director, "we're going to open one now."

"Golly!"

That little black boy took to his heels and ran farther than he had ever done before.

As in Worcester, here was the panorama of world civilisations shown by their arts and crafts, each period represented by some priceless piece or well-chosen collection. It was astonishing to find in Toledo the cloister of a French abbey with decorated capitals richly carved in the twelfth and thirteenth centuries, before America had been discovered and while red Indians were wandering about its wilderness with Stone Age weapons.

The picture galleries had an astonishing collection of the great masters from Fra Lippo Lippi to the French impressionists. Here were masterpieces by Holbein, Rembrandt, Rubens, and portraits by Sir Joshua Reynolds (a fine one of himself), Raeburn, and the eighteenth-century painters, with a grand canvas by Constable, a lovely thing by Turner.

"I have a grudge against this collection," I said to the director with a smile that let him know I was not quite serious.

"How's that?"

"So many of these pictures have come from England, taken down from the walls of English homes."

"All that leaves me quite cold," he answered. "You have so much that you can spare a little."

I dined with Mrs. Hineline, Sr., and Mrs. Hineline, Jr., and the golden cocker, somewhere near by, and a company of friendly folk. Our host was an elderly gentleman with a twinkle in his eyes. Next to me was a lady who might be called old by impertinent people who did not know that she keeps young in heart and spirit. I showed no surprise when she informed me that she was taking dancing lessons.

I had already made her acquaintance in her own house, which was surprisingly Mid-Victorian for any house in Toledo. It might have been a house in Brompton Square, London, with the pictures and furniture of the eighties. There was even a big picture of dogs by Landseer. There were other pictures of dogs by the greatest dog painter in America. There was also a full-length portrait of my hostess in the flower of her blooming youth when she had been a notable songstress. She had changed somewhat since then, I observed. One picture lured me across the room. It was a masterpiece by Teniers and worthy of any great gallery. In the rooms were some statuary, including a lovely Venus by an Italian sculptor. It was done up in cellophane like other bits of sculpture here.

Mrs. Hineline, Jr., who had introduced me to the lady of this house had brought her a bouquet of flowers. She handed them over in a casual way.

"Some stinkweeds for you," she said.

Now at dinner in a fine old club there was lively conversation until presently, after coffee, the elderly gentleman who was our host suddenly leaned back in his chair, looked round the dining room in which there were few guests, and made the following remark:

"Ain't it a bit dull here? What about getting gay?"

"Fine idea!" said the lady who kept young in spite of **Father Time**.

"What about you, Sir Philip?" asked our host anxiously. He thought I might be one of those frosty Englishmen who never unbend.

"I'm all for a little gaiety," I said.

We went gay. That is to say we drove away from Toledo, where there is a prohibition of alcohol on Sunday—at least I seem to remember that this was the reason—motored across the line of another state, and pulled up at an American road-house, in which, as presently I observed, there were dancing couples and many guests at table.

"Here," said Mrs. Hineline, Jr., "come the effete sons of the hard-worked rich, but the poor dears can't get away with anything without being observed."

She raised her hand in friendly greeting to various people in the dim light of this restaurant and at table afterwards mentioned several names in the company. They were the sons of the magnates of Toledo or their dancing sisters.

"That girl's frock is too short," she said to me, looking at one of the dancers. "A girl's knees are really not beautiful."

Our elderly host gave his hand to the lady who defied old Time and led her to the dance floor.

Mrs. Hineline, Sr., regarded them with an affectionate smile.

"Quite an idyll!" she said. "They are both such dears!"

The orchestra played a Spanish rhumba. Mrs. Hineline, Jr., danced it with grace but restraint of fire.

"I heard a good story today," she told me when she returned to the table. "It's an idiotic story, but it made me laugh quite a lot."

"Tell me," I said.

It was the story of a man who was always telling good stories but was always being told by a friend of his: "I've heard that one before, old man."

This annoyed him greatly.

One morning he saw a coloured man with a broken-down horse in the last stages of age and decay.

"I'll give you fifteen bucks for that horse," he said.

"It's yours," said the coloured man.

"I'll give you five more bucks if you bring it to my house and take it upstairs to the bathroom."

"No sir!" said the coloured man. "I'm agreeable to selling you a hoss, but I ain't a-goin' to play no tricks in nobody's bathroom. A hoss ain't meant for such doin's."

He was persuaded to take the horse home and lead it upstairs to the bathroom. But nothing would prevail upon him to turn it upside in the bath with its legs sticking up. He was scared. "Crazy stuff," he said, running down the stairs.

That evening the man who told good stories gave a party. Among the guests was the fellow who always said, "I've heard that one before, old man."

It was inevitable that in some stage in the evening he should go to the bathroom. He went and returned looking as though he had seen seven devils.

"Say," he spluttered, "what's the meaning of a horse with its legs sticking out of your bath?"

"It's a good story, that," said his host. "I knew it four hours ago. Ever heard it before?"

I refrained from telling Mrs. Hineline, Jr., that I had heard that one before.

The orchestra gave a crash of cymbals and drums. A spotlight was turned on. A group of girls scantily clad pranced in and waved their legs and gave an exhibition of step dancing.

"Lousy dancing," said a critic near to my table. "No attempt to keep time."

They departed and were replaced by a tall brunette, very nice to look upon and a good singer with a contralto voice.

Someone remarked that it was a pity she didn't keep her stomach in.

A Chinese juggler followed the lady. He was a neat little man who did the usual tricks deftly.

I smoked too many cigarettes, as usual, and between each one of them Mrs. Hineline, Jr., told me another story, grandly humorous.

One of them was about Bertrand Russell's school in the Surrey Hills. A lady rang the bell at the front door. It was opened by a little girl, completely nude.

"My God!" said the lady, greatly shocked.

"Is there a God?" asked the child.

The lights were turned off and on. The company danced again. Our elderly couple took the floor again.

No one mentioned a war going on in Europe. No one thought about it.

We drove back late at night. On our left, as we drove towards Toledo, was another roadhouse beyond some fields. It was blazing with red and orange lights.

"That's a gambling house," said Mrs. Hineline, Jr. "That's where the younger sons spend their fathers' money or where the fathers spend the money that ought to go to their families."

Before going to bed that night I read some words spoken by President Roosevelt and published in the Toledo *Sunday Times*. It was a despatch from Warm Springs dated November 29.

President Roosevelt asserted tonight that it was always possible that at next Thanksgiving time our boys in the military and naval academies may be fighting for our American Institutions.

The Chief Executive made that ominous declaration in an informal address at a dinner tonight at his Warm Springs foundation for infantile-paralysis victims. He spoke of the suffering of the people in other lands overrun and attacked, and even in countries which are attacking. Then he added solemnly: "I think we can offer up a little silent prayer that these people will be able to hold next year a Thanksgiving more like an American Thanksgiving. That is something to dream about perhaps. In days like these our Thanksgiving next year may remind us of a peaceful past. . . ."

Returning to the little white house on Pine Mountain, he found a call from Secretary Hull awaiting him and reached the opinion that he might have to leave here tomorrow afternoon and arrive in Washington Monday morning, in view of a statement by Premier Hideki Tojo that Japan would have to do everything possible to wipe out with a vengeance British and United States exploitation in the Far East.

That speech by the President was at the bottom of the page. As far as I had observed, it did not excite any emotion in the breasts of the Toledo population. No one referred to it. They went on dancing in the roadhouse.

No one referred to it at my lecture, which was followed by lively questioning about the European war and England's failure to make an invasion of the occupied countries while Germany was heavily engaged in Russia (I had to explain British difficulties of transport and material and man power) and the mystery of Rudolf Hess and the exact figures of food rationing in Britain. I think it was at Toledo that one young man, in a hurry to get a lot in, called out:

"Sir Philip, what do you think of the balloon barrage over London and the Duke and Duchess of Windsor?"

XVII

The City of Steel

You won't have so much fun in Youngstown," said Mrs. Hineline, Jr., when I parted from her at the railway station in Toledo.

She thrust into my hands a parting present which was very generous of her—an impressive package containing Old Gold cigarettes.

"I am quite certain I won't," I told her.

I was going from the City of Glass to the City of Steel. No lecturer, I was informed, quite inaccurately, I am sure, had ever gone from Toledo to Youngstown. I was given the impression that Youngstown was a very austere place into which fun never entered.

It was December 1, 1941.

In the train I met a very interesting man, as usual. He had something to do with a Chicago steel company.

I startled him for a moment by a direct question, more

important than the weather, after he had ordered a well-done steak in the restaurant car where we sat together.

"Are your people excited at all about the Japanese menace?"

"Excited?" He seemed surprised by the suggestion. "Why should they be?"

"Well, it seems to be a critical situation."

He was a big, beefy man, with good-natured eyes, amused by my English accent. When his steak came he did great justice to it, and it was a large steak.

He gave his views at greater length.

"In my view it would be a foolish thing to have a war with Japan. She's already beaten. It's hardly good form to hit a man when he's down."

"Are they down?"

He was sure of it.

"They're in a hopeless mess. They'll never master China. Their economic position is desperate. The American people are not keen on smashing a small nation out of which there is nothing to get."

He spoke with a smiling cynicism and elaborated that line of thought.

"We can't steal anything from the Japanese. It's a pauper nation. Now, if we took Canada or India, there might be something to it. But what can we get out of Japan if we do beat them? Nothing!"

He dropped his cynicism and began to talk reasonably about the changes in American life since his grandfather's days—the spread of education and so on.

"In the days of my grandfather it was very rare for an ordinary boy to go to college. Now millions go. It ought to produce some results."

His father, he said, was still a simple and old-fashioned man quite out of touch with modern developments.

"It worries him if I talk about my business or the immense munition plants I have to see. The figures of production and potential production are too fantastic to tell my old father. Either he doesn't believe them or he gets kind of bewildered. I have just been to a place where they are turning out millions and millions of shell cases. Well, I shan't worry my father about that. He's eighty. He doesn't want his mind disturbed. My word, this is a good steak!"

It was a noble steak but too big for one man, even with a hearty appetite.

At Youngstown, Ohio, I was received by three of the leading citizens, who were cordial in their welcome. They took me to the Hotel Ohio, where I was received by Mr. Courtney, the manager, who from that moment heaped courtesies upon me. In my bedroom he provided refreshment for my visitors. Flowers, magazines, the latest editions of the newspapers were already in my room.

For an hour we had a lively conversation ranging over postwar problems (as if the war were already won!) and touching upon free trade, cheap labour in Europe, the standard of living, high taxation, killing the goose that lays the golden eggs, access to raw materials, and the possible repudiation of national debt.

"The younger generation won't stand for such a burden," said one of my visitors. "They'll just wipe it out and start afresh."

Mr. Courtney, the manager of the hotel, invited me to join him in the Cascades downstairs. He would like Mrs. Courtney to join us.

The Cascades was the ballroom and barroom of the hotel. It had a steel floor, I noticed, and that seemed to me appropriate to the City of Steel. At our table beyond the dancing floor was a remarkable man who had helped to lay that floor with his own hands. Some of its plates had kept bulging up. He had had the devil of a time with it. Now he seemed to be having a good time. He knew all the ladies and treated them to liquid refreshment. He was hail-fellow-well-met with most of the hotel guests. In two minutes he was talking to me as though we had been friends for life.

The conversation turned upon Japan. That was after the arrival of Mrs. Courtney, to whom I was presented.

"There is only one discussion in the American Navy," said this new-found friend of mine. "It's whether they will destroy the Japanese fleet in three weeks or four."

Mrs. Courtney, I remember, looked at him gravely.

"I hope so," she said thoughtfully.

I looked out of my bedroom window that night and saw the panorama of Youngstown. It was a City of Steel, all right. The sky was on fire with the light of blast furnaces. I could see the black masses of immense factories. I could hear the throb and roar of engines and dynamos—or were they only in my imagination?

"Pretty grim," I thought. "Not much fun in Youngstown."

Some grim fellows, no doubt, were coming to hear me speak. I was speaking before the Youngstown Chamber of Commerce. Men were coming from all the steel towns—Detroit, Cleveland, Pittsburgh, and many others. They were the big fellows, I was told. They were directors of steel corporations, bankers, and other men associated with and dominating the entire steel industry of the United States.

I felt intimidated by these tidings. It seemed to me a very formidable affair. What could I say to these men with whom I had so little in common? How could I keep them interested —that grim crowd of steel kings? There were to be seven hundred of them, and I was scared.

I became less scared when I was introduced to many of them before a dinner at the Chamber of Commerce. They were certainly the big fellows. They were the controlling minds of American steel. Most of them were managing directors of steel corporations. But Attorney-General Herbert was among them and many banking men. They did not look grim. They were not grim. On the contrary, they were overflowing with good nature and conviviality. They chaffed each other, insulted each other, laughed at each other. Once again I saw the schoolboy spirit of American businessmen when they get together for a festive occasion.

There was one Englishman beside myself, a tall man from the British Purchasing Board in Washington. He was very civil to me.

There was also one lady. She was a very handsome lady in evening dress, with bare arms.

"Now what in the world is she here for?" I wondered. It flashed across my mind that she might be a steel queen. But she had come to sing "The Star-Spangled Banner." She sang it, superbly, before a microphone while the whole company stood up looking solemn. I felt solemn as I always do when I hear that national anthem. It is a noble tune, with a fine rhythm, but very difficult to sing as it rises rather high for the male voice.

The chairman next to whom I sat was a banker named Wilson—"the best storyteller in Ohio," somebody called him.

On my right was Mr. Weiser, director of one of the biggest
steel corporations in America, but simple and genial and keen
on things of beauty, as later I discovered. Attorney-General
Herbert had the manners of a more formal period and would
have been at home in the elegance of the eighteenth century.
There was some good conversation across the dinner table
before all lights went out and an illuminated ice pudding was
brought in—such an iceberg that it actually lowered the
temperature of the room as it passed.

The business of the evening began when the chairman
rapped with his hammer. It began with a recital of the names
and titles of all the guests from Cleveland, Detroit, Pittsburgh, and other cities. Nearly every one of them was a big
fellow in steel.

After this my fellow Englishman, Mr. Eliot, was called upon
for a few words. They were good words. He spoke extremely
well. Then it was my turn, for a terrible hour. These men, I
thought, hold the destiny of the world in their hands. Here
in this city is the raw material of all weapons of war. What
they are making here and in Pittsburgh and Detroit and other
cities of steel has had something to do with the Russian victories on the Don and with the desert fighting in Libya. In
this room are the brains behind all that. These men will control the production of that vast machinery of war which is
being planned on a gigantic scale in hundreds of plants
throughout the United States.

I made that thought the keynote of my first remarks. They
took it without contradiction. I did not underestimate their
importance, of which, no doubt, they were fully conscious.
But I spoke with complete sincerity, and what I said was true.
It was the most powerful group of men in the world today.

Late that night I sat in one of the rooms of the Hotel Ohio with a company of these men. Mr. Wilson, who had been chairman, was there, and Mr. Packard, a keen, vivid fellow, and Mr. Eliot of the British Purchasing Board in Washington, and others whose names I forget. We were speaking behind closed doors. We were speaking without veils over our eyes or gags in our mouths. The conversation was free, frank, and unrestrained.

One of the company—a hatchet-faced, dark-eyed fellow, who must have had Norman blood in him—challenged the whole structure of American life.

"We've gone soft," he said. "We're all too comfortable. We are sunk in complacency—from which one day we shall be rudely awakened. Nobody takes this war seriously, although it's our war. Who cares? The whole American population is spoon-fed. It's not told the truth, or, if it's told, doesn't believe it."

An elderly coloured man came in and spoke with a soft, whining voice to Mr. Courtney.

"I jest can't find the gen'leman nowheres."

"Look for him in the lounge," said Mr. Courtney, "and see that we have enough drinks."

"Yes sir! But I can't find the gen'leman nowheres at all."

"Take the Army," said the dark-eyed man, staring at me fiercely, as though I were commander-in-chief of the American Army.

"What's wrong with it?" I asked.

"It's all wrong. It's pampered. 'Home for Christmas!' Holy creepers! What nonsense! You can't run an army like that. 'Home for Christmas!' Like a lot of schoolboys, like a lot of sentimental brats. They ought to be treated rough.

Hardened. The modern army is full of feather-bed boys. Nice little college gents. No guts in them. They're not allowed to have guts."

Another man spoke. He was a Republican. He thought President Roosevelt had been playing a weak game, pandering to Labour, ignoring Communism.

"If Wendell Willkie had been President, we should be producing things instead of promising to produce them."

There was some talk about Mr. Wendell Willkie.

One of the company turned to me.

"Why doesn't England strike on the Continent while Germany is engaged in Russia?"

It was a question I had been asked a score of times. I had the answer but left it to another member of the company.

"England can't risk her shipping. Think what it means to transport a million men. Masses and masses of ships. Not once, but having to run a ferry service for material and supplies and ammunition and all the rest of it. Think of the inevitable losses. What a target for dive bombers, submarines, and coastal batteries. England wants to save her ships after frightful losses. Besides, her man power is heavily engaged, manning the navy and the air force, filling the factories, holding the outposts of Empire. And she is bound to keep a big army at home in case of invasion."

"Exactly," agreed the hatchet-faced man. "This war can't be won without an American Expeditionary Force. American public opinion is dead against that. American public opinion is grossly self-deceived."

The old darky came back into the room and interrupted the conversation with his soft, drawling whine.

"He ain't nowheres, Mr. Courtney. I sure can't find him."

"That's all right," said Mr. Courtney. "Bring up some more whiskey."

"I sure will, Mr. Courtney."

"There's something wrong with the German mind," said one of the steel men. "It's not merely something wrong with Adolf Hitler and Ribbentrop and Himmler and all the rest of the gang. I mean all Germans. They don't think in the same way as other people. They don't respond to the same set of ideas. They're just different, and they're just all wrong."

The hatchet-faced man drew his chair forward and put an empty glass on the table.

"The German mind," he said harshly, "must be broken to bits. There must be no soft work this time. They'll have to have hell knocked out of them. Otherwise there will be no peace in the world ever."

Another man in the company started a new theme of discussion.

"I'm darned nervous about the French fleet. It will be a major calamity for Britain—and ourselves too—if those fellows at Vichy hand it over to Hitler."

Someone in the room seemed to have special knowledge.

"It won't be handed over. Old Pétain is obstinate about that. It's his point of honour."

"Has he a point of honour—that old dotard?" asked an impatient voice.

"So far he has played a sound game," said the man who knew something about Vichy. "It's his trump card, and Hitler knows it."

He gave us a piece of news. A French general had arrived from North Africa. He had been second in command to Weygand. He was broadcasting a message to the French aviators in Morocco commanding them to fly over to the British.

"That's important," said one of the commentators.

"There's bad news tonight from Libya," said Mr. Courtney. "The German tanks have broken through the British cordon."

I had heard that news at lunch time. It lay heavily on my mind.

We went on talking. As always happens, the anecdotist gets his way on these occasions. Everyone told a funny story. They all sounded extremely amusing at that hour in the morning. There was loud laughter. Someone knocked over a glass of whiskey. He had done it twice before.

"That's all right," said Mr. Courtney, who was paying for it.

Mr. Wilson, the banker, who had been chairman of the Chamber of Commerce dinner, told the funniest story of all. He told it extremely well, but had to hark back to the beginning because he had forgotten the point. It was an excellent point.

Next day I went "on the air" in Youngstown under the direction of a young lady from the South with a soft accent. I also had to sign a number of books at the receipt of custom. I had a busy day in the City of Steel.

It was December 3, 1941.

XVIII

Canada Hears the News

It was December 7, 1941.

I was on my way to Toronto across the Canadian border. At Buffalo I had to wait an hour in its immense and crowded station. A redcap checked my baggage and promised to "take care of me" when the train was announced. I paced up and down the vast hall, eyed the bookstalls, bought cigarettes at the tobacco stall, watched the people, and listened to the music. The music was loud and sonorous. All the time I waited, except for pauses when trains were notified in a stentorian voice through loud-speakers, it blared forth enormously. March tunes. Dance tunes. Songs. Soldiers' songs. Songs of love. Silly songs. More march tunes. Along the main corridor leading to the closed tracks people were waiting, with babies and baggage. A young girl leaned her head against the shoulder of a young American soldier. Two coloured girls talked to each other in low voices. A priest read his breviary on one of the benches. A family group were discussing what they would do in the summer holidays, which seemed to me a premature discussion, in the month of December. In the restaurant, where I took a cup of coffee, men leaned with their elbows on the zinc counters from their high stools. I fell into conversation with a nice-looking boy of nineteen or so. We talked about the war in Europe. He thought his studies might be interrupted by "that kind of thing." We had a very pleasant conversation before he had to leave to catch a train to Boston.

My redcap put in an appearance.

"Yes sir!" he said, as though I had asked him a question.

He took me to the train for Toronto.

It was not a really good train, I thought—not one of those superluxury streamline trains. Indeed, it had no parlour car but was a series of coaches with hard seats. There were not many people in it. On a seat opposite to the one I took was a boy of about sixteen, roughly dressed and with tousled hair. Four lads, older than he was and smartly dressed, were ragging each other farther down the coach. The conductor, the usual type of elderly man in a peaked cap, eyed me suspiciously, I thought. But he went over to the young lad with tousled hair.

"Why do you want to go to Canada?" he asked sternly.

"My father is working there. I want to join him for Christmas."

"Oh, your father is there, is he? Let's have a look at your papers."

After examination he didn't seem satisfied.

"You'll have to step out of this train, sonny," he said. "You will have to answer some more questions."

The boy looked scared and miserable as he left the train.

I felt myself to be above suspicion, but I was wrong. The

train halted at a station which was on the Canadian border and two police officers arrived. But it was the conductor who questioned me.

"Have you your passport?"

"Here it is."

I had been informed, on what seemed to me excellent authority, that there was very little fuss on the Canadian border. A passport would take one over and back again without further questions.

I had been wrongly informed.

"Where's your White Paper?" asked the conductor.

I knew nothing of a white paper.

"Where's your authority for getting into Canada?" asked the conductor.

"My passport," I answered.

"And how are you going to get back again without the White Paper?"

"Oh, someone will arrange that!" I answered lightheartedly.

"Who?" asked the conductor sternly.

"Well," I said after a slight hesitation, "I believe I am going to the entertained by the lieutenant governor of Ontario. I daresay he'll put things right."

The conductor eyed me searchingly.

"What's his name?"

For the life of me I couldn't be sure.

"Matthews, isn't it?"

"Why do you say 'Isn't it?'," asked the conductor. "Either it is or it isn't."

He looked at my passport again.

"Do you say you're Sir Philip Gibbs?"

"I do!"

A voice spoke over the conductor's shoulder.

"That's all right. He was a war correspondent in the last war. I remember him."

It was one of the police officers. He looked at me in a friendly way. He had been with the Canadians at Vimy.

So I was allowed to proceed across the Canadian border, and presently the conductor, who seemed to be satisfied by my identity, came and whispered some words to me. They were words which changed the world and altered everything.

"The Japs have bombed Pearl Harbor in Hawaii."

I sat back as if I had been shot.

It was an act of war. It was war against the United States.

"Good God!" I said to myself.

So all that talk I had heard about the Japanese not risking war had been wrong! So all the arguments I had heard about not sending an expeditionary force, and American interests not being touched by what was happening in Europe, were utterly out of date—with all arguments, all controversies, all differences of opinion between isolationists and interventionists. War had come to the United States. They were in it, with ourselves. We were together now.

That thought: "We are together now!" was uppermost in my mind and beat in my brain like a refrain as the train jugged on. Britain was no longer fighting alone, as after Dunkirk when Churchill, in his heroic way, said, "We have the honour of being alone." Russia had broken that sense of loneliness. Russia, amazingly, had resisted the German advance, bloodily, step by step, back to Moscow. Now the American people were in, with us. So victory would be certain. Whatever happened now, the end would be victory for free peoples and for civilisation and for a decent world.

The war had flamed around the world now. It was Hitler's total war. What would happen in the Pacific? Surely the Japs had committed hara-kiri. Every American I had met had told me that the Japanese were already broken and in a rotten state. So victory was certain now. The weakness of our man power would be redressed. The potentiality of American armaments—beyond imagination—would be thrown into the scale with their own men behind them. Whatever the blood and tears ahead, victory was certain now. Victory was certain. V for victory!

I thought of all that England—and Scotland—had suffered and endured: the long bombardment from the air, the heavy toll at sea, the failure of our expeditions to Norway, Greece, and other countries because we could only send small packets of men. Even the fighting in Libya had not gone well after the first brilliant dash and victory against the Italians. Now we should have help from a nation of one hundred and thirty million people who would never quit until the end was assured.

We had held the bastion of freedom in Europe—alone—after the downfall of France. We had been hammered from the air every day and night for more than a year. Many of our cities were in ruins. Thousands of civilians—mostly women and children—had died. The American correspondents, generous in their praise of British courage, had said, "London can take it," and then, "Coventry can take it," and, "Liverpool can take it," and, "Bristol can take it." A jolly kind of slogan, as though we liked it, being so heroic. But what our people had to take was the agony on the Cross. They had stood at open pits which were the common graves of their young wives and their children. They had crawled out of the ruins of their little houses in mean streets, with all their property destroyed and nothing left but public charity. Night after night millions of them had put their babies to bed under the stairs or in the basements of flimsy little houses, one brick thick, utterly defenceless against high explosives. They had heard the crash of German shells, very close, a few houses away, or on top of them. Millions of them, aware of being in the danger zone, had readapted their lives to a subterranean habit, scuttling like rats into the subways, with a mattress and a blanket and six feet of space on a platform where trains rushed by. They were not slum folk. They were people who had had respectable homes.

They had had to part from their children. All families had been broken up. Their children now had foster parents in the countryside far away. They were forgetting their own fathers and mothers. Some of them were in America or Canada. They spoke over the radio sometimes, "Hullo, Mummy! . . . Hello, Daddy!" and fathers and mothers answered in cheerful voices with breaking hearts.

England had been wonderfully brave, taking shock after shock of defeat, failure, disappointment, without losing faith. Somehow in the end they would win! Somehow! But how no one could guess. By a miracle only. By something beyond arithmetic and the measure of man power and material forces. Hitler's attack on Russia had been a kind of miracle, saving us that year from invasion. There might be others.

Now the greatest of all had happened, by a tragedy which in the end would be turned into assured victory. The American people were with us at last. Their strength would be added to ours. Their spirit and will power, indomitable, would be put into the scales. Civilisation would not go down in darkness, after all. The lamps would be lit again one day. Beauty would come back, and decency, and liberty. The Japanese attack on Pearl Harbor, whatever its success—the success of a stab in the back or a wild-beast spring without warning—would have only one result. The English-speaking democracies and all liberty-loving peoples would thrust back the powers of darkness. One could see light ahead at last. Surely, surely!

With such thoughts in my head I came to Toronto, greedy for a newspaper.

The first headlines I saw were startling and tragic.

JAPAN ATTACKS HAWAII
1,500 KILLED IN HONOLULU AREA
PEARL HARBOR BOMBED
IN SURPRISE RAID
AMERICAN BATTLESHIPS HIT

I was met in Toronto by a small group of people among whom was a friend of mine who publishes my books in Canada—Mr. Walker of the Ryerson Press.

"What do you think of the news?" I asked.

Everyone was less excited than I had expected. They seemed to think it had been inevitable, sooner or later. They were perturbed by the amount of damage the Japanese might have done at Pearl Harbor.

"The Americans will be with us now," said one of my friends. "That makes the end certain."

They took tea with me in the Royal York Hotel, and after a hurried dinner and a change into evening clothes I was taken to Hart House to hear some music. To hear some music while the world was in flames and the United States had been attacked by Japan!

It was a strange emotional experience, that night of destiny. For here in Hart House, Toronto, the centre of university life in many of its intellectual activities, was a scene, as sharply contrasted as any might be, in a world which was now encircled by the flames of war.

I sat in the gallery, with men and women in evening dress about me, looking down upon the Grand Hall, where a quintet of musicians were discoursing the music of Mozart on a platform placed in the centre of the hall, dimly lighted except on that space. There was a full audience, mostly of students, who sat motionless until they broke into volleys of applause.

I was introduced to a lady on my right who was the wife of one of the musicians.

"Mrs. de Ridder—grandniece of Mendelssohn."

I was introduced to another lady whose husband was playing down below. She, too, had a famous name in music.

"Mrs. Hambourg."

They were playing a Mozart quintet for four violins and a clarinet. They were playing it exquisitely, as masters of their art, faultless. The clarinet was like a human voice among the strings.

"There," I thought, "is one of the lamps in the world of darkness. Tonight this is one of the little oases of civilisation in this desert of our life."

Two seats away from me was that dark-eyed lady, the grandniece of Mendelssohn, whose music was no longer allowed in Germany. Her people were being persecuted, starved, beaten up, killed, by young thugs and bald-headed brutes, merciless. It was against that spirit of cruelty and bestiality that the free peoples were fighting and dying. Against the Nazi code of intolerance and race hatred and contempt of all kindly things stood the spirit of Mozart and Mendelssohn, and all singers and poets and those who had made life lovely by their genius. How merry was this music of Mozart! How gay and light and kindly as it came back into this Canadian hall from eighteenth-century Salzburg!

What had happened at Pearl Harbor?

I lost touch with Mozart for a little while. My thoughts were haunted by the horror of what was happening out in the Pacific, away in Libya, and in the frozen snows of Russia.

De Ridder spoke to me after the concert.

"This must seem to you a little futile during a world war."

"It seems to me very important," I answered. "Men like you are keeping the torch alight."

"We can do so little to change things," he said. "Fiddling while Rome burns!"

"We need music and art more than ever," I told him.

There was a sadness in his eyes, though he smiled.

"Anyhow, it keeps me from brooding too much," he said. "There is so much agony in the world it doesn't bear thinking about."

There was curiously little reference to the news of today, the dastardly attack on Pearl Harbor.

Mr. Gillie, the deputy warden of Hart House, introduced me to Dr. Cody, president of the University of Toronto.

He spoke very warmly of a mutual friend of ours, Burgon Bickersteth, who had been Warden of Hart House for many years, doing a great work in Canada because of his inspiration to so many young men and his real genius of sympathy and leadership, which had already built up a tradition and given the right spirit to this remarkable institution, founded after the last war by Vincent Massey.

Only once did he refer to the stab in the back—that assassin deed—by the Japanese.

"You have heard the news of Pearl Harbor? It brings in the United States."

Something of the full tragedy of Pearl Harbor was in next day's papers, though full details of destruction and death had to await a government investigation. I read it all with horror and yet with that belief in a future victory whatever disasters might happen now. The whole Pacific was menaced and many places were attacked. Siam, called Thailand, had surrendered to Tokio. The Japanese had invaded Malaya. There were air raids over Hongkong. The American islands in the Pacific, defended by small bodies of marines—Guam, Midway, and Wake Island—were under aerial bombardment. The Philippines were awaiting invasion and Japanese planes were over Manila.

Something had gone very wrong in Hawaii. The American fleet had been bombed before anyone was aware of hostile squadrons approaching out of the blue. No one seemed to have been on the alert. . . .

I remembered those conversations I had had on the subject of Japan. "Beaten already . . ." "In a rotten state . . ." "We must wipe them straight out."

Something had gone wrong at the start. It would be a frightful shock to the American people.

There was a despatch from Washington which I read with an awareness that in these words the future history of mankind was to be determined.

Washington, Dec. 8. President Roosevelt asked Congress today to declare war against Japan.

He made the request after announcing that yesterday's Japanese attack on Hawaii had cost the United States two warships and two thousand dead and wounded.

"I ask," the President said, "that the Congress declare that since the unprovoked and dastardly attack by Japan on Sunday, December 7, a state of war has existed between the United States and the Japanese Empire."

There was other news that day of December 8 in those Toronto papers. But for what had happened in the Pacific they would have had the biggest headlines.

The German Army in Russia was in retreat. They were abandoning tanks, trucks, guns, and a mass of material. They had given up the attack on Moscow. The Soviet troops were pursuing and harrying them, inflicting great casualties. The German Army had been beaten by the heroic Russian resistance and by the severity of a Russian winter which prevented them from bringing up supplies. Their troops, ill clad, were suffering in the frozen snows. They were stricken with typhus. It was more than a retreat, said the Russians. It was a rout.

It was astonishing and stupendous news. The tide of war was turning in Europe. For the first time Hitler had been defeated. The myth of the Invincible German Army was destroyed. Hitler's "fanatical will power" had failed him at last. Like Napoleon's Grand Army, his broken divisions were trudging back from Moscow across the frozen snow. Like Napoleon's soldiers, many were dying in the snow. It was sensational and almost unbelievable news. A few days before, Moscow's doom seemed certain. Now all was changed.

And other good tidings came that day.

In Libya the British mechanised columns were smashing General von Rommel's tank battalions. The R.A.F. was pounding them. The corridor east of Tobruk was being cleared. British victory in the Libyan desert was now assured and British mobile columns were well on the way to Benghazi, to cut off the German retreat towards Tripoli.

In Toronto I had some glimpses of what Canada was doing in this world war. In England I had seen something of that— much of that. I had seen the Canadian armoured divisions who had come over for defence of the mother country, great numbers of hard, tough men, fully trained, perfectly equipped, keen to fight. I had seen them on the move through Surrey villages and Sussex market towns. Driving along country roads, I had passed their long columns of tanks and guns. I had seen them billeted in old country mansions. I had talked with many officers and men.

Now here in Toronto I saw one of the training depots of the Royal Canadian Air Force.

An officer called for me at the Royal York Hotel and took me to their depot, where I was introduced to the general before going the rounds.

"We have made the best use we can of all available space," said the Canadian officer.

The available space was largely provided by old exhibition buildings, some of which had been used for cattle and sheep and swine as their labels still denoted. A cynic might have seen some symbolism in that, but I am not a cynic, especially with regard to as fine a crowd of young men as any eye could see. There were six thousand of them—new recruits, getting their first papers and their first training. Every month there are six thousand new recruits to take the place of the previous batch. Seventy-two thousand a year.

"It must be difficult to handle these new lads every month," I said.

The Canadian officer agreed.

"It wants some organisation. But we have experts here, and the recruits fall into line very quickly. They're a keen crowd and discipline themselves."

Bunks had been fitted up between the iron pillars of these vast buildings which were well heated. There were rooms full of kit and supplies. There were enormous kitchens reeking with good odours. I went into the dining hall where batches of fifteen hundred were having their meal. It all went like clockwork. The young men lined up in an orderly way, passed through rails to the serving counter, and took away their first course before seating themselves at the long tables. I looked down those lines of young faces, very English, I thought, in their type, clean-cut, square-jawed, with something unmistakably British in the set of the eyes. They were just beginning their training. Where would they be a year hence? I wondered. Flying, perhaps, over the jungles of the Dutch East Indies, camped in Egyptian deserts, in island aerodromes in the Far Pacific, along the shores of the Mediterranean, possibly in China, India, Tibet, or Outer Mongolia. Fate was weaving strange, fantastic patterns on its loom. These boys would have adventures beyond the range of present imagination in places not yet to be found on the maps published in the press. They were not peering into the future with anxious eyes. There were peering into their plates laden with steak and potatoes. I heard the click of their knives and forks. They were too hungry for conversation.

After an inspection of all this and much more the Canadian officer who had taken charge of me looked at his wrist watch.

"We've only just time for our next engagement," he said.

Our next engagement was interesting. I was awaited by the Canadian Women's Auxiliary Corps who were putting up a parade for me. They were drawn up when I arrived, and I was saluted smartly by their lady commandant before I shook hands with her.

We were in a big drill hall large enough for fifteen hundred men. A Canadian sergeant who was drill instructor spoke about these young women he was training.

"No trouble at all," he told me. "They march like Guardsmen after three weeks. Keen as mustard."

He was a veteran of the last war, but a youngish veteran, full of energy and as hard as nails. Though a Canadian, he seemed to me very typical of the Cockney soldiers of the Somme and Flanders in World War I—nervy, humorous, quick, and keen.

The Canadian Women's Auxiliary Corps was drawn up at the far end of the hall. Their commandant called out orders, and they marched towards us in perfect unison, perfectly timed. Then they wheeled and marched the length of the hall, with their arms swinging out in the style of the Guards. It was a fine bit of drill and highly impressive.

"These are new recruits," said the sergeant. "They've only been at it three weeks. Not too bad, eh?"

"Pretty wonderful," I said.

They halted now in a double line facing me, and I was called upon to make a speech to them. I don't know what I said exactly, but I remember telling them of the women in England and their spirit during the great bombardment from the air. I was sure the Canadian women would be just as brave if the same ordeal came to them.

"Three cheers for England!" cried the lady commandant.

Those Canadian girls cheered heartily and with enthusiasm.

I inspected the uniform of a Scottish lassie. It was very smart indeed.

"What do you think of this war?" I asked.

She stood rigidly at attention and answered as though she were an effigy wound up and made to speak.

"It's a war we've got to win," she answered.

"What do you think of the German retreat in Russia?"

"Maybe it will lead Hitler to invade England as his last chance. I'm hoping he will. I have two brothers there. They want to see a bit of fighting."

She spoke with a strong Scottish burr, and although she still stood rigid there was a twinkle in her eyes.

I lectured that night before a big audience in the Massey Hall. I could feel something new in the way of emotional vibrations. They were excited, or at least stirred, by the world news. America was in the war with them. The Pacific was on fire. Germany was in retreat. We were smashing Von Rommel's army in Libya.

I made many references to the United States, and the audience cheered. I told them of the vast scale of armament production over the border and my conviction that when it reached its full tide no nation on earth would be able to stand up against it. I heard their cheers again. They were in a responsive mood. To these Canadians the entry of their next-door neighbours into the World War was an assurance of ultimate victory and gave them new hope.

That night after the lecture the lieutenant governor of On-

tario and his wife, Mrs. Matthews, gave a reception at
Parliament House which was a fine affair. For two hours, at
least, I stood beside Mrs. Matthews shaking hands with her
guests and having a series of quick-fire conversations with those
who passed. They all wanted to ask me questions about England and Scotland—mostly Scotland, as I noticed. Two
thirds of them had Scottish names. But here and there were
English people eager to talk about London and other cities
to which they belonged. Was Kensington much damaged?
How about poor old Chelsea? Was the Green Park Hotel still
standing? Was St. Paul's much battered?

"Now that the United States are with us," said one lady,
"there is no doubt about the end."

A hundred people said the same kind of thing, but now
and then I heard an anxious comment.

"The American people are utterly unprepared. It means a
long wait before they're ready."

"I'm afraid there was terrible damage in Pearl Harbor.
We haven't heard the full truth yet."

Mostly they were very cheerful and humorous. The tragedy
of war had cast no gloom over this assembly. I was lured away
from my stand by the side of Mrs. Matthews by people who
had many things to say and ask and who held up the long
queue.

"My dear man," said Mrs. Matthews good-naturedly, "you
are always straying away from me!"

I was getting weak at the knees. I had been standing for
hours. It was midnight in Toronto before the reception came
to an end. But I was uplifted by the spirit of these Canadians.
They were a grand crowd.

XIX

America at War

It was not easy to get back into the United States. After all, I wanted that White Paper which was being held at Ellis Island. A long-distance telephone call to New York and wires pulled by friendly people brought it to me with astonishing rapidity. It came by air mail, and I was free to go back.

"How shall I find the mood on the other side of the border?" I wondered. "How do the people of the United States take this war?"

I was anxious to get back. I wanted to see what change had happened in the American mind, now that everything had changed.

I was astonished by the calmness I found. There was no outward excitement. There was no flag-waving, no popular demonstration, no outward or visible sign that something terrific had happened in American history. The crowd in the great railway station at Buffalo looked the same as when I had left it. People were waiting quietly for their trains. The same music came through the loud-speakers. Only the dearth of newspapers quickly grabbed from the stalls indicated more interest in world affairs.

The President of the United States had spoken to his people over the radio. He said:

The sudden criminal attacks perpetrated by the Japanese in the Pacific provide the climax of a decade of international immorality.

Powerful and resourceful gangsters have banded together to make war upon the whole human race.

Their challenge has now been flung at the United States of America.

The Japanese have violated the long-standing peace between us.

Many American soldiers and sailors have been killed by enemy action.

The American ships have been sunk, American airplanes have been destroyed.

Congress and the people of the United States have accepted that challenge.

Together with other free peoples we are now fighting to maintain our right to live among our world neighbours in freedom and in common decency, without fear of assault.

The President warned his people of the grim ordeal ahead.

It will not only be a long war, but it will be a hard war. That is the basis on which we lay all our plans. That is the yardstick by which we must measure all our demands—money and materials doubled and quadrupled, production ever in-

creasing. The production must be not only for our own Army and Navy and Air Force. It must reinforce the other armies and navies and air forces fighting the Nazis and the war lords of Japan throughout the Americas and the world.

He did not hide the amount of sacrifice which would be necessary to fulfil this programme, but he called it by another name.

On the road ahead there lies hard work—gruelling work—day and night, every hour and every minute. I was about to say that on the road ahead lies sacrifice for all of us. But it is not correct to use that word. The United States does not consider it a sacrifice to do all one can, to give one's best to our nation, when the nation is fighting for its existence and its future life.

It is not a sacrifice for any man, old or young, to be in the Army or Navy of the United States. Rather it is a privilege.

It is not a sacrifice for the industrialist, the wage earner, the farmer or the shopkeeper, the trainman or the doctor to pay more taxes, to buy more bonds, to forego certain profits, to work harder, in the task for which he is best fitted. Rather is it a privilege.

It is not a sacrifice to do without many things to which we are accustomed, if the national defence calls for doing without. It is a privilege.

He spoke gravely of the tremendous responsibilities they had undertaken and made no boast. In every word was warning of tragic days ahead, in every word an exhortation to courage, will power, and the abandonment of self-interest for national safety. He ended a great speech on the most solemn note.

In the dark hours of this day, and through dark days that may be yet to come, we will know that the vast majority of the members of the human race are on our side. Many of them are fighting with us. All of them are praying for us. For in representing our cause we are representing theirs as well— our hope and their hope for liberty under God.

Those words and the news from all the fronts were being read in a train by which I travelled from Buffalo to Washington. The men and women in the parlour car were all busy with their newspapers until they had exhausted them. They looked grave and thoughtful. They talked quietly to each other. Some of them sat silently staring ahead, lost in thought.

I wanted to talk to them. These were the first Americans I had met since the declaration of war. It would be deeply interesting to find out what they were thinking about it all.

The news was not comforting to them or to me.

In the first lifting of censorship about Pearl Harbor Honolulu had reported casualties and damage to Washington. They were expected to be heavy and disastrous.

The Japanese had invaded Luzon in the Philippines with heavy forces. They had made a second air attack on Clark Field near Manila.

Hongkong was being attacked by large numbers of Japanese troops.

There was heavy fighting in northern Malaya, and Japanese forces had landed at Kota Bahru. The British reported heavy, confused, general engagements.

The Japanese were moving from central Thailand in an attempt to cut the Burma Road.

Questioned about the Japanese claims, President Roosevelt admitted that the news was "all bad" but urged Americans to reject reports of complete disaster. He described the Japanese claim to have gained naval supremacy in the Pacific as "fantastic." He believed that the purpose of these reports was to "spread fear and confusion among us and to goad us into revealing military information which our enemies are desperately anxious to obtain."

Nevertheless, that admission that present news was "all bad" was a blow to cheerfulness and confidence. Certainly the affair at Pearl Harbor must have been very tragic.

At a dinner table in the restaurant car three Americans sat down with me, all other tables being occupied.

"I heard a good English accent," said one of these men, when I had taken my place with the only one of them with whom I had previously talked. For a little while nothing was said about the war. They discussed French wines and Scotch whiskey and English beer. They seemed fairly cheerful and quite unexcited by world news. Around us the other people dining were equally calm. No one raised his voice excitedly. I had heard more noise during the baseball matches called the World Series.

Presently the man opposite me—he had an old English name going back to Saxon times—spoke of the tragedy of Pearl Harbor.

"It was inexcusable," he said. "They must have been asleep. Surely to God there ought to have been some warning before the Jap airplanes were over them. What about our air patrol?"

"The curse of this country has been overconfidence," said one of the other men. "We were all too complacent. We didn't heed the warnings. And yet the writing was on the wall, staring us in the face. Those damned isolationists——"

"We were utterly unprepared, as England was," said the man with the Saxon name. "And for the same reason. We didn't want to have a war. We shirked the idea of it. We hoped that it would not hit us—being so far away. We were very pleased to cheer on England from the side lines, and we were quite decided not to send an American Expeditionary Force overseas."

He spoke sombrely and with a dark cynicism.

"England has been pretty patient with us," he said. "We have been very slow in the delivery of munitions."

"We are grateful to you," I assured him. "We could not have recovered so quickly after Dunkirk except for aid, not only in machines but in machine tools for making them, and many other needs."

He gave me a fleeting smile.

"It's generous of you to put it that way," he answered. "Your people have been fighting our war all this time. Some of us knew it. Some of us said so. But the great mass of the American people refused to believe it and refused to do anything about it. They wanted to keep on having a good time. Now they're going to have a bad time. So are we all."

"When the truth is known about Pearl Harbor," said one of the other men, "I'm afraid it's going to be worse than anything we yet know."

"Some of those naval officers will have to be scrapped," said the man who spoke so sombrely. "When an avoidable disaster happens the responsibility must be fixed on the right shoulders and punishment given."

"They came out of the blue," said one of my companions, a mild-mannered, good-natured fellow. "War had not been declared. It was a stab in the back. I'm sorry for those fellows whose careers will be ruined."

"Who cares about their careers?" asked the man who took a sombre view. "Careers matter nothing when a nation's security is at stake."

"They couldn't expect such a thing," said the good-natured man. "One can't guard against a bolt from the blue."

"It was their job to guard against it. Hadn't they been warned? Hadn't Cordell Hull sent stiff notes? And the Japs had answered with abuse and threatened to wipe us off the map. Not exactly perfect peace without a shadow! Every man ought to have been on the alert."

They argued this question out for some time, while I remained silent.

Other people were arguing it out. From time to time I heard the words "Pearl Harbor" . . . "Pearl Harbor" above the noise of a train rushing through space and the handling of crockery by coloured waiters and the striking of matches for cigarettes. Two of the men left the table. I had a long conversation with the third man—the good-natured fellow who had first sat down with me. He took an optimistic view.

"This is only the beginning," he said. "We shall have to expect knocks, of course. It's not quite true that we are unprepared. For more than a year we have been extending our munition plants in every state. Some of them are in production. We are making almost unbelievable quantities of shells. We are turning out bombing aeroplanes, guns, and tanks in quite big numbers. The President was playing for time, while industry was swinging over to war production. I doubt whether he could have speeded it up faster, as long as we were not actually at war."

He groaned slightly and said, "Pearl Harbor is frightful. A terrible blow."

So in that train from Buffalo to Boston I saw the first impact of events upon the American mind, the minds of intelligent, well-educated men of affairs. As far as their conversation went it revealed anxiety regarding the immediate position, self-criticism because of American complacency before the war and failure to read the signs of the times, and a touch of bitterness because of the nation's weakness for immediate action in the Pacific or elsewhere. There was no word of boasting. These men stared into the face of reality without rose-coloured glasses or self-deception.

When I came back to my home base near a small town in Massachusetts, where people were beginning their Christmas shopping and the shops already were putting up their Christmas decorations, I came in touch with the mood and mind of the ordinary American folk in New England, the women, the tradesmen, the families in the country houses whose lives would be touched and changed by that need of service and sacrifice for which the President had called.

I met Lydia outside one of the shops—that girl who rides a horse down the bridle paths and has learned to fly and does sculpture; she had made a study of my own haggard head—in an old barn. She looked a little Russian, I thought, in a fur cap and a fur-trimmed jacket above her skirt and snow boots.

"How do you feel about it?" I asked.

"I feel happy about it," she told me emotionally. "There

were lots of people like me who thought we ought to be in with you from the beginning. Now we are in with you. There is no more argument about it. We are all united now. We all have to get on with the job of winning this war. I am very happy because it will pull us all together."

She spoke some words not of happiness.

"It's terrible about the *Prince of Wales* and the *Repulse*."

"Appalling!" I answered.

That news had just come through. I confess that it laid me low. I have never been quite so low, so utterly dejected, since the collapse of France, as when those two battleships were sunk by Japanese dive bombers. The *Prince of Wales* was the most modern and powerful of all our battleships. She and the *Repulse* were our main defenders of the Pacific Islands and Malaya. Their very presence would have warned off Japanese transports or put them to the bottom of the ocean. While they kept guard we should still have had the command of the sea in co-operation with American naval forces and the fortified base of Singapore. Now they had gone down, proving once again, as at Crete, that without air support the capital ships cannot stand up against aerial attack by low-flying bomber planes. Without air support! Some frightful blunder had been made about that. The *Prince of Wales* and the *Repulse* had been only one hundred and twenty miles off shore. Air support to chase off the Japanese bombers could have reached them in a few minutes. It had never come, before Admiral Phillips had given that last order of despair, "Prepare to abandon ship," knowing before his death that all was lost, his self-confidence, his pride of command, his terrific gun power, his splendid officers and men.

In this small New England town women and children were

buying Christmas gifts. I held onto the chain of a cocker spaniel who tugged at it. There was a touch of frost in the air, bringing colour to the cheeks of boys and girls.

"I was terribly excited," said Lydia, "when the news came through that the Japs had attacked, and afterwards when Germany and Italy declared war. We had an air-raid scare. It was very absurd, but it made everyone realise that we are in danger. I wouldn't put it past the Japs if they made a landing somewhere on the Mexican coast. We used to laugh about the idea of air raids and sirens in the United States because they seemed utterly unreal and imaginary, but now we know better."

"I don't think you will get bombed here," I told her. "It's too far away."

"Anyhow," she answered, "it's wise to take precautions. Everybody will have to do something. They're all volunteering."

She herself was going to do something very adventurous. She was going to join the Civil Air Patrol.

She raised her hand and went down the street, and I turned into the little shop where I get cigarettes.

"How do you do?" said the owner of that shop. "Back again?"

"Glad to be back," I told him.

"A lot has happened since you went away," he remarked. "Not very good, most of it, but the end will be all right. That's sure."

They were all sure of that.

And as I went about, meeting people in Boston and New York and in New England houses and listening to radio announcements coming through all day long, interrupted by little songs and talks advertising chewing gum, liver pills, cigars, candy, and Christmas gifts, I was struck by the similarity of this country's state of mind and activity to that of England in the first days of the war, which for us were as far back as 1939. They were calling for air-raid wardens, first-aid volunteers, ambulance drivers, fire spotters. They were arranging lectures on chemical warfare and what to do in an air raid and how to extinguish incendiary bombs. They were making elaborate plans for the evacuation of school children from danger zones. They were calling upon the young men to enlist for the Navy and Air Force. They were urging the whole nation to buy Defence Bonds and to keep on buying. Here in the United States it was happening all over again, as it had happened in England two years before—these appeals, these slogans, these civil-defence measures.

Just as we did on September 3, 1939, in London, they had a false alarm of hostile aircraft over New York and Massachusetts. Somebody had lost his head. Someone had sounded the alert. In New York millions of people had put their heads out of the windows, staring up at the sky. Children had been rushed home from school and turned out of museums, to be ordered back again by police with orders to clear the streets. Some women wept. Children were frightened. Parents were anxious. There was hopeless bewilderment and confusion of orders, until the scare passed. It was a valuable lesson in what not to do. We have all had to learn those lessons.

But on the whole the American people were keeping their heads in this first shock of war. They were astonishingly calm. At first, I think, the masses of their folk were stunned. To them it was the unbelievable which had happened. They had never believed—high or low—that the Japanese would attack. They had never believed that Hitler would declare war against them. They had never believed that the American Navy would be caught unawares. The invasion of the Philippines, with American troops falling back before the enemy, had not been in their imagination or tradition. The capture of Guam and Wake Island, defended by groups of marines left to their doom, dejected them. Those events were not according to past history in their schoolbooks.

Only one story was in line with the old tradition. It was when a message contacted Wake Island and its four hundred marines.

"Is there anything you want?" they were asked.

"Send us some more Japs," was the answer.

Good stuff that! And a pity that some days later no further word came from those marines who had fought to the end before being overwhelmed.

Because it was the unbelievable that was happening, the American people felt stunned at first, just as we did after Dunkirk and the collapse of France. There was no shouting or cheering. No excited crowds surged through American cities waving flags and yelling patriotic songs. They were very quiet and undemonstrative and thoughtful and sober. This thing that had come at them was too big for schoolboy stuff. It was going to be big and bloody. There were going to be many hard knocks.

"It is all very lucky for England," said an American lady who is a friend of mine. "It stops all further argument and all need of propaganda."

I agreed. It was very lucky for England, because that bolt from the blue, hurled by Japan and followed by the German declaration of war, had broken down that fixed and entrenched resistance in the American mind to the idea of letting their boys go overseas for fighting service. It was very lucky for England, who had borne the brunt of the war for two years, mostly alone. Now one hundred and thirty million people, grimly resolved to defeat the common enemy, would be with them, with all their industry, all their man power, all their resources. Enormous luck, but not undeserved or thrown by some freak of chance onto the gambling table of Fate. Nothing will ever rob the British people of the splendour of their spirit in resisting the enemies of freedom and all civilised ideas at a time when they had very little strength beyond their courage, and looked death in the face without flinching, and stood up against heavy bombardment, by day and night, for eleven months of days and nights, amidst their ruins and amidst their dead, unyielding and undaunted.

I went to New York for a few days and met many people there. The war which had come to the United States had taken its place in their minds and its grisly spectre had entered their homes, but they had no panic. Once again, having believed that the American people were more demonstrative than the English, I was astonished at the calm way in which they talked about these things and faced their realities.

My Negro redcap in Grand Central Station—that vast cathedral in which there is no noise as the crowds move about its vast space under the blue dome with golden stars—was the only man who seemed dejected and horror-stricken.

"This war is terrible," he said in a voice of anguish. "It's sure terrible!"

His loose limbs sagged as he carried my bags. His black face was careworn and tragic.

But out in the streets of New York the crowds looked cheerful and normal. They were preparing for Christmas. They were not going to let the war interfere with that.

In the Plaza Hotel big plants of red azaleas in full bloom were being arranged in the lounge beyond the elevators with shining brass doors, but the hotel was very empty and I dined almost alone.

"People left as soon as the war began," I was told by my waiter. "They haven't come back again. I guess they were scared."

But they weren't scared, as I learned afterwards; they wanted to be home in time of trouble. They were called back by local affairs. Many of them would be wanted to organise civil defence and other business in their own home towns, and there was also, no doubt, a disinclination to spend money in New York, having a good time when the nation had been called to war.

Everything was changed in the American mind since my last visit to that city. I saw that change when I was a guest of Dr. Potter, that intellectual humourist and most charming man, at his Faculty Club of Columbia. He was gay, as usual, and greeted his guests with amusing remarks, but as we sat in his rooms, having refreshment before a debate, the conversation quickly drifted to the war, to Pearl Harbor, the Philippines, Malaya, Russia, and Germany. On my previous visit the war had not been the main subject of their talk. They were interested in it, if one happened to mention it, but it did not haunt them. It seemed a long way, really, from their own thoughts and interests. Now it was in the centre of their minds. It was their war.

I heard some severe criticism of what had happened at Pearl Harbor, and no one disguised or slurred over the difficulties and dangers of the naval and military situation in the Pacific. These professors and scientists of Columbia University, with their wives, spoke with great candour about American unpreparedness and the immovable, unimaginative indifference of the American masses to all the warnings they had had.

"The isolationists were entrenched in the Middle West," said a squarely built man who was not a university professor but some kind of expert in technical affairs.

"Well," I said, "I failed to meet them. They did not come to my lectures and debates. I can honestly say that I didn't meet one isolationist in the Middle West or anywhere else. I seem to have missed something—including eggs."

They were astonished to hear that, but what I said was confirmed by a young American newspaperman and lecturer named Whittaker, who took part in an informal debate directed by Dr. Potter.

It was an amusing and informative evening. Four of us who were to lead the debate sat around Dr. Potter, facing a big audience who were free to ask questions afterwards. I had to open the proceedings by an analysis of the American spirit based upon my experiences as a lecturer in many states, and I brought in that bit about failing to meet an isolationist.

When Whittaker's turn came he said that he had the same experience. The isolationists had not shown up. Something, he believed, had happened, as far back as June, to change public opinion in the Middle West. They had heard the isolationist leaders and had seen the failure of their logic or the weakness of their arguments.

I was much taken by that young man Whittaker. As a public speaker he was first class, because of his own personality and knowledge of European affairs, especially in Italy. He was vivid, dogmatic, and satirical. He made very humorous faces from time to time, especially when he said something very critical of the American people. He had no bouquets to offer. He indulged in no wishful thinking. He was convinced that German morale stood high and showed no sign of cracking. He did not believe one word of the Russian war reports as regards casualties inflicted upon the Germans. He had no confidence in the loyalty of Mr. Stalin or his associates and thought they would do the dirty on us any moment if he thought it suited his purpose. At any moment he might make a new pact with Germany.

All this may have been overcynical but it was well put, and the young man's face and manner, and his little grimaces and the jerk of his head, gave a point and edge to his words.

There was another speaker who had special knowledge. His name was Eliot and he had just come from Vichy, where he had been the correspondent, I think, of the *Herald-Tribune*. What he said challenged the convictions of his audience and those of John Whittaker. He made a defence of Marshal Pétain, at least as regards his honour and his patriotism. He had no use for the old marshal's Fascist ideas, but he affirmed that Pétain was unyielding in his refusal to give up the French fleet or to surrender North Africa. They were the only cards he had to play against Hitler, and he was playing them well and with obstinate courage. Because of a million and a half French prisoners in the hands of the enemy, and because of French defeat and occupation, he had to yield a point here and there, under heavy German pressure, but on those two vital points he still held on. It was, thought Mr. Eliot, most advisable that the American State Department should bolster up this old man and not hurt his pride or act against his authority. It was most unfortunate, he thought, that the B.B.C. in England should keep on insulting him, and still more unfortunate that the Free French under De Gaulle should attack French soldiers in Syria and Africa. It would be different if they attacked Germans. Marshal Pétain had been convinced that England would be defeated and that Germany would win. Now he was beginning to think differently, and Admiral Leahy, the American Ambassador in Vichy, who was very friendly with the old man, had to keep on persuading him that the Allies would win and, with their victory, would liberate France. Any break with Vichy would play into the hands of the enemy by weakening the old marshal's will power to resist complete surrender.

This point of view seemed to me important. It was hotly questioned by members of the audience and failed to convince John Whittaker, who denounced it in scathing words. But Eliot kept springing to his feet to advance debating points and to make his meaning perfectly clear, on the evidence he had. It was an interesting debate carried on by well-trained minds, and in spite of bad news from the Pacific—always getting worse—there was no word from any of these people suggesting violence of judgment or a failure in moral poise. They were keeping their nerve. They were facing very grim realities with intellectual courage. There was no sign of wishful thinking or false heroics.

The American people had closed up together and presented a united front. The leaders of the isolationists had withdrawn opposition and lined up for national service. Colonel Lindbergh, who had resigned his commission as a protest against the President's policy, now asked to be reinstituted so that his knowledge and experience might be of use to his country.

Labour leaders had promised to be good boys. They had agreed to cut out all strikes and to allow a seven-day week for the workers. (Too much, as English experience has shown.)

But it was curious that many Americans became intensely critical of their own people. Even those who had been most hostile to the war and had tried most to keep out of it now accused the American people of selfishness and lethargy.

I met a man of that kind in the sitting room of a New England house where I took coffee one day. He is a brilliant fellow with great gifts of imaginative speech. In his best moods he startles, entrances, or convulses the company at a dinner table. He is one of those talkers who build up a thesis or an anecdote with passionate imagination, not to be taken as sober matter of fact. I found him gloomy, prophetic, and bitter in his satire. He shocked me profoundly by describing President Roosevelt as a "swindling Messiah." He shocked a lady sitting curled up in an armchair, though she knew him well enough to discount his political passion and verbal fury.

"The American people," he said with a sultry gleam in his dark eyes, "have no will to fight. They want to be comfortable. They resent this war because it interferes with their comfort and what they are pleased to call, and what is shamefully true, 'the American way of life.' "

"I like the American way of life," I told him. "I admire it."

He ignored this interruption and smiled ironically.

"This war," he said, "has been an abstract thing in their minds, utterly devoid of any grim reality. They were like children playing sham battles with little tin soldiers—English, German, French, Russian. The blood was red paint. The guns were just toy guns, fired by caps. It was all good drama for the movies and the radio. The British were doing well in Libya.

Fine! The Russians were thrusting back the Germans. Great stuff! But no stench of blood reached them, no screams of agonised men, no shrieks of mutilated women. It was as unreal as a dream or a pantomime. It didn't disturb their home comforts."

He seemed to think that the Japanese war need not have happened.

"Cordell Hull," he said, "kept on poking up the tiger with red-hot irons."

The lady curled up in the chair argued with him on this point and he accepted her rebuke meekly. I doubt whether he heard it. He was thinking inwards. New phrases were forming in his mind. He was raking up historical parallels. He had something to say about cutthroat Castlereagh and other English statesmen of the eighteenth century. He was a type to the nth degree of the intellectual and the sceptic. He, too, resented this war, not because it interfered with home comforts but because it interfered with art and beauty and human reason.

"What is coming out of all this?" he asked me presently, with that sultry gleam in his eyes, while he reached out for another cup of coffee or another cigarette. "What can come out of it except ruin, desolation, and—when peace comes—Communism?"

Extraordinarily different was a man I met in New York who came to take me from the Plaza to a suburban town called Larchmont, where I had to lecture that night. He was a tall, big fellow with a massive face. At first glance he looked "a tough guy" though handsome. Before ten minutes had passed I discovered him to be a religious-minded man with a spiritual outlook on life and a simple and perfect faith in a spiritual victory over the forces of evil.

We took a suburban train from New York to Larchmont.
It was crowded with city men going home, and one of them
kept his eye on me as afterwards he told me.

"You're a chain smoker," he said. "You lit one cigarette
from another in that train to Larchmont."

The man with faith in his heart asked me if I knew the
prophecies of Saint Odile, and after that we had an extraordinary conversation in the smoking carriage of a suburban
train. It was all about prophecies concerning the World War.
Those of the Apocalypse, and of Nostradamus, and the Egyptian pyramids, and the British Israelites. But my new friend
was most impressed by those of Saint Odile. He had a copy of
them in his pocket. He was circulating them among his friends.

"It's all coming true," he told me, "even to the exact dates.
"That's why I don't take the view that this is going to be a long
war. Hitler has had all his successes. Now he is on the down-
ward grade and doom awaits him. Saint Odile describes the
present state of the German Army, stricken with a pestilence.
Reports are coming through about that. The German soldiers
can't change their clothes in Russia owing to the extreme cold.
They can't take baths. They are bound to be verminous, and
great numbers of them are infected with typhus. It's the beginning of the end. I believe that before a year goes by something will break in Germany."

The commuters—some with their wives—put on their coats
and hats and stood up as the train slowed down. It was not
a long journey to Larchmont, though we two earnest talkers
had travelled in our conversation from the beginning of history
to the future beyond the veil.

Mr. Barrett took me to his club, where I put on evening

clothes before dining downstairs with a group of his friends, among whom were three or four ladies.

The conversation turned inevitably to the war and especially to Pearl Harbor. The men were very severe on those responsible for that disaster. The women were full of sympathy for the naval officers who.had been dismissed.

"A naval officer who loses his ship is court-martialled and punished," said one of the men. "Even if it wasn't directly his fault, he has to take the responsibility. That's a good rule. It's naval discipline."

"In the case of Pearl Harbor," said another man, "there was certainly gross negligence. They were all asleep! It was inexcusable."

"I can't see it," said a lady. "The Japs came out of the blue. There was no declaration of war. No one expected it. One can't guard against an assassin's blow."

"It seems to me pitiable," said another lady, "that distinguished men should have their careers ruined because something happened which they couldn't foresee."

"They ought to have foreseen it," said one of the men. "There couldn't have been any reconnaissance. Where were our scouting planes?"

So they argued rather bitterly over that tragic episode.

That evening I gave my last lecture in the United States. But it was the first lecture to American people since they had been at war. I scrapped everything I had previously talked about and made an impromptu speech lasting for an hour. "The Spirit of Britain" was to have been the title of my talk, but I changed it to a broader view of the war and to the spirit of the American people.

It was a big audience for a small town, and I could make

no complaint about their attention and enthusiasm. It was good to hear their cheers, though I had refrained from any false heroics. For the last time I answered the fire of questions which had reached me so many times from so many people. I remember a few of them.

"What about Russia after the war? Will Russian Communism invade Europe?"

I answered that in my belief Russia would become more democratic after the war, with a more liberal system of government. The Russian people who had fought with such heroism for their country would not go back tamely to the old tyranny. They would demand a greater share of self-government. They would, I thought, demand more individual rights and liberties. Stalin might institute a new constitution more in line with that of England and the United States. In any case Communism had been greatly modified in Russia since its first rigid tryout, which had failed.

"How has the war affected religion in England?"

That was a poser, but I answered that in my belief and experience the war had made most people in England more spiritual in their outlook on life. With death so near, and with so much suffering and self-sacrifice, most people turned to religion for consolation, or, if they had no definite faith, were more aware of the spiritual side of things and tried to find some faith beyond the material illusion.

"Why was England so unprepared?" asked a woman's voice, repeating a question addressed to me a score of times.

One answer would have been easy and justified now.

"Why is America so unprepared?"

I did not make that answer but spoke of the English desire for peace, the failure of appeasement, which I had supported, the hope that Hitler would not betray his pledges, the popular support of the League of Nations—too long, perhaps—and a thousand other hopes and ideals which had been betrayed.

Many people came up to speak to me afterwards.

One was a French lady.

"Did England do enough for France?" she asked. "It may be untrue, but many French people like myself, without knowledge, cannot help thinking that England did not come to our aid with sufficient strength and abandoned us at a critical time. I should be so glad if you would tell me the truth."

I told her the truth as far as I knew it. We had sent all we could to France. We believed that the French could hold their lines. They had told us they could. Our expeditionary force was left in the air and cut off when the enemy broke through at Sedan and drove its armoured columns to Boulogne. Before France capitulated Churchill had offered everything—common citizenship, federal union, complete financial support, all our resources in a common pool, if France would go on fighting in Africa and join her fleet with ours. We did all we could for France.

I don't suppose that lady was convinced, but she was polite. And these American people who surrounded me were like so many others in so many states to which I had been on that lecture tour—warm in thanks, eager to express their admiration of the British people, courteous, kind, and friendly to an elderly Englishman who had come to talk to them. In spite of all fatigue, hard travelling, nervous tension, I was sorry that that would be the last time for me to meet this warmth of the American spirit, this contact with the American mind. I had had a wonderful experience in a great country.

There was one thing different in this last audience of mine. They were no longer looking at the war as a thing apart from them. They were no longer "cheering England from the side lines," as one of them had said. They were in it. It had caught up with them. They were our allies. The last limits of "Aid to Britain" had been passed. We were now fighting together for the common goal of victory, and before the end they would have to make the same sacrifices, endure the same anxieties and tribulations, pay the same costs, in blood and money and tears, as we in Britain.

They knew that. Some of them said so.

"It's our turn now," said an elderly man who held my hand for a moment. "We shall never quit until those fellows are beaten. There will be a lot of bad news before good tidings. But your people have given us inspiration by their courage and their faith in the darkest hours. I doubt whether we shall get bombed like London or your other cities. We shall be spared that, perhaps."

"God bless England," said an old lady. "England led the way."

"God bless America," I answered. "And God bless the American people now and in this year to come."

The year that was coming would be a great testing time of this American civilisation, with its great strength and hidden weaknesses, with its mixture of nationalities, not yet completely merged in the great melting pot, with its high standard of living now to be lowered, with its mixture of idealism and self-interest, with its variety of character and temperament in all its different states, with its mass-production methods of industry and intelligence and mass psychology. For them it would be the year of Destiny. How would they face it? How would they stand the test?

Having seen and studied them in many of their states, I am certain that they will emerge from their ordeal, whatever its agony and its price, nobly. They will drive their chariots through Armageddon to the sunlit plains of peace beyond. Their sons will struggle through jungles and swamps, over sun-baked deserts, across old battlefields in Europe. Their blood will soak into the soil of foreign lands. The American Eagle will go with the British Lion and the Chinese Dragon into strange places. American college boys, now smooth-faced, will be hardened and thinned down, and their eyes will see frightful things. They will sail over the Seven Seas with the black bats of death above them and the snakes of the sea below them and about them. They will drive great tanks over dead bodies which once were living men. They will sit above strong wings in flights above crowded cities and oceans, and their squadrons will race across the sky on moonlit nights, and their loads will be lightened when they fling their fury upon the enemy below. They will be like avenging angels, those American boys, so nicely educated, so tenderly brought up. They will look different afterwards, for they will know what hell is like—this man-made hell of world war. And the American people will be different, for the American way of life, with its demand for a thousand luxuries which now seem needful, will undergo a change during this great struggle. The thirty million cars will be worn out and not replaced because there is greater need for guns and tanks and armoured trucks. One by one the little luxuries will go—no more chewing gum, no more radio sets, no more tailor-pressed suits, not many razor blades, no more shopping for the mere sake of buying. The American people are going to be taxed, cut down, and skinned in their way of life. They will become as shabby as the English with their coupons for clothes. They will be reduced to the bare bones of life, as England has been. Their wealthy classes will have all their wealth taken away from them, as in England. They will face a lean, hard time, with no superfluity of good things.

But they will not whine. The pioneer spirit is still a tradition with them. They will laugh, if need be, and make a joke of it. They will go through this grim business grimly, with an unyielding will power and the usual wisecracks. They will win through and come out of it like fine steel, hard pressed and tempered.

I believe that.

XX

American Christmas

THERE WAS something tragic in the American celebration of that 1941 Christmas. It was in such gleaming, twinkling, fairylike contrast to the dark business in hand. Behind it all was Pearl Harbor, and invasion of the Philippines, and the capture of Wake Island, and the black-out on the Pacific coast.

Britain has had three Christmas days since this war began, and they were saddened and darkened—away from the children—by war thoughts and circumstances and by the frightful contrast between the message of Christ to humanity and the murderous things being done by mankind.

But the Americans make more outward show of Christmas than the English. The decorations are not only in their homes but in their streets. Their Christmas trees are not only indoors but out of doors, and each house, in New England above all, has a holly wreath on the front door and coloured lights for all passers-by to see.

The first time I saw this was in the town of Taunton, very typical of all small towns in New England. I was astonished and dazzled by the illuminations. Christmas trees alight with fairy lamps lined the sidewalks. There were triumphal arches of coloured lights. Stars glittered above the highest buildings. The Court House was floodlit. Every shop was elaborately illuminated. Most of the houses in residential streets were decorated with Christmas emblems, shining forth brilliantly. Santa Claus in his scarlet coat drove his sleigh, drawn by reindeer, between the pillars of the Town Hall above the balcony in Middleboro, not far away. Every city in the United States, including New York, had their display of Christmas trees and stars and fairy lights.

These things are done not only for the children but for the child in the heart of every grown-up American—the hard-boiled businessman who is often very soft inside and the "tough guys" who are not nearly so tough as they look. At Christmas the ordinary American man and woman become children again and must have their Christmas tree, whatever their age may be.

We had one in my own family for the children, and early that morning I heard their shouts of "Happy Christmas!" and the scampering of their feet upstairs.

Somebody turned on the radio. One item of news that came from it was startling.

Winston Churchill was at Washington conferring with the President. On Christmas Eve they had both made Yuletide messages to the nation.

Churchill's words held a grim reminder of war, though he spoke of the Christmas spirit and its gladness.

"This is a strange Christmas Eve," he exclaimed, speaking

after the President. "Almost the whole world is locked in deadly struggle; armed with the most terrible weapons which science has devised, the nations advance upon each other . . . Here in the midst of war, raging and roaring over all the lands and seas, creeping nearer to our hearths and homes, here amidst all these tumults, we have tonight the peace of the spirit in each cottage home and in every generous heart. Therefore we may cast aside, for this night at least, the cares and dangers which beset us and make for the children an evening of happiness in a world of storm. . . . Let the children have their night of fun and laughter. Let the gifts of Father Christmas delight their play. Let the grownups share to the full in their unstinted pleasures before we turn again to the stern tasks and formidable years that lie before us, resolved that by our sacrifice and daring these same children shall not be robbed of their inheritance or denied their right to live in a free and peaceful world."

Fine and rolling phrases delivered on the spur of the moment! Churchill's gift of oratory never fails him.

But other words came over the radio on that Christmas morn in frightful contrast to the spirit of the day, and I listened to them while children were laughing and playing with their toys.

An outnumbered American Army, commanded by General MacArthur, was grimly fighting against a pincers movement by the Japanese. Manila was gravely menaced.

Japanese submarines were sinking American merchant ships along the California coast.

British troops were losing ground in Malaya and falling back to new lines.

Almost every hour over the radio came a message warning

all civilian-defence workers to be on the alert during Christmastide to prevent the possibility of sabotage in factories and other places of importance.

"Remember Pearl Harbor!" said the announcers before turning to Christmas carols.

> *Hark! the herald angels sing,*
> *"Glory to the newborn King . . ."*

The old hymns vibrated through the air with their beautiful cadences while little yellow men were pushing their way through jungles and swamps, firing at British and American soldiers, heavily outnumbered, while machine-gun bullets sputtered about them and the trees were slashed by shellfire.

That morning before the Christmas feast I walked with two children to Hill-top Farm of which I have written. We had a few gifts to deliver but found no one at home.

"Perhaps they're in the Fuller House," suggested Martin, who always has bright ideas.

The Fuller House is like an English dower house in the same park as the old mansion, but it is inhabited by Lydia who wears wings. It was moved there, I believe, from some distance away, but it is an old eighteenth-century house in the New England style, built of wood, with little rooms and big fireplaces and old panelling and old floors.

Martin was quite right. The family was there, and the parlour was in a litter of silver paper and coloured paper and cardboard boxes and coloured string.

"We've been opening our Christmas stockings," said Lydia.

Her father had had a Christmas stocking filled with sweets and toys and comic things.

"America has another visitor besides Santa Claus," said

Lydia's mother, that wise woman who had told me so much about American politics and personalities with a liberal, free, and humorous mind.

"Yes," I answered. "Winston Churchill is here. I heard it over the radio. What do you think about it?"

"We are hospitable," she answered. "We like to have visitors. It pleases our sense of hospitality. But it is doubly good when at such a time as this we get a visitor like Winston Churchill. I think it's wonderful! We all think it wonderful. It is a great tonic to us."

That evening I went to a party on this first Christmas of America at war. It was in the town of New Bedford, which still has old eighteenth-century houses and old families settled there for many generations. There were no children present, but a crowd of elderly and young who gathered round a giant tree, with gifts from all to each other.

My host had been busy with this all day long.

It was heart-warming inside this room. There were shouts of laughter and delight as the Christmas parcels were opened. I was given a New England calendar with many fine photographs of New England scenes. I was also given a pocket torch, dainty and serviceable. Food was abundant. Drink flowed. All was very merry and bright. Most of these people were related to each other. It was a privilege to be among them. There was Jo, who had gone with me up the Mohawk Trail uttering screams of ecstasy. There was Weezy, her tall, dark sister. There was Lydia, their cousin, and many others. The spirit of Christmas prevailed. War was shut out from this pleasant room. Its grisly spectre was not at the feast. Not visibly. Not with the touch of a bony finger to chill one down the spine or spoil the laughter or put sadness into merry eyes.

"No one is thinking about the war," I thought to myself. "No one remembers Pearl Harbor tonight. That is good. We are like that in England on Christmas Day."

But a young man leaning against the banisters in this old-fashioned house mentioned the unmentionable thing. He had a glass of rum punch or some such liquid in his hand.

"You know," he said, "I was all wrong!"

"About what?" I asked.

"About this war."

"In what way?"

"Well, you know, my wife has been spending a lot of time in civil-defence work and all that. Air-warden stuff. First aid and all that. Helping to organise things in this small city. I used to say to her, 'It's all absurd. Why do you tire yourself out like this for perfectly useless things? There won't be any air raids. We're not going to be touched by this war.' Then Pearl Harbor happened. God-awful!"

"Frightful."

"Well, I said to my wife, 'I take it all back. You were right and I was wrong.' That's what I said, and that's what I mean."

He looked at me gravely before taking a sip out of his rum punch or whatever was in his glass.

Then he laughed.

"This is Christmas," he said. "I said to my wife, 'I give you twenty-four hours. That's for Christmas. After that we're going to take this war seriously.' I'm in it—up to the neck."

He put his hand up to his neck, marking the exact spot up to which the war had reached him.

He was a fine-looking fellow, and his factory was already

doing war work with government contracts to keep them busy. Presently he spoke about Churchill's visit.

"It's very gallant of him to come," he said. "We should feel very nervous if President Roosevelt went to Europe."

We drifted back into the sitting room.

"I have some good news for the family," said Lydia's sister Helen, a pretty girl sitting back in an armchair with a little sausage at the end of a stick.

"What's that, my dear?" asked my host, who was her uncle.

"It's going to happen in June, Uncle Tom."

"Well done, my dear. That's fine."

There was another girl present, equally pretty, equally young, Patty by name, who soon would be presenting my host with his first grandchild.

No one said: Isn't it a bad time to bring babes into the world? Is one justified in bringing a little innocent into this life which is so murderous and so full of evil and agony and death? That thought crossed my mind and then was thrust away. Perhaps these children, shortly to be born, would escape all perils and be the heirs to a New Age after World War II, when human intelligence may have decided to prevent such a thing happening again, ever, and may have planned out a better way of life for everyone, with a fair share of life's gifts in comfort and decency and beauty and spiritual values. In any case women bring their babes into the world with faith and joy, whether there be wars or plagues or famines, because of that vital urge, that desperate human heroism which ensures survival to the human race.

"You're eating nothing and you're drinking nothing," said Jo quite untruthfully, offering me one glass on a tray of glasses.

It was a good Christmas party. Charles Dickens would have liked it.

On the morning after Christmas Day, for the first time in American history, there was an extraordinary session of Congress called by the President to hear an address of a distinguished stranger.

That "stranger" was the Right Honourable Winston Churchill, Prime Minister of Great Britain.

The address was given in the Senate Chamber before both houses. The galleries were crowded with a distinguished audience of foreign diplomats, judges of the Supreme Court, cabinet ministers, and officials of state.

Churchill was in good form. That is to say he was marvellous, as an old orator who is a master of the art of playing on human emotion, rolling out sonorous phrases, building up a vivid picture of world affairs, scarifying his enemies, inspiring his friends, and giving a touch of magic to a simple phrase. These senators and congressmen of the United States are not without their own gifts of oratory. They, too, can move a public audience in their own states. But here was a man who held them spellbound. It was a triumph for him. He held them in deep attention as he outlined the critical phases of the war with candour and clarifying truth. They vastly enjoyed his irony, his ridicule, and his bitter characterisation of their own enemies and his. They were thrilled by his confidence in final victory balanced by his frank and terrible admissions of present weakness and continuing disaster. He exalted them, after casting them down. He was very much at ease in this American assembly. He spoke to them in a language they understood, because half his blood was theirs. He knew the American mind and mood and yet spoke as an Englishman and as the leader of the British people, who had turned to him in their darkest hours and had faith in his courage and defiance when all seemed lost.

It was not oratory alone, divorced from action. This "stranger" who stood before the representatives of the United States was a man of action. In two world wars he had taken command, moved ships and men about—not always with success—thought out plans of strategy which had failed at times because subordinates did not think so quickly and lagged behind his orders. For forty years he had been behind the scenes of history and playing a great part on its stage, an impetuous Hotspur, a daring Rupert, adventurous as soldier and statesman, always ready to take great risks.

I had seen the energy of this amazing man in private life and out of office before World War II. I had spent a day with him in his country home when I had some facts about the weakness of our Air Force, deeply alarming, which I thought he might want to have—and then found he already had them. He was restless and untiring, smoking cigars continually as he walked me round his estate, showing me the lakes he had cemented with his own hands and the walls he had built with his own hands. Wherever there was a nice paddock he had built a high wall round it, for the fun of laying bricks. He had built his own studio, where he paints pictures with passionate enthusiasm. "I regard a day as ill-spent," he told me, "unless I have painted two pictures." Two pictures! Most professional artists would be content with painting two pictures in two months, but not Winston Churchill, who has written more books than most authors, while getting his material for them as Sea Lord, or Chancellor of the Exchequer, as Cabinet Minister or Leader of the Opposition, as Secretary for War, or political free lance.

Now, as Prime Minister of England, he faced the American Senate and House and told them the things they wanted most to know.

He paid a tribute to the American nation for the calmness with which it took the first shock of war.

I should like to say how much I have been impressed and encouraged by the breadth of view and sense of proportion I have found in all quarters over here to which I have had access. Anyone who did not understand the size and solidarity of the United States might easily have expected to find an excited, disturbed, self-centered atmosphere, with all minds fixed upon the novel, startling, and painful episodes of sudden war as it hit America. . . . But here in Washington I have found an Olympian fortitude, which, far from being based upon complacency, is only the mark of an inflexible purpose and the proof of a sure, well-grounded confidence in the final outcome.

Reviewing the past, he did not shirk the admission of British weakness.

We have indeed to be thankful that so much time has been granted to us. If Germany had tried to invade the British Isles after the collapse of France in June 1940, and if Japan had declared war on the British Empire and the United States at about the same time, no one can say what disasters and agonies might not have been our lot. But now, at the end of December 1941, our transformation from easygoing peace to total war efficiency has made very great progress.

He described the building up of British war production and its increasing weight and power.

Sure I am this day that now we are the masters of our fate, that the task which has been set us is not above our strength, that the pangs and toils are not beyond our endurance.

He spoke sombrely of the dangers ahead both for Britain and the United States and more than hinted that disasters would happen in Malaya and other regions of the Pacific because the victories in Libya had been attained only by sending all the available weapons there, as well as to the aid of Russia.

After an analysis of those limited resources and difficulties of their disposal in the right places at the right time he dealt with "the life line of the Atlantic," the hope of the dawn to come, and the general strategy of the war. Then suddenly he turned again to the broader issues and spoke noble stuff worthy of remembrance.

Members of the Senate and members of the House of Representatives, I will turn for one moment more from the turmoil and convulsions of the present to the broader spaces of the future.

Here we are together facing a group of mighty foes who seek our ruin. Here we are together defending all that to free men is dear.

Twice in a single generation the catastrophe of world war has fallen upon us. Twice in our lifetime has the long arm of fate reached out across the oceans to bring the United States into the forefront of the battle. If we had kept together after the last war, if we had taken common measures for our safety, this renewal of the curse need never have fallen upon us.

Do we not owe it to ourselves, to our children, to tormented mankind, to make sure that these catastrophes do not engulf us for the third time? It has been proved that pestilences may break out in the Old World which carry their destructive ravages into the New World from which, once they are afoot, the New World cannot escape.

Duty and prudence alike command, first, that the germ centers of hatred and revenge should be constantly and vigilantly curbed and treated in good time and that an adequate organisation should be set up to make sure that the pestilence can be controlled at its earliest beginning before it spreads and rages throughout the entire earth.

Five or six years ago it would have been easy, without shedding a drop of blood, for the United States and Great Britain to have insisted on the fulfilment of the disarmament clauses of the treaties which Germany signed after the Great War.

And that also would have been the opportunity for assuring to the Germans those materials, those raw materials, which we declared in the Atlantic Charter should not be denied to any nation, victor or vanquished.

The chance has passed. It is gone. Prodigious hammer strokes have been needed to bring us together today.

If you will allow me to use other language, I will say that he must indeed have a blind soul who cannot see that some great purpose and design is being worked out here below, of which we have the honour to be the faithful servants.

*It is not given to us to peer into the mysteries of the future.
Still I avow my hope and faith, sure and inviolate, that in the
days to come the British and American people will, for their
own safety and for the good of all, walk together in majesty,
in justice, and in peace.*

That speech of Winston Churchill was heard by millions
of Americans over their radio sets. They liked it. It was, I
was told by some of them, a tonic to them, and very hearten-
ing. It was also thought-provoking.

"What we like about Churchill," said one of my friends,
"is his refusal to paint in rose-coloured tints the chances of this
war. He does not spare us the ugly truth. During this Christmastide we are not dwelling on that side of the picture. We
are allowing ourselves a little forgetfulness for the children's
sake and our own. It may be the last Christmas for some of
us—for many of our young men. But tomorrow we must face
all those grim things of which Churchill spoke. He is a great
man. It is splendid to have him here. It is a pledge for the
future comradeship of our two nations. One day we will make
a peace together, as now we make war."

So the American Christmas of 1941 came to an end. The
children had had their day. The sleigh bells of Santa Claus
faded out.

XXI

The Year of Fate

I SAW THE NEW YEAR IN with my family and friends in Lakeville, Massachusetts, in the old house of my brother and his wife.

There were a few visitors from the outside world—the well-known playwright Russel Crouse and his wife, Alison Smith; a French girl, Denise, who had come over as a refugee, and two young men from Harvard.

My brother brewed some rum punch, very comforting on a cold night. The playwright, assisted by the young men from Harvard, and other volunteers were busy for quite a while with the ancient custom of popping corn over a fire of blazing logs. He burned his fingers but held on heroically to the end of the corn-popping machine, which was like a toasting fork with a steel cage at the end of it. Someone held a paper over his head to shield his face.

The beautiful Phoebe, sister of Lydia, edged her way to a corner of the fire to cook marshmallows on bits of stick. The fun of the thing is to snatch the marshmallow from the stick without getting a sticky mess on one's fingers. The delight of the thing is to pop it into one's mouth regardless of wood ash or cinders.

We played some games of questions and answers. The playwright and I took handfuls of popcorn from time to time. What was the good of cooking popcorn and burning one's face and hands unless somebody ate it?

I looked around this room with its shaded lamps and its open hearth fire and its friendly company. What would the New Year bring to each one of them? Those two Harvard young men would be tagged for the Army or Navy. In a year's time they might be fighting in the Dutch East Indies or Syria or France. Lydia, with those long, sensitive hands, would be an airwoman. Phoebe would lose her friends. They would be elsewhere. This sanctuary in Massachusetts, this old house of peace, upon whose walls my brother had hung many of his own paintings of blue skies and hilltop towns in France, was no longer outside the zone of war. War had flared up to the American coast line. The price of war would have to be paid even in Massachusetts. There would be no peace of mind in the coming year, no restfulness.

It was nearly midnight when my brother moved towards the radio.

"In a few seconds . . ." he said.

We stood waiting. At the turn of the switch the noise of New York came through to this firelit room. They were dancing and singing and shouting in Times Square. Bells were ringing. Crowds were cheering. One could hear the noise of the tumult.

All over the United States people were waiting for the

coming of the New Year. I thought of all those cities I had visited—San Francisco; Fort Worth, Texas; Lexington, Kentucky; Oklahoma City; Chicago—and many more. In my mind I had the vision of all those people I had met, all the seething crowds in the streets, all the vastness of this American continent with its variety of races, colour, types. A mighty people. A mighty big nation. A hundred and thirty million souls awaiting a Year of Fate. They were aware of that. There was no longer any illusion in their minds. All those doubts, uncertainties, and evasions of reality which I had met on my travels had now gone with the wind. They knew now that this coming year would be filled with grim drama touching their lives closely, taking their lives, perhaps, taking their sons. Never before, since the Civil War, had the American people stood on the threshold of a New Year so fateful as this. The Civil War itself was not so stupendous in its test of courage and endurance as this call from Destiny. The United States were challenged and menaced by world powers devilish in their purpose and ruthlessness. Already they had scored the first hits, below the belt at Pearl Harbor. Anything might happen. Invasion. Bombing raids over American cities. Naval battles off the American coast.

There was silence in the room, and the crowds in New York were hushed. Clocks struck twelve.

"Nineteen forty-two!" said my brother, looking into my eyes.

We joined hands and sang, very feebly and inharmoniously, "Auld Lang Syne."

"Nineteen forty-two," said the playwright. "What does it mean to us?"

One of the women gave a little, deep sigh. It was my sister-in-law, Jeanette, our hostess. She was deeply moved, I think, but tried to laugh it off, this sense of emotion.

"Why do we make so much fuss about an arbitrary date in the calendar?" she asked. "The Chinese have a different New Year's Day. It makes no difference."

What would 1942 mean to the American people?

That question was answered by President Roosevelt, on January 6, in a speech which excited and staggered the world.

He had been conferring with Winston Churchill on the grand strategy of the war. He had conferred with his admirals and generals and many of his experts. He had made great plans, there in the quietude of the White House. With Winston Churchill he had agreed on unity of command in the various war zones. He had drawn closer the bonds of alliance with Russia and China. Twenty-six nations had given him the allegiance of their support in the common cause.

He had made plans for his own people and for the part they would have to play in the World War. He told them exactly what 1942 would mean to them.

The war, he said, would be long and hard and bloody.

The enormous potentialities of American production would have to be put into complete and total fulfilment.

This production of ours in the United States must be raised far above present levels, even though it may mean the dislocation of the lives and occupations of millions of our own people. We must raise our sights all along the production line. Let no man say it cannot be done. It must be done, and we have undertaken to do it.

The President then announced concrete figures, staggering to the mind, vast, audacious. Terrific in their tremendous scale.

When that speech ended President Roosevelt was acclaimed with wild enthusiasm. His greatness stood revealed. No one again could call him a "swindling Messiah." No one could say, "Here is a man of words without action, a man with a charlatan mind." His words rang true as steel. They were like a trumpet call to his people. He had proved his courage, his vision, his audacity. No man ever in the world, in all history, had announced such vast plans, given such tremendous orders, called for so much toil, wealth, service, and sacrifice from a great people. Behind the words was the power of fulfilment. They were words of power. He commanded; he did not plead. "This must be done," he said. "It will be done. We have undertaken to do it."

He called for toil—toil and sweat, seven days a week, twenty-four hours a day, in blast furnaces where men would stand above molten metal, in its heat and light and roar; in machine shops where men would bend over delicate tools needing precision and skill of hand and eye; in league-long plants where men, and women, would stand by the assembly lines awaiting their moment to screw a bolt or hammer a rivet while the track moved on; in shipyards noisy with hammering at hulks, for a new armada of merchant ships; in dockyards with high derricks and moving cranes, loading or unloading the raw material for this monstrous machine of war, loading or unloading the finished guns, tanks, aeroplanes, and engines; in steelyards, foundries, workshops, railway yards, warehouses. Terrific toil, gruelling toil, for American men and women. It would make their limbs ache, their brains dizzy. Women would faint at their work. Men would sweat themselves weak. They would be strained in every fibre, muscle, and nerve. It would be the toil of a demoniacal energy demanded of them.

And he called for sacrifice of all luxuries and all delights. The American people would have to give up their wealth, their leisure, their thousand-and-one desires. This programme would mean to them the abandonment of their motorcars, the surrender of their purchasing power. There would be very little to buy. The great stores would empty. The era of advertising, on the radio and on the streets, would pass or have a moratorium. No use advertising goods which could no longer be made. No more luxury articles. No more temptation to spend beyond one's means. Everything would be cut down, or cut out, because of all energy directed to war industry.

The President called for attack beyond defence, wherever the enemy could be reached and hit. That would mean not one expeditionary force but many expeditionary forces. It would mean that millions of young men would be sent overseas to fight all round the world by sea, land, and air. A long, hard, and bloody war. American mothers would be weeping for their sons. American boys would be slain on many battlefields before final victory. They would crash over flaming cities. They would be torpedoed and shelled and dive-bombed in all the Seven Seas. They would fling themselves on rocky coasts, storm their way through forests and swamps, fight hand to hand with yellow men, with fair-haired Germans, with dark-eyed Italians. They would stand on the cliffs of Dover and the coasts of Scotland, Ireland, and Wales. They would be part of an Army of Invasion, driving through Europe to liberate many peoples rising in revolt to join them. They would see horrors unspeakable before the end came. They would fall in foreign lands while their comrades went on or fought to the last man in many mantraps of death.

The American educational system, with its widespread

opportunity of knowledge and culture, would for a time—for the duration of this war—be wasted or applied to primitive instincts by which a man kills his enemy, by every means of cunning and craft, lest he be killed himself. The alumni of Harvard and Yale, Brown and Princeton, Columbia or Ann Arbor would lie in ditches under machine-gun fire and be ragged, bearded, dirty men, covered by tank oil, with blood-stained bandages on their heads and eyes deep sunk in hollow sockets. Their bodies would be crawling with vermin, these young American gentlemen from nice homes where they were taught to wash behind their ears.

Elderly men, beyond active service abroad, would be guarding railways, munition plants, power stations, observation posts, on nights when the temperature drops below zero, when the cold wind cuts them like a knife, when frozen snow is cold to the feet, when ears and noses are frostbitten.

Young American girls who wanted to have a good time, and had had it, would find themselves in factories, sorting, packing, tying, and labelling, for long hours, until their backs ached and their fingers were cramped and fatigue attacked their nerves. "Keep at it, Miss Smith. No loafing here! There's a war on." Seven days a week. No respite. No letting up. What did the President say?

It must be done; we have undertaken to do it.

That, and much more, was the meaning of the President's speech to the American people on January 6, 1942. He had put a heavy burden on them. And they were willing to take it, in loyalty, in courage, in endurance, because in them was the spirit of their pioneer forefathers and the ghosts of American history, hard, tough, and heroic.

XXII

The Leaders of the Nation

I. GRAVE NEWS IN WASHINGTON

W‍ASHINGTON was crowded when I went there two months after the declaration of war. Every train entering Union Station brought new contingents of state officials, contractors, subcontractors, directors of industrial companies, and all the horde of men engaged in the business of war.

A picture in the *New Yorker* caricatured the overcrowding of the capital. "Planning to be in Washington long?" asked a man sleeping with three others in the same bed.

It was almost as bad as that. Having been put up at the Metropolitan Club by the kindness of my friend Mr. Coert du Bois, American Consul General in charge of the Caribbean islands, I had to vacate my room after two nights (I did not worry him about that) because of a prior claim, and I failed to find another room after ringing up eleven hotels. I was saved from sleeping in Rock Creek Park on a frosty night (better than a jungle in Malaya) by a generous-hearted friend of mine who had a cot put up for me in his bedroom at the Wardman Park Hotel.

Since my first visit to Washington on the eve of war much tragic history had happened, and its shadow lay darkly on the minds of many people with whom I talked in the capital, and especially those of my own nation serving on British missions and commissions. I arrived there at a time when the war in the Pacific was going against us, terribly. Our forces in Singapore, which we had regarded as our strongest bastion, were making their last desperate stand against overwhelming forces of the little yellow men. The city was being bombed incessantly, and women and children were being evacuated under that fire from Japanese dive bombers. Our air bases in Malaya had been captured or destroyed. Our men, fighting and dying in that shambles, had but little air support. Only a few heroic boys challenged the flocks of Japanese airmen who came over by day and night with new loads of high explosives. The promise of reinforcements, constantly made, had not been fulfilled to any extent which would make a difference to the beleaguered garrison, told to fight to the death and obeying orders with a knowledge of doom—boys who had not had their fair share of life. For most of them it was only a question of days or hours before they died in that mantrap. How had it happened? What ghastly blunders had been made? Had the Brass Hat mind, with its incurable overconfidence, its belief in the old school tie, its contempt of those damned little yellow men, failed to foresee the danger or prepare for it? So friends of mine in Washington were asking each other, angrily and bitterly, and, I think, unfairly. It was only two months since the disaster at Pearl Harbor and the Japanese attack. It takes three months for a

British ship to reach the southwest Pacific by way of the Cape.

General Douglas MacArthur was making a heroic last stand in the Philippines, holding on to Corregidor against immense odds. He, too, had received no reinforcements, and every day the Japanese were extending their line of attack, with raids and landings on many islands of the Dutch East Indies and a threat to the Burma Road. The Allied Fleet had sunk many enemy ships in the Macassar Straits. American flying fortresses had done good work here and there, but the picture of the Pacific was one of Japanese supremacy by land, sea, and air, and the American nation was shocked and dismayed by this revelation of their own weakness and failure to strike back. It was not in line with their tradition. They suspected that the report on Pearl Harbor, frightful though it was in its admission and condemnation of unpreparedness and inefficiency, had not revealed the full truth of naval losses. (That rumour, whispered in Washington when I was there, was denounced by the President as a wicked lie.) The man in the street was bewildered and distressed by this humiliation of national pride.

I listened to the comments of the man in the street in Washington when I was waiting to see the President of the United States and other leaders who are deciding its destiny. The taxicab drivers of Washington, like those of New York and Chicago, are hard-thinking fellows and very chatty at their wheels.

"I find only one comfort in the war news," said one of them, "and it's very comforting."

"I wish you would tell me," I answered, not having found that comfort.

"We've reached rock bottom," he said. "That's a comfort! When you've got as low as that you can't get any lower."

I was not so sure that we had touched rock bottom. Before I left Washington there was the news that the *Scharnhorst, Gneisenau,* and *Prinz Eugen* had slipped out of Brest and got through the English Channel and the Straits of Dover. Before I left Washington friends of mine were talking about the menace to India, gloomily.

Sitting in a deep chair in the Metropolitan Club, I overheard a conversation between two Americans, unaware of the proximity of an Englishman.

"Winston Churchill repeats himself too much," said one of them, looking up from his newspaper. "One Dunkirk after another. One evacuation after another."

"Surely to God," said the other man, "they might have evacuated those women and children months ago. I can't bear to think of it—embarking under storms of bombs. The English seem to have no foresight, and they are always in retreat."

It was President Roosevelt, with whom I had the honour of an interview, who was most generous in his defence of England and the English when he spoke of these things. He knew more about them than those gentlemen in the Metropolitan Club. He had no word of blame.

Nor did the coloured porter outside the Metropolitan Club, who seemed to think it necessary to speak some words of comfort to an English visitor.

"Don't you worry, Mr. Gibbs," he said. "Everything am coming all right for your folks and mine. There's bad news over the radio, but it don't deject me. No sir! The Bible must sure be fulfilled. The Lord will take care of this war. Yes sir!"

His brown hand gripped my arm in a friendly way. Perhaps he thought I looked downcast. I was, not only on account of world news but because I had just lost my checkbook.

On my way to the Senate Office Building to see Senator Byrd of Virginia another cabdriver was good enough to give me the benefit of his knowledge and wisdom.

"We were caught unprepared," he said. "We're still unprepared, because it takes time to catch up. And our people don't understand yet. They're all asleep. Everything seems such a long way off. The Philippines? What do they know about the Philippines? Of course they get a kick out of General MacArthur's great stand. Fine stuff for the radio! They want to make him the next President. Mr. Wendell Willkie wants to make him Commander-in-Chief or something of the kind. The Glamour Boy of the American people. That's all right. He deserves it. But they don't understand that their lives are in danger. They don't understand that we're going to lose this war unless we take it more seriously. They don't understand nothing. They'll have to get it into their heads somehow— harder work, more suffering, lots of blood, everything different in their lives, before the end comes."

2. SENATOR BYRD OF VIRGINIA

There was a cloudlessly blue sky and bright sunshine over Washington, though a cold wind blew, when I went up the long flight of white steps leading to the Senate Office Building, where I had an appointment with Senator Byrd of Virginia. I found myself in a great marble hall with long corridors leading out of it. A clerk at a desk gave me the number of the senator's room, and I sat only a few minutes in his antechamber, being early for the time appointed, before I was taken to him.

I knew him to be a keen critic of the Administration, because of its long delay in preparedness and its failure, as he thinks, to fulfil the production pledges. He is a youngish, middle-aged man with a fresh-complexioned face and keen eyes. In the background of his life there is the fresh air of Virginia and its warm sun over miles of apple blossoms. After a brief career as a newspaperman in a farming district he became one of the biggest applegrowers in his state, and that open-air life has touched his skin and given him a fine physique. So it seemed to me when I shook hands with him. But he served in the Virginia Senate for ten years and was governor from 1926 to 1930, doing fine work, I am told, in cutting down expenses and promoting efficiency. Now he is Chairman of the Rules Committee and a member of the Finance, Civil Service, and Naval Affairs committees and gets all the facts behind the scenes.

He had read some of my books and seemed to have liked them, and we had not talked for long before another man came in to shake hands with me because he was also one of my readers. He was a tall, lean Virginia congressman named A. Willis Robertson.

"There are no more Cities of Refuge in this wicked world," he said, alluding to one of my novels.

After that pleasant interruption—it is good to have made friends through one's books—I was left alone again with Senator Byrd, whom I found both charming and impressive, with an alert mind, critical but constructive, with no other purpose than winning the war.

"I have never been hostile to the President's foreign policy," he told me. "But ever since this war began in Europe I felt that the American people moved in a sense of false security and were not awakened to the grim facts of our unpreparedness. The facts and figures about our munitions production then seemed to me deplorable if one really knew them, but they were not made available and the President's high optimistic estimates were not realized in the actualities of production. He could have had the people with him two years ago, after the fall of France. We should have driven ahead then in making aeroplanes and tanks. But we let the years pass."

I was reminded of Winston Churchill's campaign in the House of Commons for a stronger Air Force and his cry of regret for "the years that the locusts have eaten." This senator of Virginia had uttered the same plea and the same warnings. He summed up his previous warnings in November of 1941, a month before Pearl Harbor, in an article for the *Reader's Digest* showing the poor results of American production up to date and startling the big American public—"fifteen million people read that publication," he told me—by this revelation, which was completely opposed to the optimism and propaganda with which they had been supplied by officials.

"My figures were never seriously challenged," he told me. "They could not be denied."

They were alarming figures then, and the weakness of the United States when attacked by Japan was due to their significance. The supplies to Great Britain were "pitifully inadequate," he declared. In spite of all the money voted generously by the American people, only a few scanty products had actually reached England—in dire need of bombers, tanks, merchant ships, and antiaircraft guns two years after the war had begun. For American home defense and war needs no more had been done. In September 1940 the American forces had only fifty-six four-engined heavy bombers. In the year that followed, said Senator Byrd, only two hundred others were produced, although the President announced five hundred a month as the goal.

As regards merchant ships, Senator Byrd said in his *Reader's Digest* article that in the two years since Hitler invaded Poland the American Government had produced no more ocean tonnage than Great Britain had lost in two months of war. In the second year of World War II the United States had produced only fifteen hundred light tanks and no heavy tanks whatever.

"We talked big," said Senator Byrd, "but we did not deliver the goods. We preferred business as usual to production at war speed. Up to a few weeks ago the automobile industry was producing millions of luxury cars while the world was in flames."

All this was a review of the past—"the years that the locusts have eaten"—but I questioned Senator Byrd about the present and future.

"Production is stepping up," he said. "We really only got busy after the Japanese attack. Give us six months for production and it will begin to tell."

But I was disappointed to hear him say it was doubtful whether the President's figures—60,000 aeroplanes this year, 45,000 tanks this year, 8 million tons of merchant shipping—could really be fulfilled. They might be overoptimistic, he thought.

"What is going on in the minds of the American people?" I asked. "What do they think of the present situation?"

"They are stunned and shocked by what has happened in the Pacific," he answered. "They cannot understand it. They were told by a very high public official that we should clean up the Japs in ninety days."

He laughed a little bitterly, but there was no mirth in his eyes.

"Why was this done?" he asked. "I was told it was to keep up British morale, but there was no need of that. The British can take the truth. They have proved it. They don't want to live in a fool's paradise. Nor do the American people. That is why I tried to awake them to the real facts."

We spoke of the future. In that quiet room in the Senate Office Building in Washington, on a day when Singapore was fighting desperately in the last ditches, this senator of Virginia looked ahead at the shape of things to come with a clear, candid vision unclouded by any rose-coloured spectacles.

"The British are hard pressed," he said. "They are losing bits of their Empire already. There may be worse to come. Their shipping losses hamper all their efforts, and our own production of merchant ships is not too fast."

He asked me a question.

What will be the future social state of England after the war?

We spoke about the possibility of state socialism and a swing to the Left. The idea did not appeal to him.

"Would you not lose your liberties?" he asked. "Would not state socialism break up all your traditions?"

"What about Russia?" he asked. "We regard Russia's war contribution as priceless, and we must back Russia to the limit during the war, but our inherent opposition to Communism is going to make post-war dealing with Russia a very delicate problem."

Because of future political troubles, amounting to social revolution, he thought the President made a mistake in "slamming" his critics and going down into their states to attack them. "He may need us to defend the Constitution."

"After the war," he said presently, "there should be a closer co-operation between the United States and Great Britain. We must act together to prevent economic chaos and shape out a decent peace and world order."

He spoke of American industry and the wartime conditions and criticised the amount of profit being made by the manufacturers.

"Ten per cent profit on each contract is far too much," he said. "The plan of fixing the percentage of profit on each individual contract pyramids the net profits of the corporation itself, so that the actual profit on the invested capital, which is the true criterion, may be many times more than ten per cent."

I give only a brief summary of our conversation, which covered many topics. I found it deeply interesting, for here was a man who was a truthteller, very candid, very critical, and yet with a constructive and liberal mind, not cramped by political prejudice or poisoned by personal ambition. I was very much impressed by Senator Byrd of Virginia. He is one of the leading minds in the United States. He will help to make its history. Before this war ends, and afterwards, the world will hear much about him, I think. He has a fine personality, being fearless and fair-minded in his pursuit of truth and efficiency. He is a gentleman of Virginia, and that is a good type. In his apple orchards he had time to think, and something in his character, perhaps, its straightforward simplicity, is due to the soil and the toil which brought him close to nature, beyond the fever of the cities. Like his brother, Admiral Byrd, the arctic explorer, he is a man of action and a man of courage. That, anyhow, is my impression of him.

3. THE LEADER OF LABOUR

It was half-past nine in the morning, with a bleak wind blowing, when I went round to the United Mine Workers Building in Washington to see a man named Philip Murray, at the head of the C.I.O. (Congress of Industrial Organisations), generally regarded as the most advanced wing of American Labour and—by big business and defenders of capital—as a revolutionary organisation very dangerous to the American way of life when under the leadership of John L. Lewis.

Philip Murray was born in Scotland. It is curious that several of the American Labour leaders were born in the British Isles and came out in their youth to the United States before joining the Labour movement there. I suspect they owe a good deal to the Trade Union tradition in England, Scotland, and Wales.

"Here is a true-born Yorkshireman," said Mr. Murray, introducing me to his second-in-command. "Every day at lunch he orders roast beef with potatoes, Brussels sprouts, and natural gravy. 'Don't forget the natural gravy,' he tells the waiter."

I had a friendly reception in the United Mine Workers Building. Strange as it may seem, these men had read my books. Because of that—or in spite of that—they were exceedingly kind and cordial to me. I found Mr. Murray a square-shouldered, ruddy-complexioned Scot with most pleasant manners, a sense of humour, and a candid way of speech. The American women who are afraid of the C.I.O. as a revolutionary body would fall for him and lose their fear.

"Tell me something about American Labour conditions,"

I asked him presently. "How are they affected by this war?"

"The chief effect," said Mr. Murray, "is the temporary displacement of labour owing to the switch-over of industry to war production. About four million men are affected. There are now six million unemployed in the United States. As a matter of fact, there were five million before the defence programme, still left over from the depression. This transition period will last from two to eleven months. Meanwhile we are claiming an unemployment benefit of twenty-four dollars instead of sixteen dollars as at present allowed. That's what we are pressing for in Congress, as you may have seen. We don't want to raise wages unfairly to an inflationary level, but American industry can well afford that."

He spoke about the variations in wages in the United States owing to the differences in climatic, agricultural, and racial conditions. Down South, of course, they are especially noticeable—and deplorable—owing to coloured labour and a poor standard of living. The C.I.O. wants to eliminate these discrepancies and raise the poorer communities to the general level. That is part of their programme.

Remembering the opinion of Senator Byrd that industry was making too much profit out of the war, I asked Mr. Murray what his own views were on this point.

"Industry is getting outrageous profits," he answered, "sometimes as much as 15 to 20 per cent. The government subsidies of war industries really amount to a theft from the nation. There is profit taking all down the line—contractors, subcontractors, brokers, and middlemen, piling up the cost to the consumer. Take a big corporation like Bethlehem Steel. It gets 3½ million dollars in contracts and makes a profit of 9½ per cent. All this makes it impossible for a factory hand, faced by rising prices, to reconcile his own scale of wages with these immense profits. It is bound to lead to bitterness and bad blood—which we don't want."

I asked Mr. Murray about public opinion, especially in labour ranks, regarding the war and its increasing menace. He answered with good-humoured frankness.

"Before December 7 the mass of the American people were utterly unaware of any threat to the United States. They just couldn't realize it. It was beyond their imagination. Isolationist spokesmen and glib talkers helped that ignorance to prevail by loose speech. 'America isn't menaced,' they said. 'Hitler isn't too bad. In any case, that war is a long way off and none of our business. Make peace in the Pacific with the little yellow man. Why bother about the Philippines? They've always been a darned nuisance. What the hell? Let the Philippines go. Let's keep out of war and get on with our own job.' That's how a lot of people talked. . . .

"The Government didn't tell the truth to the people over here. They built up a false picture. They didn't let the people know the facts. They could have taken the truth all right, just as the British did."

Labour is behind this war. The C.I.O. is urging all the workers to invest in government bonds and has piled up enormous sums in that way. There is no pacifism or lack of driving energy in the one grim purpose of winning this war, come what may. In agreement with the A.F. of L., American Labour adopted a resolution that there should be no strikes for the duration of the conflict. The workers will never quit, however much sacrifice is demanded from them. They know now—after Singapore—that they are in for a life-or-death struggle.

I had an idea that they were being overstrained in the munition industries and working a seven-day week, but Mr. Murray put me right on that point. "The newspapers have given a wrong impression about that," he told me. "We are still working a forty-hour week."

We discussed the future, and our conversation took the same line as that I had had with Senator Byrd. He foresaw an internal political struggle in the United States and in England.

"There are certain groups who have funny ideas over here," he said.

He did not go into details about those "funny ideas," but I guessed that he meant Communists on one side and Fascists on the other—people who have lost their faith in democracy and believe in the despotism of the Right or Left.

He seemed to think that some form of state socialism was inevitable in England, owing to the necessity of pooling wealth and resources for national survival.

"That would be more difficult to establish in the United States," he said. "There are great varieties in the character and interests of our forty-eight states. England is more industrialised. American farmers own their own land and are strong individualists. Nevertheless, that struggle is coming. Nothing will stop it."

I read the character of this Scottish president of the C.I.O. as a man of moderate views, not out for any kind of revolution and believing in the old Liberal method of gradual progress in the lifting up of social conditions to a good level for all workers, by fair play and justice and progressive organisation.

"May I ask an indiscreet question?" I said as I rose to go, after a longer conversation than I have here recorded.

He laughed and said, "Why not?"

"How are you getting along with the American Federation of Labour?"

My question did not shock him as a great indiscretion.

He laughed at my timidity in making this enquiry.

"We have established a working agreement," he told me. "We are having meetings twice a week to draw up a programme on behalf of Labour for the President. We have been getting on quite well. I can get on with anyone!"

He laughed again at this touch of self-analysis, and I felt sure that he was telling me the truth. I can well imagine that President Murray of the C.I.O. can get on nicely with anyone. I know that he got on very well with Lord Halifax, who invited him to lunch at the British Embassy with one of the other Labour leaders.

There is a friendly truce now between the two Labour organisations. A proposal to amalgamate into one federation was turned down by the C.I.O. because, however desirable it might be, it would lead the unions from questions affecting the welfare of the nation to a Kilkenny cat fight over jurisdiction and position within a single Labour movement. But Mr. Murray himself is giving a strong lead towards unity within the Labour ranks and, as far as I can judge after my conversation with him, I am convinced that President Roosevelt will have the full, willing, and dynamic support of American Labour in the production of the war machine and the way to ultimate victory. Anxiety about all that has "gone with the wind," I imagine. To Great Britain, as well as to the United States, the will to win of American Labour is a fact of major importance in this deadly struggle for survival.

4. THE VICE-PRESIDENT

I had the privilege of a conversation with Mr. Henry Wallace, Vice-President of the United States. Before I entered his room at the Senate Office Building at five o'clock one afternoon I knew something about his mind and ideas and liked what I knew. I had read a remarkable article of his in the *Atlantic Monthly* called "The Foundations of the Peace." It revealed a liberal, far-seeing mind, untrammelled by narrow national interests and constructive in its practical suggestions for a fair deal to all nations and renewed prosperity and order after transition from war to peace. He wrote:

Thinking of the future peace is not searching for an escape from the stern realities of the present, nor taking refuge in airy castles of our minds. From the practical standpoint of putting first things first, at a time when there are not enough hours in a day and every minute counts, planning for the future peace must of necessity be a part of our all-out war program. . . .

It seems almost certain that sometime within the next few years another peace will be written. If it should be a Hitler peace no one but Hitler and his henchmen would be allowed any part in writing it. But if, with this country's determined participation and support, the allies are successful the world will have a second chance to organise its affairs on a basis of human decency and mutual welfare.

It was a courageous article. This Vice-President of the United States did not hesitate to point out the frightful blunders of the last peace made by his own and other nations.

"The United States, newly become a creditor nation,

adopted tariff policies which only a debtor nation could hope to live with and in so doing helped make it certain that the world would go through hell."

Reviewing the mistakes of the past, Mr. Wallace laid down the basis for good international relationships in a more reasonable future.

His first point is the universal necessity of access to raw materials and the need for an economic arrangement to protect the raw-material producers of the world from such violent fluctuations of income as took place after World War I.

Another is the indispensability of markets for goods produced.

A third is the present existence in all countries of tariffs and other barriers to imports.

A fourth is the use of gold as a base for national currencies and as a means of settling international trade balances.

A fifth is the place of credit for stimulating international trade.

A sixth is the close relationship between stable national currencies and the exchange of goods and services. A seventh, and most important of all, is the essential role of adequate purchasing power within the various countries that are trading with each other—for full employment within nations makes broad trade possible with other nations. All these facts and factors are of prime importance in determining the state of the world's health, and they will naturally form some of the main ingredients of postwar economic planning, if it is to be done on a comprehensive scale.

I have cited enough to show some of the main ideas in the mind of the American Vice-President which, in his article in the *Atlantic Monthly,* were developed in a very practical and, at the same time, idealistic way, far beyond the average thought of his own people, even in high places. It was with that knowledge of his ideas that I met him in the Senate Office Building.

Here is a man, I thought, who would make a good peace in the world, if any good peace is possible in the coming years. He had written that article a month before Pearl Harbor, which had postponed the possibilities of peace.

I found Mr. Henry Wallace a man of charming manner. Occasionally in his eyes there is an aloof, far-off look, but he has a sense of humour, and our conversation was with the realities of the situation, very grim that day when Singapore was doomed, beyond all doubt, and when the Japanese were becoming masters of the western Pacific.

"Do the American people understand?" I asked him.

He smiled at me and shook his head.

"Not yet. It will take a series of shocks to awaken our people to a full sense of the menace ahead. Pearl Harbor woke them up, but they went to sleep again. I believe the loss of Singapore will have more effect upon them than Pearl Harbor."

He seemed to think that the American people were still being lulled into a false sense of security by the newspapers and news commentators. They were rather apt to exaggerate the importance of small successes. "American planes had scored a victory by destroying two Jap planes for the loss of one of ours." Somewhat out of proportion.

He thought it would be a good idea if the Government took over the air for fifteen minutes every day and told the straight truth to the people.

"Raymond Gram Swing does a fine job," I reminded him. "There is no lullaby about his talks. He does not hide the truth, however painful."

Mr. Wallace agreed.

"Yes, and people follow a man they learn to trust."

I spoke about his article in the *Atlantic Monthly* and the work of the Economic Defence Board which had been set up to study those problems.

Mr. Wallace had a smile in his eyes when he answered.

"I don't find the Conservative mind in England very receptive of those ideas. I find a resistance to them."

"Is there a Conservative mind in England?" I asked, thinking to myself that it had been killed by recent history.

Mr. Wallace was slightly startled and amused, I think, by that question.

"It still exists!" he answered. "The English people have been fine, but they have lacked leadership. How is that?"

I said we had lost the fine flower of our youth in the last war —our future leaders—but he did not seem satisfied by that explanation.

"The other boys grew up," he said. "They weren't all killed."

He said some amusing and interesting things about the traditional mind in England. It was an answer to my question on that subject.

"I am sorry for the English country gentleman. He is a good type, with a good code, but he must find himself out of place in this ill-mannered world with its unpleasant people who refuse to play the game in the old style. He couldn't bring himself to believe that Hitler and the Nazis were such dirty dogs. He finds himself stranded between the past and the future. He has no place anywhere, and taxation will wipe him out. That is sad, in a way."

"The ax will strike lower down this time," I said. "The well-to-do middle class will be destroyed."

I told him about a report by a group of American bankers on England's financial condition after the last war. The first line of it said that in four and a half years of war Great Britain had expended as much as in two and a half centuries previously.

Mr. Wallace nodded.

"Even with a different social system England will find great difficulty in feeding itself after this war. Some form of totalitarianism or state control may be forced upon the English people for national survival. There will have to be some hard thinking by good brains to restore general welfare and world trade. I doubt whether Winston Churchill could handle that situation. He is not interested in economics. Perhaps that is a good thing."

He thought a friend of his—a man named Harris in Boston—might be useful in countries forced to restrict their diet. He had worked out a perfectly good diet giving all requirements for health at a cost of twelve cents a day.

He laughed at some reminiscence of his own.

"When I was working as a newspaperman in Iowa I used to experiment on the side with scientific ideas. I worked out a diet for myself and lost ten pounds very quickly. The necessary vitamins were lacking, but I had great fun with it. I can claim that I increased the number of bushels of wheat per acre by other experiments which I found amusing."

Now, as Vice-President of the United States, he is doing

other work far removed from the problems of the good earth and scientific research.

I brought him back to his ideas of a new economic order including the lowering of tariffs and the distribution of raw material, including wheat and other foods. He thought it would be necessary, by government purchase, to keep up the price of agricultural produce so that there would not be the distress of farmers and growers which followed the last war.

"Is the imagination of the American businessman equal to all that?" I asked. "Having been used to a high-tariff system, will he abandon it?"

"There will be a tough struggle ahead," he admitted. "Big business and vested interests will put up a fight. But they are being educated."

He believed that the future of the world would be decided by a closer co-operation between Great Britain, the United States, and Latin America. It all depended on that.

Throughout this conversation I had in my mind the grim realities of the present, and they cast a shadow over this vision of a decent and intelligent peace. Would that ever be possible?

"How are things going now?" I asked. "Will the President's figures of production be fulfilled in time?"

He was fairly optimistic, I found, about the state of American production and its potentialities, though he did not answer my question directly.

"In the long run we are bound to overtake the Japs," he said. "Like in Russia, there will be a comeback. It is only a question of time."

I rose and he took me to his door, and we stood there for a few moments talking on other points. He looked a little tired and overworked, I thought, and he admitted with a smile that he had "plenty to do" as chairman of many committees.

We looked into each other's eyes while he held my hand in a friendly way. Things had been left unsaid, terrible and tragic things. The world was making things very hard for idealists and scientists like Mr. Henry Wallace, Vice-President of the United States.

That man is one of the rare souls, I thought when I went away from him.

5. FRIENDS OF MINE

I met many people in Washington, some of whom were old friends of mine. For "everybody" goes to Washington in this time of war, and some of them have jobs there. Valentine Williams, the novelist, said "Hullo!" one day from a chair in the Metropolitan Club. As an officer of the Guards in the last war, a first-class journalist, and a writer of exciting stories, he is one of my oldest friends, and I was glad to find him here.

I called on Raymond Gram Swing, who years ago had introduced me to Stresemann in Berlin and then, years after that, had been a neighbour of mine in a Surrey village to which he lost his heart. Now I found him in some office rooms at the Roosevelt Hotel looking busy and looking tired, as well he might be. For two years he has been a wonderful interpreter of the United States to Great Britain every Saturday night over the B.B.C. All intelligent people in England listened to him, impressed by his fairness of mind, his balanced judgment, his illuminating way of recording the week's history in his own country before it came into the war. He kept us patient, when we might have been impatient, with the aloofness of the American people while we were in a life-and-death struggle, under heavy bombardment from the air. He was an advocate of President Roosevelt's foreign policy and showed us how the President was leading his nation step by step to greater aid for Britain and to the awareness of the peril to all liberty. He took us through American Labour troubles, through presidential elections, through the labyrinth of American politics and bewilderments. He did a "swell job." Now, when I saw him in Washington, he had been a fine commentator on the war, using his analytical mind to give his listening public the real facts and their underlying significance as far as he was able.

"Give us some good news!" I told him after a friendly talk.

"I wish I could," he answered. "But I can't."

There was no good news, outside of Russia.

I met an old friend of mine named Lowell Mellett, who laughed and called me Phil when he came out to me from his Office of Government Reports. Once he had been a war correspondent with me in World War I. Once, when I came to Washington after that war, he had been my fairy godfather and waved a magic wand for me. I did not understand the magic by which in one afternoon he had taken me to see the President of the United States and many of the senators who were leaders of the nation at that time. Such things are not done in England.

"Anything I can do for you, Phil?" asked Lowell Mellett when I met him this time in World War II. "Do you want to see anybody in Washington?"

"I would like to see the President," I told him with some diffidence. I also mentioned other names.

Mellett used his telephone. He knows everybody in Washington. He called them by their Christian names. They were very obliging indeed. It was entirely due to this good-natured friend, staunch and true after many years, that I was received into many rooms in Washington not easy of entry. One of them was a room in the White House where President Roosevelt sat.

"Do you remember that dinner party I gave when Princess Bibesco came as a fairy queen?" asked Lowell Mellett.

I had forgotten the details.

It was in the old days. I was going to dine with Elizabeth Asquith, who was Princess Bibesco, but Mellett was "throwing a party" and insisted that I should come. He rang up Elizabeth, explained the situation, and said, "Come too." "I shall be in fancy dress," she told him. "I'm going to a ball." "Fine," said Mellett, "that will be good for my party." He was surprised when she arrived with her husband. He had not invited the husband, who made the fourteenth guest. Mrs. Mellett, informed somewhat tardily of this dinner, was distressed. The arrival of the prince was the last straw. "Don't you worry, ma'am," said the coal-black maid. "Jest make the cocktails twice as strong and the party will go fine."

It was a merry party in a small apartment.

Lowell Mellett is no longer a newspaperman. He is in government service and hard worked. Like most others in Washington—except the President—he looked tired and overstrained. But he kept his smile and sense of humour, except for a moment when he spoke about the war with tragic gravity. The news that afternoon was terrible.

Up in the woodlands of Chevy Chase, on the outskirts of Washington, I met two American friends whom I had known in London, and the lady kissed me when I came into her apartment because so many sad things had happened since last we had met. She introduced me to her guests, and we talked until nearly midnight. We were people talking in a flame-swept world. This was a little oasis of civilisation amidst the furnace fires creeping closer.

There was an argument about the awareness, or the ignorance and complacency, of the American people.

"I don't believe in all this accusation of complacency," said a young man. "I believe the American people are wide awake to the dangers and the sacrifice. It's just newspaper stuff and loose talk over the radio."

He was challenged by his friends, but I leaned a little to his side of the argument. Up to December 7 American public opinion had been, as I have shown in this book, incapable of realising a direct threat to the United States. But now it seemed to me that the man in the street was conscious of the menace to his own national life and liberties. Anyhow, they were all getting into something. Labour was pulling its weight. Perhaps the Vice-President and Mr. Murray and others were underestimating the awareness of the people to the need of service and sacrifice. They seemed to know all about it in one small town in Massachusetts where I talked to the people. They were getting scared. The women were getting frightened.

Some of my English friends in Washington were also getting scared, I found. Certainly they were very gloomy in their conversation about the war. They could see no gleam of light ahead, now that Singapore was doomed to fall.

"It opens the way to India," said one of them.

"Australia is in danger," said another.

They were disappointed with the rate of American production.

"The President's figures cannot possibly be fulfilled," said another. "He plucks them out of the ether. They have no reality."

They were days when gloom was unavoidable by most minds. The fall of Singapore—that strong bastion—was a staggering blow. The escape of the *Scharnhorst* and *Gneisenau* and *Prinz Eugen,* under the very guns of Dover, was no help to cheerfulness. It needed great faith to look into the future with confidence and certainty of victory.

I met a man of faith at a tea table in Washington. It was a tea table in the British Embassy, and the man was Lord Halifax. He had just come back from Springfield, where he had attended an anniversary celebration of Abraham Lincoln, who had begun his career as a young lawyer in that city.

"It seemed to me a historic moment," said Lord Halifax, "for a British Ambassador to give an address on Abraham Lincoln. I was glad to go there, and I had a thrill when I saw the Union Jack and the Stars and Stripes floating above Springfield Town Hall. The audience sang 'God Save the King'—look, it's printed on the back of the program so that everybody might sing the words—and then 'Drink to Me Only with Thine Eyes' and 'There'll Always Be an England.' "

Lord Halifax was not a gloomy Englishman that afternoon though he alluded to the bad news. When his tall figure came into the room I could see that he was not steeped in depression. He was quite cheerful over the tea table and not unduly dismayed by world events. He spoke of his contacts with the American people. Mr. Philip Murray, president of the C.I.O., and one of the other Labour leaders had been to lunch with him one day, and he was glad to meet that type of man. He liked the Americans and hoped he had established friendship with them, in spite of the usual criticism. He gave me a copy of his address on Abraham Lincoln, and I found it an interesting psychological study of that great man, written with

sympathy and understanding and admiration, which I am
certain is completely sincere.

There are many passages in it I should like to quote, for
the spirit of Lincoln is greatly needed now, but the following
extract reveals the lesson which Lord Halifax himself drew
from his study of Lincoln's life and spoke of to the people of
Springfield when their nation had received the hard knocks
of war.

*In these stern days there is much for our generation to
learn at the school of Lincoln and great need to learn it. To a
world trained to think of toleration as a mark of enlighten-
ment and virtue, it is wholesome to remember how sharply for
Lincoln the line was drawn between the things where compromise for the sake of peace was possible and those where
peace so gained would deny the cause to which his loyalty
was pledged.*

*In all the struggle to preserve the Union, he thought and
spoke and acted as one whose principal concern it was to preserve something that might, long after his name had passed
into history, still exercise a potent and healing influence upon
the whole future of the human family. Mr. Robert Sherwood
has spoken of this in words that seem to have the sum of the
matter in them. "The reason that Lincoln lives today, and
still inspires so many men everywhere with the will to shake
off their chains and find freedom and opportunity in the
brotherhood of life, is that he was essentially a citizen of the
world." As Lincoln himself said as he entered upon his first
term as President, "I have often enquired of myself what
great principle or idea it was that kept this Confederacy so
long together. It was not the mere matter of separation of the*

colonies from the motherland, but that sentiment in the Declaration of Independence which gave liberty not alone to the people of this country, but hope to all the world, for all future time." Assuredly Lincoln would not have been slow to recognise the utter impossibility of compromise with the evil philosophy that now seeks to impose itself upon mankind. Nor would he have reckoned any cost too great to preserve the world from the spiritual death that must accompany the destruction of those values by which its real life is sustained.

But the cost will be great indeed: and as in every crisis of human destiny there may for many be times when the issue seems almost beyond the compass of human strength. Those so tested would do well to remember Lincoln's indomitable faith, as through four long and lonely years he carried almost singlehanded the future of this great Union.

Among his many photographs there is one which more than any other reveals the beauty of Lincoln's character. It is a portrait taken on the 10th April, 1865, and it was the last one ever taken. Lee had surrendered. The war was over. The Union had been saved. The work of reconciliation could at last begin. The face of Lincoln is strained and weary; the struggle had left its mark upon his forehead and in his greying hair; but the gaunt face is touched by the glow of an inward smile. There is again a spark of humour in the eyes, and in their depths a warm light shines. It is the light of a far brighter day than Lincoln lived to see, a day which might have known no dawn but for his unconquerable soul.

6. THE PRESIDENT

Shortly after ten o'clock in the morning I drove to the gate of the White House. President Roosevelt was going to attend one of his press conferences, and by the magic wand of Lowell Mellett, my good friend, I was to obtain admission. Afterwards I was to be introduced to the President, and I was keyed up to a slight state of nervous tension. Being an incurably shy man, in spite of having been battered about the world in a journalistic career, I am always anxious and nervy before an interview of this kind. But I was very keen indeed to see the man who, more than any other, perhaps, holds the fate of the world in his hands, for victory or defeat, for liberty or enslavement. For his leadership of his own people I had respect and admiration, in spite of all the criticism hurled at him by his political opponents, now mostly silenced.

I was challenged at the gate of the White House and was taken to a small lodge where I gave my credentials and mentioned the name of a Mr. Hassett, which had been given to me as the password by Lowell Mellett. It acted like a charm, and in a very brief time I was given a pass which admitted me to the White House, to which I walked up the drive. Two or three newspapermen preceded me, and I followed them into a large hall with white pillars. Out of it was a press room where the Washington correspondents assembled and hung up their hats and coats as I did, and stood about smoking cigarettes, as I did too. I looked around for familiar faces, but the crowd I had known had made way for other and younger men. One of them talked to me, and I found that he had married the daughter of an old friend of mine in England.

I also introduced myself to Mr. Hassett, who was master of ceremonies in these press conferences. He came and sat beside me for a time and we talked about England, which he knew well, and many mutual friends in Fleet Street.

"There will be a rush when the President is ready," said Mr. Hassett. "I will take you in at the right moment."

He gave me an advantage by leading me ahead of the queue and taking me into the room where the President was to receive us. He was already seated at the table when I took a chair in front of the other correspondents, who were mostly standing.

We were in a circular room, perfectly white from floor to ceiling, in the Adams style of the eighteenth century. It was very light and airy, looking out to the grounds of the White House. There were flowers on the President's table. At my elbow close to my chair was another table, and on it I noticed was a toy horse with long ears—a comic-looking fellow—and another horse of ebony or some black stuff, and other toys and gadgets. I had heard that the President was amused by such toys, like a boy.

My eyes roved only for a moment. They came to rest on the President himself as his rich voice rang out. Franklin D. Roosevelt. Many times in England I had been thrilled by that voice and stirred by the words he spoke across the world by the miracle of the microphone. Now here I was sitting within a yard of him, seeing him in the flesh, able to study his personality at close range.

He looked very handsome sitting back in his chair. He is better looking than his photographs depict him, having a fine ruddy complexion in contrast to his white hair. He has a massive torso, deep-chested and broad-shouldered. He looked the picture of health, I thought, and I paid homage in my mind to the courage and spirit of the man who has over-mastered his physical infirmity by a miracle of will power.

World news was bad that morning, but the President of the United States had no dark shadow on his brow or in his eyes. He was smiling, genial, and cheery. He made play with his hands, well modelled and graceful in their gestures. He chaffed these correspondents from time to time but answered their questions seriously and candidly.

It was a little disappointing to me that most of their questions dealt with domestic questions instead of with world affairs. Only one man asked about an international subject.

"Mr. President, what do you think of the present relations between the American Government and Vichy?"

"Better ask the State Department," said the President.

Questions arose about a poll tax of two dollars or so which was to be paid by registered voters before they can vote. Down South the coloured folk and the poor whites cannot afford to pay this tax and are thereby prevented from voting.

"Mr. President, do you think this tax is a hardship in certain parts of the country?"

"I do," answered the President. "I have always been hostile to the poll tax."

He had an amusing and ironical minute or two on the subject of cutting down the staffs of civil-service bureaus in Washington.

"Some of you bright boys," he said, "come to me with suggestions that I should cut down these numerous staffs. Fine idea! I am all for economy and reduction of needless offices. But it is also so vague. I want details and concrete suggestions. Take, for instance, meat inspection. That employs quite a

large number of people. It costs quite a lot of dollars. It would
be quite easy to reduce the number of people employed in
that work. But supposing I were to do so? What would be
the result? Some of you gentlemen would suffer from meat
poisoning. The health of the nation would be seriously affected.
No, these suggestions by the glib boys don't work out."

He answered other questions more seriously, one concerning
the present state of things in the training camps for young
unemployed men. It was suggested that some of them were
capable of military service. The President said it would be a
good idea to go down and find out, with an enquiry into why
the young men were there and what was their condition.

The press conference lasted about twenty minutes.

"Well, thank you, Mr. President," said several voices.

The newspaper correspondents filed out. The President had
a short talk with a visitor. I was beckoned forward by a
gentleman whom I knew as Mr. Stephen Early, the President's
right-hand man. The visitor left. I was left alone with Franklin D. Roosevelt.

"I am very glad to see you," he said with a charming smile
and a wave of the hand to the chair by his side.

"I have been doing these press conferences twice a week
for nine years," he told me. "I enjoy them."

I put some question about the state of American opinion
regarding the bad war news, and he answered good-naturedly.

"The American people are more awake now than they have
been before. But they need to be frightened. It's hard for them
to understand. I would like to talk to them when they have a
globe or a map before them. They don't understand distances
or time and how the whole war is governed by those two
factors. Time and distance. Distance and time. It takes three

months for a British ship to reach the southwestern Pacific, round by the Cape of Good Hope. There has to be time for assembling material, for loading, for getting the ship away. All that makes for delay. It is only two months since the Japanese attack. I doubt whether the British or ourselves could have done much better in the time. It was difficult to get reinforcements out there in two months. The time factor was against us."

We spoke of the Japanese successes.

"They are putting up the cry of Asia for the Asiatics," said the President. "Many people out there may be tempted to believe that. That is why I have ordered General MacArthur to make a last stand and why Winston Churchill has ordered his forces at Singapore to hold out to the end. Otherwise the Asiatics may say the white races are abandoning us. They are quitting. There is to be no evacuation, except for women and children."

The President had no patience with people who were demanding the recall of MacArthur.

"They don't understand," he said. "They have no international background. They just don't know."

Presently he began to speak about the figures of production which he had announced—those staggering figures which I have quoted in this book.

"When I gave out those figures," he said, "they seeped through into Europe. They couldn't be kept out. They discouraged the Germans and heartened our friends. All the enemy could do was to jeer at them. 'It is impossible!' they cried. But it is not impossible. We are doing it!"

He spoke those last words with cheerful confidence. "We

are doing it!" He was President of the United States. He had all the reports in his hands. He was untouched by doubt.

For a moment, perhaps, his mind was aware of criticism such as Senator Byrd of Virginia had directed to the long delay in preparedness during those two years which had followed the opening of World War II.

"It was impossible," he told me, "to drive ahead in time of peace. We had to wait until we were in the war. American public opinion was slow in moving to an awareness of what was happening. Now things are being stepped up. Naturally people are impatient. They read the appropriations for planes and ships and tanks, and at the end of two weeks or so they ask: 'Where are they?' "

The President laughed at this simplicity and this impatience.

"We can't get them in two weeks," he said. "But they are coming along. They are coming along!"

He spoke for a few minutes of the escape of the three German battleships and made a generous defence of the British Navy.

"It was easy for the enemy," he said. "The Germans chose their weather. They made their dash when there was bad visibility and they could not be seen thirty yards away."

He did not think this episode increased the dangers of an invasion of England.

"That is a very different thing," he said. "It would need a constant stream of ships, not having the initial surprise and under the fire of British guns and bombers."

I remember a few more of his words.

"I get on very well with Winston Churchill. We understand each other."

"I am Dutch-Scot. That is a tough ancestry!"

He spoke a few things "off the record" and then gave me his hand and the friendliest of smiles. I had had a good conversation with him and thanked him for the privilege.

"Come again!" he said genially, with a farewell wave of the hand.

So I left him, deeply impressed by his personality, his charm, his spirit. Friends of mine were gloomy in Washington, but there was no gloom in the mind of the President of the United States. The war news was truly terrible, but Franklin D. Roosevelt faced it buoyantly and undismayed. He looked at the future with bright eyes. He waved away the failures of the past.

"We are doing it!"

That was the cause of his confidence, his belief in ultimate success.

The English-speaking peoples of the world, the captured nations, the lovers of liberty, depend upon this man, above all, for their hopes and chances in this desperate struggle with powerful enemies. His optimism, his calm acceptance of temporary disaster, his faith in final victory, his strangely radiant spirit in the darkest days are great gifts at a time when many men despair. The personality of President Roosevelt, touched by a kind of boyishness and yet masterful and strong in his decisions, gives him a power of leadership which in spite of criticism puts a spell upon his own people and upon all who come in touch with him. If his own faith is fulfilled and victory attained after all defeats, by the enormous power now being forged in American factories and directed by his will, his place in history will be supreme among world leaders.

When I left his presence I had a sense of having left a man touched by some magic, very human and yet queerly supernatural, or what the Scots call "fey." I had found a radiant personality in a world on fire, with disaster and tragedy and infinite peril coming closer to the last strongholds of our defence.

Since then, when I sat by his side that day in Washington, there has been no respite, and our best hope is to gain that time which President Roosevelt knew as his pacemaker in this race for life or death.

America Speaks. In this book there is something, I hope, of the spirit of a great people who, after bewilderment and unawareness, because of time and distance and a reluctance to change their way of life, as we were all reluctant, have now awakened to the full knowledge that their own destiny is at stake. I am certain that that spirit and will power and dynamic energy and unrivalled mastery of mass production will never slacken or falter through the coming years. If the British people can hold out against all assaults, all losses, and all the stupendous peril which bears down upon them, the people of the United States will fling their mighty strength into the scales of fate. Give us Time, O Lord!